ALSO BY BETTY ROHDE

So Fat, Low Fat, No Fat

More So Fat, Low Fat, No Fat

Italian So Fat, Low Fat, No Fat

MEXICAN SO FAT, LOW FAT, NO FAT

Betty Rohde

A FIRESIDE BOOK
Published by Simon & Schuster

Rockefeller Center
1230 Avenue of the Americas
New York, NY 10020

Designed by Katy Riegel

Manufactured in the United States of America

1 3 5 7 9 10 8 6 4 2

Library of Congress Cataloging-in-Publication Data

Rohde, Betty.
Mexican so fat, low fat, no fat / Betty Rohde.
p. cm.
"A Fireside book."
Includes index.
1. Cookery, Mexican. 2. Low-fat diet—Recipes. I. Title.
TX716.M4R62 1998
641.5'638—DC21 97-29292
CIP

ISBN 0-684-83525-8

To Bob

How can I tell you how much you mean to me? You have had a very heavy load these past four years; with the death of both my parents, all the new endeavors we have faced, the new life we lead, it seems like we only see each other occasionally. You are always there with your arms open. Your shoulder is always ready to catch my tears of joy or sadness. You laugh with me and at me, you cry with me and for me. You hardly ever miss a television appearance; you leave work for a twelve-minute segment, go to a friend's to watch, or have one of the boys call you and let you listen to me over the phone when you can't watch. When it's permitted you travel with me, sit in airports, stand in lines, with never a word of complaint.

The real test comes when you taste-test everything I create. Your palate knows not what to do.

You are my Gentle Giant! God bless you. I love you.

Betty

Contents

Introduction

To cook Mexican food, to write about Mexican food, to understand better the techniques of cooking, blending, mixing, matching, marrying of the spices, the peppering of the peppers—before I started this book I knew I should go for help. What nicer, prettier place than Santa Fe? I knew I did not want to go into Old Mexico. I am not a Mexican nor can I cook the real authentic Mexican style, nor can the average American housewife who enjoys preparing and eating Mexican food. Everyone thinks, Well, no more Mexican food for me if I am going to cut out the fat. Not so. Here is your answer: *Mexican So Fat, Low Fat, No Fat.*

I hope you enjoy using this book just a fraction as much as I did writing it. The research was very pleasant, the tasting was delightful, the company was excellent. You're in for a great treat with some of these recipes, so let's take a look. By the time you are halfway through the book you will be on your way to the grocery store to stock up on tortillas and frijoles.

Healthy, happy eating!

Searching for the Seasonings

No matter how old an old dog gets, she can always learn new tricks. When the possibility of a Mexican book came up with Simon & Schuster I thought, Oh, that will be easy. Little did I think about the many, many different seasonings, peppers, regional dishes, and other things that would be involved. I never go into anything without giving it some serious thought, and studying has become a way of life for me.

I sat down to give some serious meditation as to just how I would tackle this, as I did with my last book, *Italian So Fat, Low Fat, No Fat*. Hopefully you have read my story in that book, "Two Short Blocks to Red Pepper Soup," and enjoyed the Italian low-fat recipes.

I try to treat each and every recipe just as if I were going to make it for my family, and I do, every night. This is what Bob survives on: experiments. I know that the majority of you are normal-cooking, regular-eating people just like we are. Most of us do not have nor do we want a gourmet pantry, or a gourmet chef (now that is a lie—I would love one and I know you would also). Back to the story—we do not have the budgets for that kind of cooking. We have regular groceries on the shelf, and a lot of you like myself live in a small area like Gore, America. We have one small grocery store, as I have mentioned in previous books. I say, "If I can get it here in Gore, America, you can get it anywhere."

I did not have the availability of the authentic native cooking or restaurants here, so I made the decision to go to Santa Fe, New Mexico, to some cooking classes and to study the subject in all aspects.

Since Bob is my secretary, notetaker, taster, tester, tease, and fun to take home, I thought I would take him along to help out.

You first must understand what taste you are trying to achieve and then make it taste as near the same as possible without the fat. The challenge: We look for what spices, what flours, what flavors, which cheeses; we investigate how hot the peppers; we study the presentation; and we put all this together without the fat.

On an educational trip through the gourmet restaurants and shops of New Mexico, Bob and I knew we could only taste and not pig out—ten pounds would be on us before we could say "Scat"! This was a research trip and not a vacation.

We arrived in Albuquerque and sampled the breakfast menu at the hotel. Naturally, everything on the menu had a Mexican name. We each ordered different items so we could taste, discuss, and make notes on everything. The waiter thought we did not understand the menu and were making a large mistake. He explained, These are two large breakfasts; you must be awfully hungry? We tried to explain this was a research project. His disbelief was showing on his face as he looked at us like we were two crazy people.

We realized we could not identify the spices by taste, so I would talk to as many of the chefs or cooks as I could. Bob was doing some heavy-duty tasting by this time. *No, No*, Honey, this is a tasting project, not a pig-me-out contest. He would laugh and say, Yum, this is good, and go back to the tasting and comparison we had started. We laughed and had a ball doing this.

We made our way toward Santa Fe early. The balloon festival was starting that morning and we were in some heavy traffic going out of town; we had to pass right by it as we drove to Santa Fe. Beautiful.

When we arrived we looked up the cooking school and I enrolled in some classes. I returned at the time designated for my first class. The biggest challenge was the different peppers; there are hundreds of them. I tried to use my head and put myself in your place: Now, will my ladies be able to get this in their area of the country? If not, I'll pass. I hate nothing in the world more than trying to make a recipe and it calls for something from outer space. If I jump on the space shuttle and find the spice three hours later, it sits in my pantry from then on. Fifteen years down the road I will look at it and wonder what the heck that was. If I use a native spice in the recipes that follow, I have given you substitutions that will work.

The classes were wonderful. Bob roamed the city while I worked, and he told me of all the things he saw and how beautiful they were. Wait a minute! That's not nice. He gave me that killer smile. Well, I guess you were bored. OK, I am happy you found entertainment. More classes, more touring for Bob. *Heh!* We did manage to go to the opera in Santa Fe; it is an outdoor opera open only during the warm months. The opera suggestion was made to me by the lady who bought my first book at Simon & Schuster, Marilyn. Bob has told me, "You always thought Marilyn could walk on water." She is no longer with S&S. She and her husband moved to Santa Fe. *Left New York!!*

We took another trip in the fall to attend more classes. I had made arrangements and enrolled in advance this time. I insisted that Mr. Bob go to the classes with me: If you are going to be my secretary and personal assistant, you need to help me take some notes and not do so much sightseeing. He, being Bob, said, "OK, whatever makes you happy." That is the answer I always get from him—well, sometimes we do have just a tiny bit of a difference of opinion, but not too often. He sat up there in class and raised his hand, asked more questions than anyone in the room, had a ball, and is ready to go to more cooking classes.

Let me be the first to tell you this little story about Bob cooking. I was working late about twenty years ago at a little craft store in Tulsa before we moved here, and Bob decided he would cook dinner. *Yikes!!* When I came in the door I could smell something burning. He was talking on the phone to his mother. Before she died they would talk every two or three weeks for sometimes an hour to get caught up; it was very hard for me to break myself from saying, "You need to call your mother," after she passed away.

I walked into the kitchen where he was sitting at the counter talking to Mom. He had a bottle of wine he had opened and was sipping. Nothing wrong with that. He had cut up some potatoes ready to cook and left them on the counter, forgetting what he was doing. They were black. He had some sausage patties patted out, ready to fry; they were mushy. The cauliflower was burnt to a crisp and smelled like rubber tires burning. The bread was hard as a rock. Need I say more? I started laughing and begged him, Please darling, leave the cooking to me. We agreed for sure on that one.

Back to our trips to Santa Fe. We benefited tremendously from the classes, and we got to spend some time with Marilyn and Sandy. They have become very special friends of ours since my beginning at Simon & Schuster, have visited us two times in our home in Gore, America. We have been to their home in Santa Fe, were treated to a wonderful dinner, all low-fat, enjoyed some side trips, etc., etc. She also gave me much needed information about different things associated with cooking Mexican. We discussed spices, herbs, peppers, delving deep into the Mexican cuisine. We found a large flea market outside Santa Fe and had a wonderful time—you can buy fresh herbs, spices, ristras, almost everything there. (The shipping charges to send it all home were very expensive.) We also shopped for some very nice Mexican pottery, a serving bowl, platters, and Bob's rooster. Look on the cover of this book and see Mr. Rooster. He is a magnificent bird.

I have the dishes all displayed on the cover with wonderful food in them. Look in the background behind the bird. There is a beautiful wreath made in New Mexico, special order. You will also see two Mexican pitchers, one on each side of me. These were purchased in Old Mexico, one by Mother when I was in the second grade on our first trip, the other while visiting my Aunt Juanita in Alamogordo, New Mexico, on a trip over the border. The scarf the bird is standing on was bought from some weavers in New Mexico on one of our trips with Marilyn and Sandy. Look at the beautiful hen bowl I have the cornmeal muffins in, right in front of me. She is also a magnificent bird. Bob calls her "the old hen." *What?* As you can well tell, Bob and I have a lot of fun together. Don't be afraid to have a good time, ladies—*smile;* life is short. I try to make sure that every day of my life, I laugh, smile, and do something fun, if it is no more than hiding behind the door and grabbing Bob when he arrives. (He likes that too.) Every night after we have dinner, we play one hand of cards—gin. He beats me quite regularly. Sometimes the tide turns; when it does, he draws a little picture of a skunk by the score. Says, That was a stinker. We miss that while I travel, but make up for it when I get home.

Have *fun* making these dishes. Know that a part of our life is involved with each and every one. Try and imagine when and where this was thought up, and travel along with us in your imagination.

Healthy, happy eating!

Betty

Steps to Losing Weight and Gaining Self-Control

1. *Make up your mind:* You really need to sit down and seriously think about what you want to do. Is it just to lose a few pounds? Is it to look prettier? Is it your *health?* Is it all three? If it is just a vain thing alone, the chances are you're treading in very shallow water. If you are concerned about your health to the point that you are very worried about the condition you're in, and thinking as I was that you may be shortening your life expectancy, you're probably getting in up to your knees. When the situation gets deep enough for you to be up to your bottom in concern, you're likely to really put this thing into perspective. *First* and most important of all is your health. This is probably the most important point and highest-rated positive thing you will ever do. *Make up your mind!* You have to make up your mind. If you don't, you're wasting your time. If you just say, "Oh I think I will try eating low-fat for a couple days to see how I like it," you won't last two days. Make up your mind that you need to make a very dramatic change in your life to save your life. Tell yourself, "OK, I know I need to do something to get some of this weight off and better myself for whatever reasons." Even if it is that you have a new friend in your life, I think that is a pretty strong reason: he or she

will be very impressed that you like them enough to concern yourself with the way you look and the condition of your health, and to start a fun, interesting, and exciting new way of thinking, cooking, and eating. I have had a ball—still am—and I have lost a total of 85½ pounds since 1993. The most exciting thing is that I have kept it off; I had never been able to do that before. *Yay!* I never am hungry, I don't exercise. I wish I had time to walk; the only walking I get is in the airports, running from plane to plane. My life keeps getting more exciting every day. I wish I had a couple weeks; I would tell you all about the goings-on in my life.

2. *Decide:* You need to really think and talk to yourself. Some of us do that anyway, then some of us answer ourselves occasionally. Well, yes, I do, when I am really busy, don't you? Sure you do! Ha ha, caught you!

Decide on what you want to do. How do you want to handle this problem? I talked to my doctor; he advised me that cutting down to 30 to 50 fat grams a day would be normal, and I would start to lose weight and better my health by lowering my fat intake to these numbers. I stopped, just as I want you to do, thought about the day before, what I had eaten, how many fat grams, roughly. Wow, was I shocked! If you, like me, never really thought about it, just ate them, stop and count them. It more than likely will shock you to a state of *This can't go on.* I truly hope it does.

You don't need to do everything the first day, week, or month. I only counted my fat grams. My doctor told me, when I asked about counting calories, that if I would watch my fat intake I would do fine, because that is where the calories come from. So I was going to go into this the easiest way I could.

3. *Ease:* I thought, Count the calories, count the fat grams, weigh every bite I eat, exercise, cut my portion sizes, and cut my sugar. Since I am a sweet freak, I will never do it, because I am over fifty (quite a ways), I am set in my ways, and I just am not going to do all of the above. I know it and

you know it. Oh, I might have had good intentions, maybe lasted two weeks, if that long. In my mind, I could hear myself telling Betty, "Lady, you have been there, done that" more times than once. Been on every diet in the knowledge of fat people (that's another thing you will need to admit, I am fat, I know it and I do care, no matter what I keep telling myself). I use to tell one of my best friends, who was always starving herself, I know I am fat, but you know what? I don't care. I am happy and Bob is happy with me.

Ha! Little did I know. I was miserable. I would stand in front of the mirror and hold my hands over part of my tummy and think, I wonder what it would be like to be thin again? Bob was too much of a gentleman to say anything. He loves me whatever the situation. Is that not great, two people married twenty-five years by the time you read this and still in love? On our anniversary last year, our twenty-fourth, he proposed to me all over again. We are planning to be married in February of 1998. No, I am not going to wear a big white gown. Sounds like fun, but better be sensible about this, just like the weight thing.

Oh yes, I was thin when Bob and I got married—little, young, feisty. What a great time, young, feisty, flitting, and meet the man I did, Bob Rohde. I better get on with my story before I get on the subject of Bob. I could write you a complete book about this fellow I married, and maybe I will someday.

I am now—well, not young, not thin, but still feisty, I guess so. I am also still fifty. I am busy as a cranberry merchant. How busy is a cranberry merchant? I have heard that all my life. Why are they so busy, that is what I ask Betty Rohde. Why are you so busy? The answers please me, I love it.

I have a new career, when I thought I was Fat, Fifty, and Finished. You know that situation. Kids are all gone out of the nest, you and hubby are comfortable enough, making ends meet, as always, so lay back and rest, slide the rest of the way out, eat all you want of whatever you want, lay around, sleep, take it easy. *Not!* I have a couple of aunts—the ones I told you were all over the kitchen in the first book, *So Fat, Low Fat, No Fat*—who are an inspiration to me. They both walk, run all over the country, go every where, do *not* sit home and feel sorry for themselves, look great and are great. One is youthful enough that she had a facelift in her younger years. Man, I wish I had the nerve to do that. She looks wonderful. You won't ever need to worry about me doing it. I faint at the sight of a needle. If I could just be put to sleep at home and wake up back at home with it all over, I would consider it. But I just don't have time to sandwich it in between my flights. One doctor told me he would meet me at the airport and give me a routine test. I was getting ready for a couple years ago. Of course he was teasing.

I suppose I could put myself in the category of Fun, Flying, and Still Fifty, unfortunately. No, I take that back, I don't want to go through the raising of my kids, losing my parents, etc. etc. etc., that I have had to do. I like it just the way it is, I love my private time with Bob and the new adventures we are experiencing. I am sorry that most married couples are not as happy as we are after twenty-five years together.

I am very happy that I decided to do something about the state my health and body were in. I know that Bob likes what he sees better, although he would never say anything of a criticizing nature. He supports me in any and all that I do, or try to do. He has as much input as I do in what we do—if no support, no success. Be a support to your mate, tell him or her you love them, you are there for them, you are behind them in whatever adventure you both take on.

4. *Start:* After you have given yourself a long talking-to—have decided that you must do something, that you are going to do something—the next step is to decide the way you will be most comfortable, what you think will fit your

personal situation best. Then you are ready to start. Go to the store and start reading labels. It takes a little longer to shop at first, but you will be amazed at the things you find without fat these days, and at the number of products that sit next to each other on the shelf that are fat-free and fat-full. Always make it a habit to flip the item over and check the label; sometimes you pick up what you thought was free of fat grams and it isn't !

5. *Beware:* As you get started in this new fun, fascinating, and challenging adventure, be aware also of your sodium intake. Bob has high blood pressure and a very stressful job, so I need to be aware of the amount of salt or sodium in what he eats. Now that I have been watching what I cook and eat, I realize that if I eat something salty, like pretzels, because they are fat-free, the salt is too much for me and I am swollen the next day. If I eat something fat-full, it makes me ill; within thirty minutes, I have the stomach cramps so bad, and then the back-door trots. (That is the language of the country: people had outhouses many years ago, and you had to run out the back door to go to the convenience parlor.) Read "Carter Red" in one of my future books. I loved that chicken. Still do and still tell the story every time I get a chance.

6. *How many grams:* You need to make the decision as to the number of fat grams you think you will be happy with. Once you get started you will be amazed at how much you can eat with so few fat grams. I cut mine lower than 30 grams—cut down to 10. You think that is very drastic. It really wasn't. You can eat almost totally fat-free. But I do *not* want you to think for one minute that I advise you to do that. You need a certain amount of fat for your body to operate properly. You must *not* totally stop having any fat. You will become sick from that also. Find yourself a happy medium.

7. Now that all that is mentally logged into your computer, let's go!

Staples for the Freezer

Healthy, handy, helpful, hurry-up, and happy things to keep in your freezer for ease, convenience, and speed: good tasting as well as good for you. I feel that is the lifestyle of today. I style almost all of my recipes for this type of preparation.

shoepeg corn This is a small, crisp-kernel corn, called just that, shoepeg. Found in all local grocery stores, it is usually supplied by canning companies such as Green Giant. It can also be found in the freezer department—but that I cannot find in Gore, America. Need to get out of town again, don't I? Adds just a very interesting taste as well as appearance with a nice texture to almost any soup, chili, salad, or vegetable dish.

frozen onions, peppers, or a mixture of onions and sweet peppers Keep these in your freezer for convenience. Many recipes use these to save time and energy. They are just as good, and you and I don't have time to chop anymore. I wouldn't if I had time. We just don't cook the way we used to. If it takes very long to make, forget it. We live in a frantic and busy world now in the 90's. I suppose you could classify us as 90's Ladies.

chicken tenders Also listed or bagged with the title of "boneless skinless breast tenders," these are small tender strips from the breast area. They are very low in fat. Four pieces equal ½ gram of fat—or ⅛ gram each. Hey, I can live with that. They can be found in large wholesale-type places, frozen in large bags; only take out as many as you need per meal. Very convenient; keep them available for quick, late, or hurry-up times.

frozen cooked cubed chicken white meat You can find this in your large wholesale-type stores, such as Sam's. It is very quick to fix, useful in many recipes; use your imagination or use my recipes. Very convenient to keep in the freezer.

potatoes Frozen cooked potatoes, cubed, chunked, shredded, wedges, any way you can find them frozen, without any fat. *Read your labels! Always.*

green peas Frozen peas add a wonderful color, healthy and good. No need to thaw, just pour into a salad.

cornmeal mix If you make cornbread or muffins, this is very convenient for quick, fat-free hot breads, for family dinners or guests. You can add many different spicy touches. Check some of my recipes. Oh, I love hot cornmeal muffins, with a little onion and peppers, or some spices. Yum! Yet there's just a trace of fat from the cooking spray. Notice the large hen bowl full of spicy cornmeal muffins on the cover. Good to the last crumb, and that crumb is good too.

Bake, broil, boil, grill, or dry-fry in a nonstick pan. This is the way we must all learn to cook. No oil! Sauté in water, or quick-fry, dry-fry, or bake-fry. The food still has the appearance, the texture, and the taste, and you still have your health.

Hopefully this will get your attention enough to get you started thinking, "What is best for my health, my family, and my friends?" If I did it, *so can you!*

Glossary

adobo seasoning A dry seasoning with a Latin blend of salt, garlic, pepper, and oregano. It is very good for using with meats, seafood, and poultry. Usually found in grocery stores, even in Gore, America.

black-eyed peas These are actually the seeds of cowpea, an annual vine. They are tan, with a black dot on the skin that is the "black eye."

burrito (bur-EE-toh) A tortilla rolled around a filling of meat, refried beans, onions, salsa, cheeses, or just about whatever you desire. Fold the ends in before rolling into a long narrow package. *Mexican So Fat, Low Fat, No Fat* leaves out the meat or else substitutes chicken or turkey.

cheeses Mexican Monterey Jack, Cheddar cheeses, small amounts of Parmesan, and authentic Mexican cheeses, usually not found in area stores, are all used in Mexican cooking. I also use feta cheese, soaked for an hour or so in cold water and drained.

chilaquiles (chee-lah-KEY-lehs) A casserole of tortilla strips, baked with a variety of sauces and fillings.

Christmas sauce A mixture of red chile sauce and green chile sauce is known as Christmas sauce.

cilantro (sih-LAHN-troh) Much like flat-leaf parsley in looks, cilantro's flavor is entirely different. It is strong, fresh, and tangy. It needs to be stored in the refrigerator, as does any fresh herb. It may also be found in the dried spices section of your supermarket.

cinnamon A Mexican cuisine must, cinnamon is used in everything from chili con carne to sweet and/or savory sauces. It comes in tightly rolled sticks as well as ground. The sticks are great for decorations and also for flavoring your hot cocoa or coffee.

coriander This spice is the seed of the plant that gives us **cilantro.** It's commonly used whole in Mexican cooking as well as in many other cuisines, such as Indian, Scandinavian, and Caribbean. (It's also available ground.)

cumin (KYOO-mihn) Powerful, sometimes dominating, spice used mostly in Mexican cooking. Available both as whole cumin seed and ground cumin. Don't leave it out of a recipe.

El Asador (ah-SAW-dor) Trade name for a nonstick grill or trivet made of heavy metal mesh, with two wooden handles, available in $10\frac{3}{4}$-inch size, used to roast peppers and other vegetables, warm pita bread, bagels, etc. (See page 40.)

enchilada (en-chee-LAH-dah) A corn tortilla rolled around a filling of refried beans, cheese, or meat and served hot with salsa. Normally these are fried, but now we must bake. Just as good tasting and much better for you, using fat-free ingredients.

fajita (fa-HEE-tah) Flour tortilla rolled around sliced steak, pork, chicken, or shrimp. In this book, you can expect chicken, along with fat-free cheese, beans, lettuce, tomatoes, onions, just whatever you desire or have on hand. It's sort of a "mustgo." Ever had mustgos for dinner? I have. They're anything in the refrigerator that "must go."

frijoles (free-HOH-lehs) Spanish for beans.

Great Northern beans Large white beans with a mild flavor, sold dried and canned.

green chilies Anaheim or green chile peppers, also known as California or long green chilies. May be found fresh or canned, whole or chopped.

ground red pepper This may be a variety of different peppers: cayenne, red chilies, Chimayo peppers. But try not to use habanero peppers; they are very hot, and mainly used in sauces. There are too many peppers to name. Remember—a little is good, a lot is *hot.*

hominy Dried corn kernels that are soaked and lightly cooked until the outer coating can be removed. Whole hominy is found canned mostly.

jicama (HEE-kah-mah) A bulblike vegetable with brown skin, often called Mexican potato. Its crunchy white flesh is eaten both raw and cooked.

Mexican oregano A strongly flavored oregano grown and harvested in New Mexico, sold fresh or dried at local stands. I am sure that it is available in dried form all over the country; it adds a wonderful flavor to almost anything.

Mexican seasoning A dry seasoning containing chile pepper, salt, onion, sweet pepper, garlic, cumin, oregano, and red pepper. Found at any local grocery store, even in Gore, America.

nachos (NAH-chohs) Crisp chips, usually pieces of corn tortillas, topped with cheese, salsa, and chilies and baked—a category of appetizers, although some people make a meal of nachos alone. Amend the ingredients and you are off to a wonderful taste, using fat-free cheese for instance. See the recipe on page 34.

pinto beans (frijoles) These are speckled, with a brown and pale pinkish background that turns brown when cooked. No, you are not going to be eating pink beans. Relax.

posole (poh-SOH-leh) A thick soup always cooked with **hominy.**

taco (TAH-coh) A tortilla, crisp or soft, folded in a half-moon shape, leaving the center open, filled with a meat filling and topped with shredded lettuce, onions, and tomatoes.

tomatillo (tohm-ah-TEE-yoh) About the size of cherry tomatoes but a brilliant green, these grow in a paperlike husk. If starting to turn yellow, they are too old and have lost some of their acidic freshness. They can be fresh or canned. Great in salsas.

tortilla (tor-TEE-yuh) A round flat unleavened bread made with cornmeal or sometimes flour, the tortilla is the basis of Mexican cookery. Tortillas are rolled, fried, baked, soaked, twisted, turned, chopped, filled, munchy, crunchy, wedges, chips, dips—just about every Mexican meal has them in some way.

Chapter 1

Dips, Appetizers, and Snacks

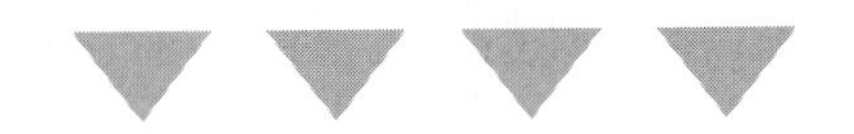

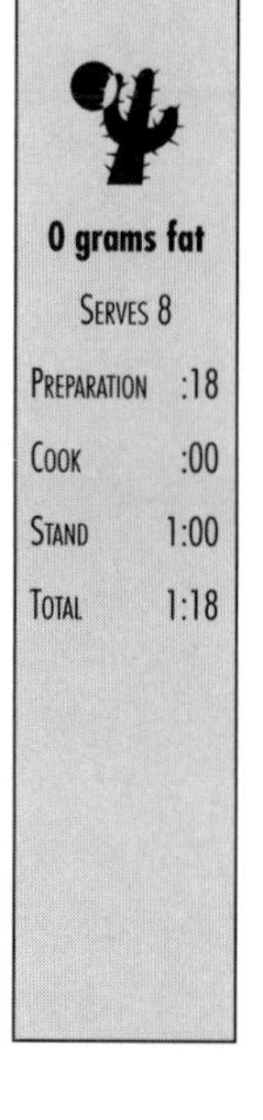

FIESTA DIP

¼ cup finely chopped dill pickle
1 teaspoon green salsa (commercially prepared)
1 (16-ounce) carton fat-free sour cream
1 (4-ounce) can water chestnuts, chopped fine (may use pine nuts or pumpkin seeds, toasted, but will add fat grams)
1 green onion, chopped fine
1 (11-ounce) package Fiesta Ranch party dip mix
1 (15-ounce) can black beans, drained and puréed in blender or 1 (16-ounce) can fat-free refried black beans

Combine in a medium-size bowl the pickle, salsa, sour cream, water chestnuts, green onion, and dip mix. Stir in the puréed beans. Mix with a wire whip until well blended and smooth. Cover with a lid or plastic wrap and let stand in the refrigerator for at least an hour.

0 grams fat
MAKES 2 CUPS
PREPARATION :05
COOK :00
STAND :00
TOTAL :05

RED-HOT FIVE-MINUTE DIP

You may use your imagination on added ingredients. As noted earlier, "Some like it hot, some not." With that thought in mind, you could divide the recipe and make one half hot, the other mild.

1 (8-ounce) brick fat-free cream cheese
1 (8-ounce) jar picante sauce (see Note)
Jalapeño pepper rings, chopped fine, for garnish
Baked tortilla chips for dipping

Let the cream cheese come to room temperature. In a medium bowl, carefully stir the cream cheese with a wire whisk. If you beat the cream cheese too hard, it will break down and become too thin. Continue gently creaming as you add the entire jar of picante sauce. Stir with a spoon just until well blended. You may garnish the top with chopped jalapeño peppers, and serve with nice low-fat or no-fat baked tortilla chips.

Note: For the picante sauce, use mild or medium or hot salsa. You could even use green salsa.

CHEESY RED-HOT DIP

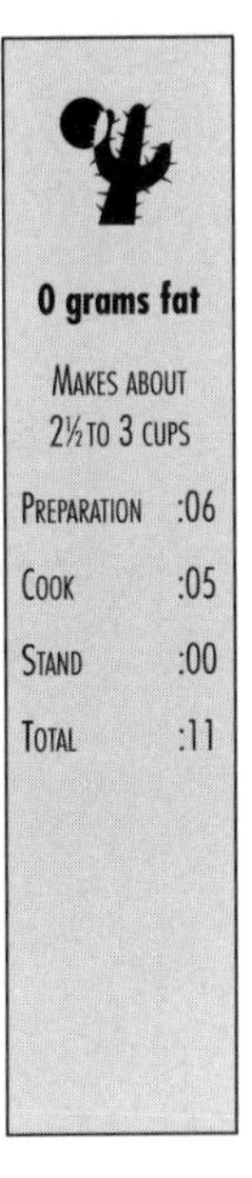

Serve this in that fondue pot we all had to have twenty years ago that is now collecting dust. Keep on low heat and your dip will stay warm throughout the evening. Stir occasionally.

1 (16-ounce) brick processed fat-free cheese, such as Healthy Choice (comes in 1- or 2-pound packages in a long green box—looks like Velveeta)
1/4 cup skim milk
1 (10-ounce) can Ro-Tel diced tomatoes with green chilies, drained and juice reserved
Baked tortilla chips or veggies for dipping

Cut the cheese into 1-inch cubes (or smaller cubes for quicker melting). In a microwave-safe dish, combine the milk and cheese. Pour half the Ro-Tel over and stir until mixed. Cover with plastic wrap (leaving a corner opened for venting) and microwave for 2 to 3 minutes. Watch for it to start melting. Stop, stir, and return to the microwave to continue melting. Repeat this process until the cheese is melted and the Ro-Tel is well blended. The milk is to give it a little thinner and smoother texture. If the dip is thicker than you like it, add a little more milk or juice from the Ro-Tel.

Taste the dip. If you want it hotter, now is the time to add more of the Ro-Tel. I usually just add the entire can, juice and all, but you may choose to be a little more cautious.

Serve with baked tortilla chips, and/or a tray of fresh vegetables to dip.

TAMALE DIP

1.75 grams fat per serving

SERVES 8

PREPARATION	:15
COOK	:25
STAND	1:00
TOTAL	1:40

1 (15-ounce) can chicken tamales
1 medium-size onion, chopped
1 clove garlic, minced
1 (10-ounce) can diced tomatoes and green chilies
1 ($10\frac{3}{4}$-ounce) can tomato sauce
½ cup diced celery
1 ($1\frac{1}{4}$-ounce) package taco seasoning mix
1 medium-size fresh tomato, diced
½ cup shredded fat-free Cheddar cheese for garnish

Empty the can of tamales into a colander and very gently rinse off all the sauce. Try not to crush them. You are going to chop these tamales but not smash them. Transfer to a shallow dish and chop the tamales into small pieces. Set aside.

Place the onion, garlic, tomatoes and green chilies, tomato sauce, and celery in a large nonstick saucepan. Simmer for about 20 minutes, stirring several times.

Add the taco seasoning mix and the tamales, stirring until heated. Place in a serving dish. Stir in the chopped fresh tomatoes. Sprinkle a little of the shredded cheese on top of the dip.

Serve with a basket of low-fat baked tortilla chips and a small bowl of shredded cheese alongside.

GUACAMOLE

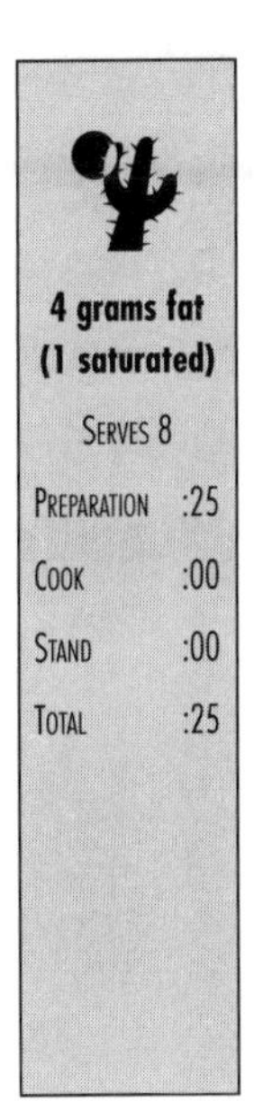

1 (20-ounce) package frozen green peas, thawed and drained
3 tablespoons lime juice (fresh squeezed is better but bottled will do)
2 tablespoons chopped fresh cilantro
1/2 cup minced onion
3 tablespoons chopped green chilies (canned)
1 medium ripe avocado, peeled, pitted, and cut into small chunks
2 medium tomatoes, diced fine
1/4 cup picante sauce or salsa
Salt and ground black pepper to taste

Process the peas in a blender, adding the lime juice, cilantro, onion, and chilies and blending until smooth. In a bowl, mash the avocado, leaving it a little coarse for a nice texture.

Transfer the blended pea mixture to the bowl with the avocado; stir to blend. Add the diced tomatoes, picante sauce, and salt and pepper to taste. If you prefer a little spicier taste you may add a drop of hot sauce, but add only one drop at a time, then stir and taste. You can ruin your dish in a New York minute by using too much hot sauce.

Serve as a dip with baked tortilla chips.

2 grams fat per serving

SERVES 4

PREPARATION	:10
COOK	:00
STAND	:00
TOTAL	:10

LAZY DAZE GUACAMOLE

2 large ripe avocados
½ cup thick and chunky salsa
1 teaspoon lime or lemon juice
½ cup chopped onion

Peel and pit the avocados. Put the avocado in a serving bowl and mash with a spoon, leaving it somewhat lumpy. This gives some texture to the dish.

Add the salsa, lime juice, and chopped onion.

Stir to mix well. Place the avocado seed in the middle of the guacamole until serving time to keep the dip from turning dark. Remove at time of serving.

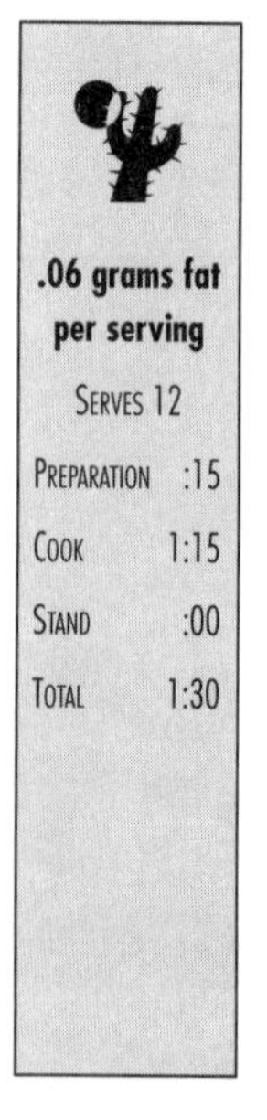

PARTY POTATO SKINS

Prepare the potatoes a day ahead and refrigerate them until needed—or they may be prepared on the day you need them.

6 medium-size baking potatoes
Garlic powder to taste
½ teaspoon ground red pepper, such as Chimayo or cayenne
Ground black pepper to taste if desired

Scrub the potatoes well, pierce with a sharp fork so steam can escape, and bake in a 425 degree oven for 45 to 60 minutes, until tender. (Do not cover them with foil.)

When the potatoes are cool enough to handle, cut them in two lengthwise, making a boat effect, and scoop out the centers, leaving about ¼ inch intact with the skin. Put the scooped-out potato aside to use for another day, another recipe.

Lightly coat the potato shells inside and out with butter-flavored cooking spray. Sprinkle a little garlic powder and pepper over the inside of the shells. Place them skin side down on a baking sheet and bake at 425 degrees for 15 minutes. Turn the skins over and continue to bake, open side up, for another 15 minutes or until lightly browned and beginning to crisp. If you like them crispier, bake a little longer on both sides.

Serve with your favorite dip, salsa, or a seasoning of your choice.

TORTILLA CHIPS

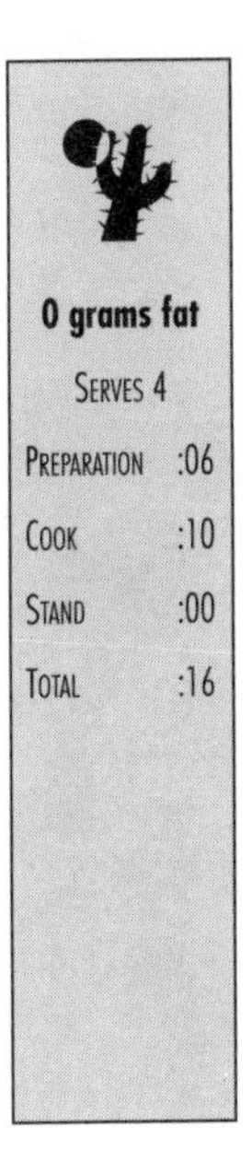

If you are looking to make something healthy for snacks, try sprinkling these chips with sugar and cocoa powder, or cinnamon. For a spicy snack, use Mexican seasoning, red pepper (lightly), or garlic and cheese sprinkles. Let your imagination help you.

6 fat-free flour tortillas, or corn tortillas (1 gram fat each)

Preheat the oven to 400 degrees. Stack your tortillas one on top of the other; cut into 6 wedges. Arrange in a single layer on a baking sheet lightly sprayed with vegetable oil cooking spray. Spray the tops slightly, just a tiny bit to brown nicely. You may do this without any spray if desired. After spraying, if you care to have different flavors such as spicy, sweet, etc., you may add those spices at this time and the spray helps the spice to stick evenly.

Bake for about 5 minutes; turn the chips over and bake an additional 5 minutes. Watch them closely; don't let them burn.

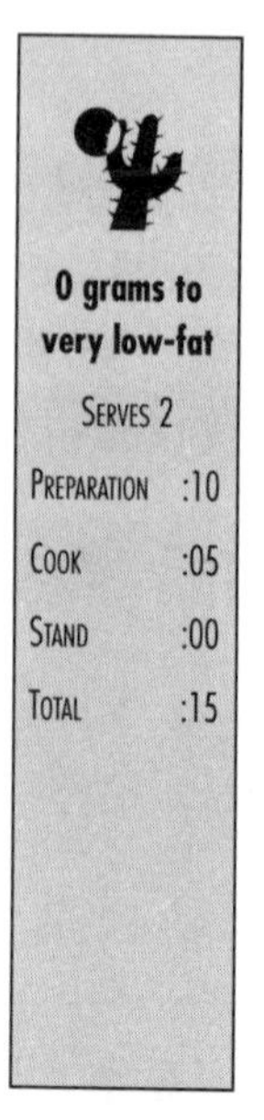

NACHOS (TORTILLA CHIPS WITH CHEESE AND CHILIES)

1 recipe tortilla chips (page 33) or about 3 dozen low-fat commercial chips
2 cups shredded fat-free Cheddar cheese or grated fat-free processed block-type cheese such as Healthy Choice (comes in 1- or 2-pound packages in a long green box—looks like Velveeta)
Jalapeño chile slices (canned or bottled)

Preheat the oven to 400 degrees.

Arrange the tortilla chips on a heatproof platter or shallow baking dish. Sprinkle with cheese and top with slices of jalapeño. (Use the desired amount of chilies.)

Bake until the cheese is melted, about 5 minutes (or you may microwave for about 1½ minutes). Serve immediately. These are also good with salsa or fat-free sour cream on the side.

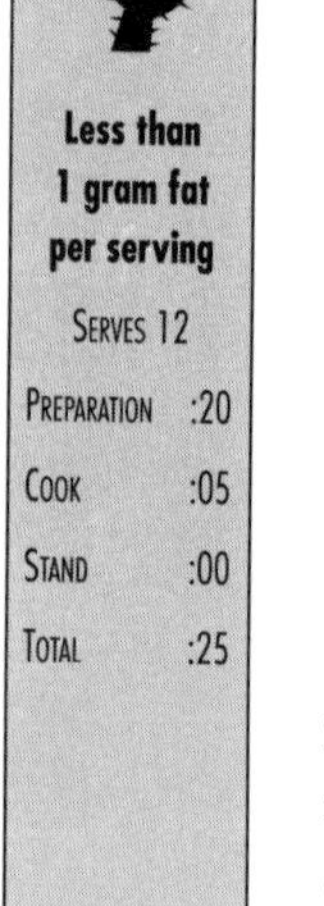

NACHOS OLÉ

24 low-fat baked tortilla chips (pick unbroken ones)
1 (15½-ounce) can fat-free jalapeño-flavored refried beans
¼ cup thick and chunky salsa
¼ cup fat-free shredded cheese (your choice)
Ripe olive slices to garnish (optional)
¼ cup thinly sliced green onions to garnish (optional)

Preheat the broiler.

Lay out the chips in a single layer on an ungreased cooking sheet. Warm the beans just enough to make them more spreadable. Spread a spoonful on each chip. Top each with ½ teaspoon of salsa, then with ½ teaspoon of cheese.

You may garnish with sliced olives—be careful to read

he label; they are full of fat grams—or sliced onion pieces. Broil 5 to 6 inches from the heat source for about 2 minutes, until the cheese melts.

You may choose to top each with a small dollop of fat-free sour cream.

VEGETABLE TORTILLA ROLL-UPS

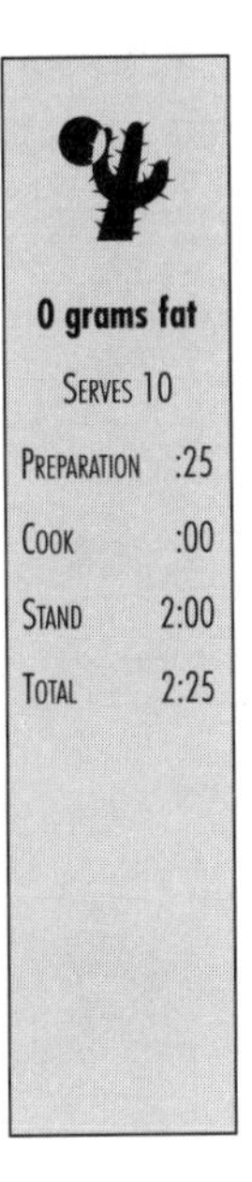

Great appetizers for entertaining.

1 (8-ounce) package fat-free brick cream cheese, softened
1 envelope dry onion soup mix (check for 0 fat)
2 green onions, chopped fine
1/4 cup finely chopped red bell pepper or drained pimiento
1 tablespoon chopped green chilies, drained
Tabasco to taste
6 (8-inch) fat-free flour tortillas

In a mixing bowl, gently stir the cream cheese with a wire whisk until it starts to become creamy (not too much or it will break down and be too thin). Add the soup mix, onions, bell pepper, and chopped chilies, and start to add Tabasco, one drop at a time. Taste to make sure you are not getting it too hot for your guests.

Place the tortillas on a flat work space and spread the cheese mixture evenly over them all the way to the edge. Roll up like a jelly roll. Place seam side down in large shallow dish. Refrigerate the rolls for at least 2 hours before slicing; this lets the onion soup and the other ingredients marry well before serving.

Remove from the refrigerator; cut into slices about 1 inch thick. Continue to store in the refrigerator until serving time, covered with plastic wrap.

CHEESE QUESADILLA

0 grams fat

Serves 1

Preparation	:05
Cook	:05
Stand	:00
Total	:10

During my research for this book, I discovered that quesadillas (keh sah-DEE-yahs) were traditionally a finger food, eaten as a snack held in the hand as you walked about the Mexican markets doing your shopping.

1 (6-inch) flour tortilla
½ cup shredded fat-free cheese (Cheddar, Gouda, Monterey Jack, Muenster, Mexican, or a mixture)

Preheat the oven to 400 degrees. Place the tortilla flat on a baking sheet; cover half the surface with shredded cheese. Heat until the cheese is melted, about 5 minutes. Remove from the oven and fold in half immediately.

The quesadilla may also be made in a nonstick skillet. Place the tortilla flat, top with cheese as above, and heat until the cheese is starting to melt. Fold and continue to heat until the tortilla is lightly brown and the cheese is melted, turning once to ensure even melting. Serve with salsa or fat-free sour cream.

Warming tortillas: Fat-free flour tortillas and low-fat corn tortillas are available at the time of writing. By the time this book is out, fat-free corn tortillas will probably be available. When grilling, lay the tortillas next to each other right on the grill and warm just until hot. Overheating will cause them to be tough. Another suggestion is wrapping a stack of tortillas in foil and placing the package on the top rack of the grill just until hot.

TOMATO-ONION QUESADILLAS

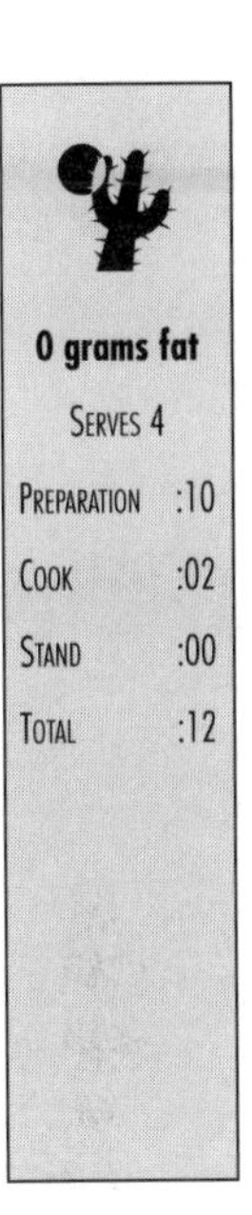

4 fat-free flour tortillas
1/4 cup grated fat-free Cheddar or Monterey Jack cheese
1/4 cup chopped onion
2 jalapeño pepper rings, chopped fine
1 medium tomato, chopped fine

Preheat a nonstick skillet or griddle or El Sador until very hot. Moisten your tortillas very slightly. If you have a mist bottle, mist lightly, or dip your hand in water and rub over the tortilla. Place a tortilla on the hot griddle and heat for just about 5 seconds. Remove the tortilla and layer one half with cheese, onion, pepper, and tomato (divide each of these ingredients into fourths, using a fourth on each tortilla—and use rubber gloves with the pepper).

Lower the heat slightly, then return the filled tortilla to heat about 15 more seconds. Fold, using tongs, a knife, or a spatula, while it is on the griddle; pat the quesadilla closed. Turn the quesadilla over, and heat the other side for approximately 15 seconds or until the cheese begins to melt. Repeat this with each quesadilla. Keep them warm with foil or a cloth until serving time. Reheat on the griddle if necessary.

Serve as part of meal or cut into thirds or fourths and use as appetizers.

Variation: Use corn tortillas instead of flour. You will add a fat gram for each tortilla, unless fat-free ones are available by the time this book comes out.

CHILE-CHEESE QUESADILLAS

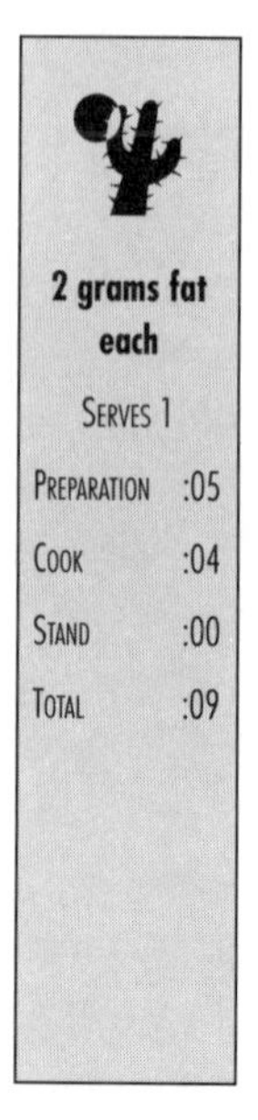

2 (6-inch) corn tortillas
2 teaspoons fat-free ricotta cheese
2 tablespoons shredded fat-free Monterey Jack cheese
1 teaspoon diced mild green chilies
Vegetable oil cooking spray

Spread the ricotta cheese over the entire surface of one tortilla. Sprinkle with the Monterey Jack cheese and diced chilies. Top with the second tortilla. Spray a nonstick skillet or griddle with vegetable oil cooking spray and place over medium heat. Cook the quesadilla about 2 minutes on one side or until golden brown; turn and cook about 2 minutes on the other side or until golden brown. Remove to a serving dish, cut into 4 wedges, and enjoy.

To make additional quesadillas, multiply the recipe times the number of quesadillas desired.

QUICK FRESH TOMATO SALAD

0 grams fat
SERVES 4
PREPARATION :15
COOK :00
STAND :10
TOTAL :25

This is a quick and tasty salad, or it could be used as a salsa with chips.

4 medium-size ripe tomatoes
1/2 cup chopped fresh sweet banana peppers
(about 3 peppers)
1/2 cup chopped onion
Tabasco jalapeño sauce (green) to taste
1/2 teaspoon lemon pepper

Peel and chop the tomato, moving the chopped pieces aside before putting them in a bowl, to eliminate some of the juice. Discard the seeds and juice, as much as possible. You should have about 2 cups of chopped tomato.

Combine the chopped peppers, onion, Tabasco to taste (add one drop at a time), and lemon pepper in a small bowl. Toss gently to blend the seasonings well. Let stand about 10 minutes. Combine with the tomatoes.

TOMATO SALAD

4 cups cubed fresh tomatoes (about 8 medium tomatoes)

DRESSING:

1 teaspoon olive oil
2 tablespoons balsamic vinegar
2 teaspoons fresh lemon juice
Dash of salt (optional)
Dash of ground black pepper

Drain the tomatoes. Mix the dressing ingredients in a large salad bowl, add the tomatoes, and toss gently to coat evenly. Let stand about 15 minutes to let the seasonings blend. Serve on a leaf of lettuce if desired.

7 grams fat entire dish

SERVES 4–6

PREPARATION	:10
COOK	:00
STAND	:15
TOTAL	:25

ROASTED (ANAHEIM) GREEN CHILE PEPPERS

0 grams fat

Preparation	:10
Cook	:06
Stand	:05
Total	:21

This roasting method can be used for any fresh pepper, including red and green bell peppers. Anaheim chilies are also called California or long green chilies. They are used in stews, sauces, soups—almost any dish is enhanced with the right amount of this chile. They are also excellent stuffed (rellenos). There is a red Anaheim chile, very decorative to liven up your dish, but used mostly to make ristras, which are the long hanging clusters of red peppers you see in magazines, pictures, movies, and of course in Mexico and New Mexico. They are also dried, ground to powder form, and sold as "chile colorado" or ground red pepper.

Roast your peppers on El Asador (see Note) or directly over your gas burner, turning to keep the roasting even. The smell is wonderful. Roast the peppers until blackened, about 3 or 4 minutes on each side, watching closely and turning with tongs. You may also roast them under the broiler, 2 to 3 inches from the heat, for 3 to 4 minutes on each side.

As the peppers are roasted, place them immediately in a plastic zipper-lock storage bag. Close tightly and allow them to steam for 5 minutes or longer. Very carefully peel off the charred skin. Use thin rubber gloves—and don't rub your eyes or nose!—if the peppers are even mildly hot. Cut off the stems, remove the seeds, rinse the peppers under cool running water, and blot dry with paper towels. Slice or chop fine. Store in the refrigerator or freezer.

Note: El Asador, described on page 23, can be ordered from Santa Fe School of Cooking, 116 W. San Francisco Street, Santa Fe, New Mexico 87501. Telephone: 505-983-4511; Fax: 505-983-7540. The price is around $20.

ROASTED RED PEPPER DELIGHTS

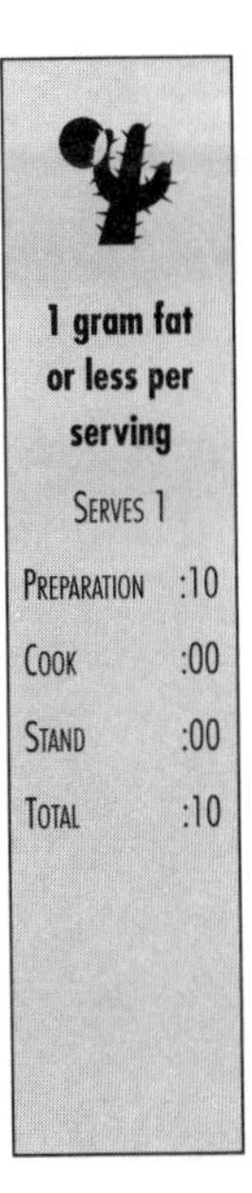

/3 cup drained roasted red bell peppers, purchased or following recipe on page 40
4 tablespoons fat-free brick-style cream cheese, softened
Pinch of crushed Mexican oregano or regular oregano (about 1/8 teaspoon)
Dash of garlic powder
1 low-fat bagel, wheat or any grain
Sprouts for garnish (optional), or shredded lettuce or chopped fresh spinach

Blend the peppers in a mini food processor or mash to a paste in a small mixing bowl. Add the cream cheese, oregano, and garlic powder. Stir to mix well. Don't stir cream cheese too vigorously or it will get thin and runny. It has a water base and breaks down easily.

When blended to a smooth paste, spread evenly over a bagel cut in half. Serve as an open-face sandwich, garnished with sprouts, lettuce, or spinach. Or cut into bite-size pieces and serve as an appetizer with your own choice of garnishes.

0 grams fat

MAKES
1¼ CUPS FILLING

PREPARATION :30
COOK :00
STAND 2:00
TOTAL 2:30

STUFFED VEGETABLE APPETIZERS

Clean and prepare your vegetables a day ahead; store in plastic bags. Prepare the cream cheese filling and when ready for entertaining, put cheese mixture into vegetables.

VEGETABLES FOR STUFFING:

Cucumbers, cut into slices to be topped with cheese or halved, hollowed out, cut into half-moon chunks
Celery stalks, cut into short pieces
Cherry tomatoes, centers scooped out
Mushrooms caps (stems popped off)
Zucchini slices about 1/4 inch thick

1 (8-ounce) package fat-free brick cream cheese, softened
2 tablespoons grated fat-free Parmesan cheese topping
1 teaspoon skim milk
1 teaspoon Mexican seasoning
2 jalapeño pepper rings, chopped extra fine
Touch of ground black pepper

Prepare vegetables of your choice.

Combine in a small mixing bowl the cream cheese (careful—stir gently so it doesn't break down), Parmesan topping, milk, seasoning, jalapeños, and black pepper. Cover and refrigerate for at least 2 hours before serving.

Use a pastry bag to fill vegetables (it makes the job a lot quicker and easier). If you have no pastry bag, put the mixture into a small sandwich-type zipper-lock storage bag, close, cut a very small hole off the corner, squeeze down tight, and use just like a pastry bag.

MEXICAN HATS

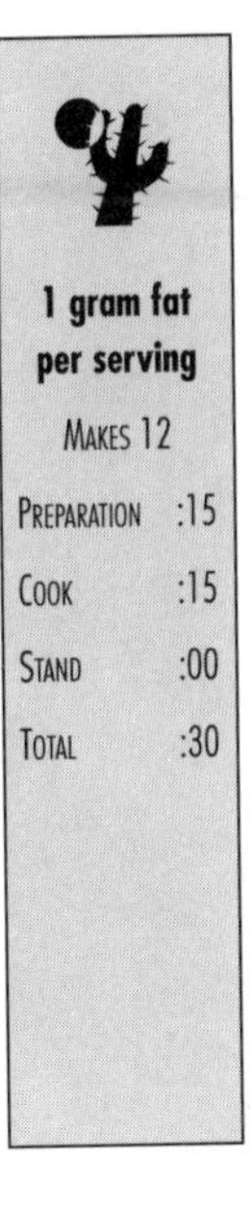

1 gram fat per serving

MAKES 12

PREPARATION	:15
COOK	:15
STAND	:00
TOTAL	:30

Filled mushroom cap appetizers—baked or broiled

12 large mushroom caps—stems removed
1/2 pound fresh lean ground turkey
1/3 cup finely chopped onion
1 tablespoon minced cilantro
3 tablespoons egg substitute
1 tablespoon Dijon mustard
1 clove garlic, minced
1/2 teaspoon Mexican oregano or regular oregano, crushed
1 teaspoon Mexican seasoning
1 teaspoon low-sodium soy sauce
Ground red pepper for garnish

Preheat the oven to 350 degrees, or turn the broiler on to 400 degrees. Spray a cookie sheet lightly with vegetable oil cooking spray.

Clean the mushrooms: brush with a mushroom brush or wipe them with a damp paper towel.

Combine the ground turkey, onion, cilantro, egg substitute, mustard, garlic, oregano, Mexican seasoning, and soy sauce. With clean hands, mix as you would a meat loaf or such. When mixed evenly, fill each mushroom cap with the meat mixture. Place on the cookie sheet, hat top down, meat filling up. Sprinkle each very lightly with red pepper.

Bake for 10 to 15 minutes or until the meat is cooked through. If you choose to cook under the broiler (which is faster when you are entertaining), broil for 6 to 10 minutes. Watch very closely. You don't want to serve burned Mexican Hats.

MANGO DRESSING

0 grams fat

Serves 4

Preparation	:25
Cook	:00
Stand	:00
Total	:25

Makes about 2 cups.

2 cups very ripe mango chunks
1/3 cup lime juice
1/4 cup fresh orange juice
1/4 cup cider vinegar
1/2 teaspoon grated orange peel
Pinch of ground ginger

In a blender, combine all the above ingredients and whirl until very smooth. Use on a nice green salad or a fruit salad. Will keep up to a week.

Fat-free salad dressing can be used in a variety of ways, as marinade, as barbecue sauce, and, mixed with other ingredients, as a flavorful way to bake meats. Try this one: An envelope of dried onion soup, a small jar of apricot jam, and a regular or large, depending on the amount needed, jar of salad dressing, such as Catalina. Mix together and pour over baked and drained meat, such as chicken. Bake for 10 to 15 minutes longer; serve over a bed of rice. Wonderful! It has a sweet and sour taste—you could have worked all day making this.

GREEN GODDESS DRESSING

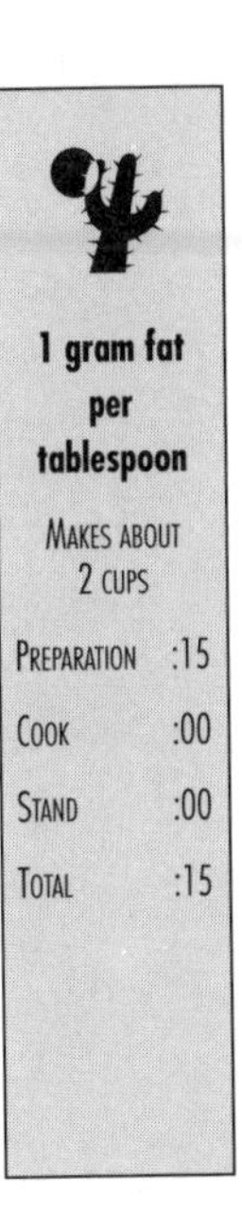

This is a great salad dressing, but also can be used as a dip for veggies at any entertaining event.

2 ripe, soft avocados, peeled and pitted
2 tablespoons lime juice
2 teaspoons Tabasco jalapeño sauce (green)
1 clove garlic, minced
3 tablespoons green salsa, bottled
4 green onions, chopped very fine
1 cup fat-free sour cream, or fat-free plain yogurt

In a shallow bowl, with a fork, mash the avocados with the lime juice. (Save the avocado pits.) Add the pepper sauce, garlic, and green salsa, stirring all in well. Add the green onions and sour cream or yogurt. Continue to stir with a fork until all is nice and blended and smooth.

If using this as a dip, you may want to thicken it just a little with fat-free mayonnaise. Add 1 tablespoon at a time until you get the consistency desired.

Variation: You can substitute mayonnaise for the sour cream or yogurt if you use this for a salad dressing. You may want to thin it just a little, for pouring consistency. If so, add 1 teaspoon of nonfat skim milk and stir.

Jalapeño Jelly

Jalapeño jelly has become very popular. It is delicious on toast, bagels, English muffins, just about anything you care to put it with. A favorite for entertaining, quick and easy.

Spread it lightly on low-fat crackers. Or put a thin layer of fat-free cream cheese on a cracker and top with a dollop of jalapeño jelly. There are red and green jalapeño jellies. They are very festive during the holidays to use alongside each other, or to top every other cracker or appetizer on a platter with a different color. Trim a holiday cream cheese cake, or a regular cake with vanilla frosting, with a small amount of jalapeño jelly. Plain cookies with a little low-fat frosting on top become fancy when touched lightly with a small amount of jalapeño jelly.

Be careful when handling jalapeño peppers, you can burn your skin very easily. Let me tell you about making jalapeño jelly.

Jalapeño Pepper Jelly

You have probably read about my dad's gardens and how large they were. One year Dad had a bumper crop of little bite of beets in while feeding him, he would spit them out as fast as they went in. They are very good for you in vitamins, iron, etc. Have you ever noticed how many they serve in the hospital, or in nursing homes? Mother liked beets; she would eat them for us. She was in the nursing home just six months after Dad died.

Mother was a lot like a jalapeño pepper. Sometimes she was sweet and spicy; sometimes she would bite you, just like a jalapeño pepper will do.

Mother died May 15, 1996.

Chapter 2

Soups

Less than 1 gram fat per serving

SERVES 4

PREPARATION	:35
COOK	:00
STAND	2:00
TOTAL	2:35

GAZPACHO

2 large cucumbers, peeled and seeded
12 Roma tomatoes
1 cup chopped green bell peppers
½ cup chopped green onions
1 cup fat-free chicken broth
⅓ cup low-sodium vegetable juice cocktail
½ teaspoon dried thyme leaves, crushed
3 tablespoons red wine vinegar
¼ teaspoon hot pepper sauce (more if desired)

Chop 1 cucumber and 8 tomatoes. Combine the chopped cucumber and tomatoes with ½ cup of the chopped peppers, 2 tablespoons of the green onions, the broth, vegetable juice, and thyme in a food processor or blender. Process until puréed. You may need to do this in two batches. In that case, combine all the ingredients in a mixing bowl and divide into the blender or processor.

Pour the puréed vegetables into a fine wire strainer; rub with the back of a wooden spoon until only skins and seeds are left. Toss the remains and continue the process until all has been done. Skim any foam from the juice and discard.

Chop the remaining cucumber and tomatoes. Combine with the remaining chopped pepper and green onions. Add this vegetable mixture to the puréed mixture. Add vinegar and hot sauce and mix well. Cover and chill at least 2 hours or up to 24 hours before serving in chilled bowls.

CHICKEN VEGETABLE SOUP

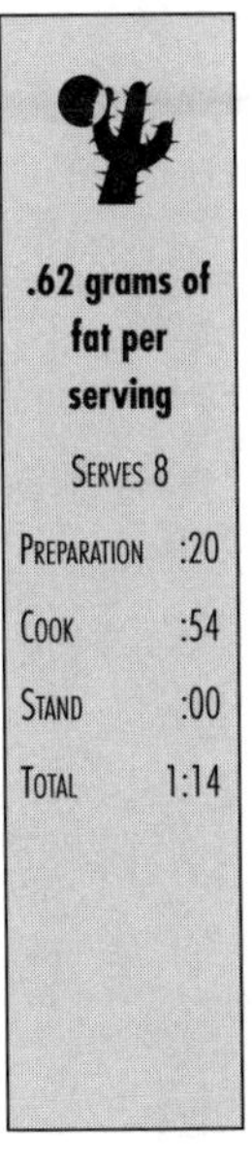

Serve with nice hot cornbread, crackers, or tortilla chips.

3 chicken tenders, cut into bite-size pieces
3 quarts water
1 medium onion, cut into bite-size pieces
1 medium green pepper, cut up (about 1 cup)
2 tablespoons chopped canned green chilies
2 cups frozen mixed vegetables, such as peas, carrots, beans, etc.
1 cup sliced celery
2 medium potatoes, pared, cut into bite-size pieces
1/4 teaspoon Mexican seasoning
1/4 teaspoon dried thyme leaves, crushed
1/4 teaspoon dried basil, crushed
1/2 teaspoon Mexican oregano or regular oregano, crushed
2 tablespoons chicken-flavored bouillon
1 (11-ounce) can white shoepeg corn
1 1/2 cups chopped raw cabbage
1 cup cooked pasta, your choice

Place the chicken tenders in a large saucepan or Dutch oven. Cover with water, about 3 quarts, place over high heat, and bring to a full boil. Lower the heat to a medium boil, continue cooking.

Add the onion, green pepper, and chopped green chilies; stir. Add the frozen veggies, celery, potatoes, seasonings, chicken bouillon, and corn. Let boil for about 15 minutes. Lower the heat to a nice high simmer and continue cooking for about 25 minutes. Add cabbage and cook another 6 to 8 minutes, until cabbage is crisp-tender. Add the cooked pasta and let simmer about 6 more minutes. It's ready when you are.

TORTILLA SOUP

Less than 1 gram fat per serving

SERVES 6

PREPARATION	:30
COOK	:58
STAND	:00
TOTAL	1:28

1 fresh Anaheim chile, roasted (see instructions page 40)
3 medium-size ripe tomatoes, blanched
1 clove garlic, chopped fine
1 pound chicken tenders or boneless skinless breast meat, all fat removed
3/4 cup chopped white onion
1/2 cup finely chopped green onion
1 cup finely sliced or chopped celery
6 to 7 cups water
1 (16-ounce) can fat-free chicken broth
1 teaspoon Mexican oregano or regular oregano, crushed
1 1/2 to 2 fresh fat-free flour tortillas (6-inch)
Salt and pepper to taste
Fresh cilantro (optional)

Purée the roasted chile, blanched tomato, and garlic in your blender or food processor. Set aside.

Brown the chicken over medium-high heat in a medium to large (5- to 6-quart) saucepan, turning frequently. (I usually take the kitchen shears and cut the chicken into bite-size pieces after cooking, or you may leave whole until seared to seal in the juices.)

Add the white and green onions and celery; sauté this mixture until the onions are crisp-tender. Stir in the water and broth. Bring to a boil, cover, reduce the heat to medium-low, and cook for about 15 minutes. Add the chile-tomato purée and oregano and mix well. Cover and cook an additional 15 to 20 minutes. Add salt and pepper to taste if desired.

Make tortilla strips while the soup is cooking: Cut the tortillas in half, then cut into 1/2-inch strips. Arrange them in one layer on a baking sheet and place in an oven preheated to 300 degrees. Bake for 5 minutes, watching closely so little bite of beets in while feeding him, he would spit them out as fast as they went in. They are very good for you in vitamins, iron, etc. Have you ever noticed how many they serve in the hospital, or in nursing homes? Mother liked beets; she would eat them for us. She was in the nursing home just six months after Dad died.

Mother was a lot like a jalapeño pepper. Sometimes she was sweet and spicy; sometimes she would bite you, just like a jalapeño pepper will do.

Mother died May 15, 1996.

Soups

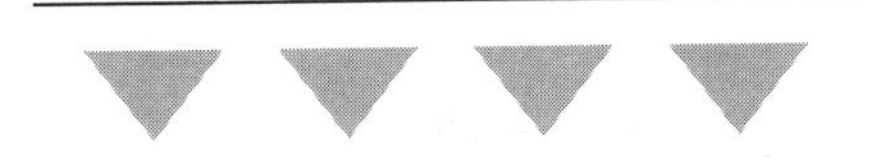

Less than 1 gram fat per serving

SERVES 4

PREPARATION	:35
COOK	:00
STAND	2:00
TOTAL	2:35

GAZPACHO

2 large cucumbers, peeled and seeded
12 Roma tomatoes
1 cup chopped green bell peppers
1/2 cup chopped green onions
1 cup fat-free chicken broth
1/3 cup low-sodium vegetable juice cocktail
1/2 teaspoon dried thyme leaves, crushed
3 tablespoons red wine vinegar
1/4 teaspoon hot pepper sauce (more if desired)

Chop 1 cucumber and 8 tomatoes. Combine the chopped cucumber and tomatoes with ½ cup of the chopped peppers, 2 tablespoons of the green onions, the broth, vegetable juice, and thyme in a food processor or blender. Process until puréed. You may need to do this in two batches. In that case, combine all the ingredients in a mixing bowl and divide into the blender or processor.

Pour the puréed vegetables into a fine wire strainer; rub with the back of a wooden spoon until only skins and seeds are left. Toss the remains and continue the process until all has been done. Skim any foam from the juice and discard.

Chop the remaining cucumber and tomatoes. Combine with the remaining chopped pepper and green onions. Add this vegetable mixture to the puréed mixture. Add vinegar and hot sauce and mix well. Cover and chill at least 2 hours or up to 24 hours before serving in chilled bowls.

CHICKEN VEGETABLE SOUP

Serve with nice hot cornbread, crackers, or tortilla chips.

.62 grams of fat per serving

SERVES 8

PREPARATION	:20
COOK	:54
STAND	:00
TOTAL	1:14

8 chicken tenders, cut into bite-size pieces
3 quarts water
1 medium onion, cut into bite-size pieces
1 medium green pepper, cut up (about 1 cup)
2 tablespoons chopped canned green chilies
2 cups frozen mixed vegetables, such as peas, carrots, beans, etc.
1 cup sliced celery
2 medium potatoes, pared, cut into bite-size pieces
1/4 teaspoon Mexican seasoning
1/4 teaspoon dried thyme leaves, crushed
1/4 teaspoon dried basil, crushed
1/2 teaspoon Mexican oregano or regular oregano, crushed
2 tablespoons chicken-flavored bouillon
1 (11-ounce) can white shoepeg corn
1 1/2 cups chopped raw cabbage
1 cup cooked pasta, your choice

Place the chicken tenders in a large saucepan or Dutch oven. Cover with water, about 3 quarts, place over high heat, and bring to a full boil. Lower the heat to a medium boil, continue cooking.

Add the onion, green pepper, and chopped green chilies; stir. Add the frozen veggies, celery, potatoes, seasonings, chicken bouillon, and corn. Let boil for about 15 minutes. Lower the heat to a nice high simmer and continue cooking for about 25 minutes. Add cabbage and cook another 6 to 8 minutes, until cabbage is crisp-tender. Add the cooked pasta and let simmer about 6 more minutes. It's ready when you are.

TORTILLA SOUP

Less than 1 gram fat per serving

SERVES 6

PREPARATION	:30
COOK	:58
STAND	:00
TOTAL	1:28

1 fresh Anaheim chile, roasted (see instructions page 40)
3 medium-size ripe tomatoes, blanched
1 clove garlic, chopped fine
1 pound chicken tenders or boneless skinless breast meat, all fat removed
3/4 cup chopped white onion
1/2 cup finely chopped green onion
1 cup finely sliced or chopped celery
6 to 7 cups water
1 (16-ounce) can fat-free chicken broth
1 teaspoon Mexican oregano or regular oregano, crushed
1 1/2 to 2 fresh fat-free flour tortillas (6-inch)
Salt and pepper to taste
Fresh cilantro (optional)

Purée the roasted chile, blanched tomato, and garlic in your blender or food processor. Set aside.

Brown the chicken over medium-high heat in a medium to large (5- to 6-quart) saucepan, turning frequently. (I usually take the kitchen shears and cut the chicken into bite-size pieces after cooking, or you may leave whole until seared to seal in the juices.)

Add the white and green onions and celery; sauté this mixture until the onions are crisp-tender. Stir in the water and broth. Bring to a boil, cover, reduce the heat to medium-low, and cook for about 15 minutes. Add the chile-tomato purée and oregano and mix well. Cover and cook an additional 15 to 20 minutes. Add salt and pepper to taste if desired.

Make tortilla strips while the soup is cooking: Cut the tortillas in half, then cut into 1/2-inch strips. Arrange them in one layer on a baking sheet and place in an oven preheated to 300 degrees. Bake for 5 minutes, watching closely so they don't burn. You may want to turn them halfway through cooking time.

Serve the soup piping hot from a tureen garnished with the tortilla strips. Add a tiny garnish of minced fresh cilantro if desired.

RED SALSA SOUP WITH VEGETABLES

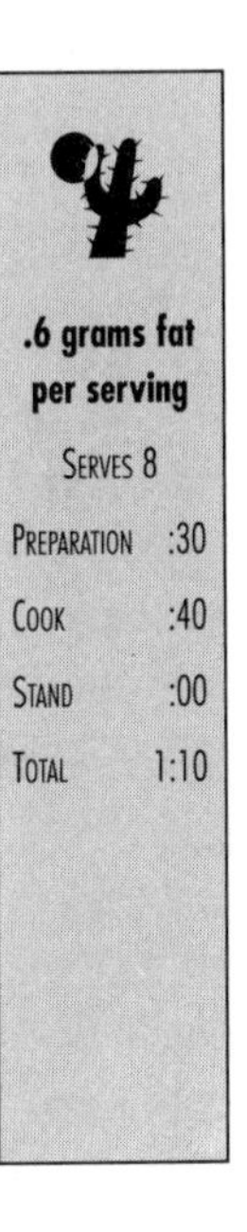

.6 grams fat per serving

SERVES 8

PREPARATION	:30
COOK	:40
STAND	:00
TOTAL	1:10

Keep a plastic container in your freezer and add any leftovers as you have them. When you make a soup, add the entire container.

Great to cook in the summer when the vegetables are plentiful from "Dad's garden." I sure do miss my dad and our gardening together.

8 to 10 cups liquid (fat-free chicken broth, water, vegetable broth, or a combination of any of the above)
1 1/4 cups thick and chunky tomato salsa
1 cup chopped celery
3/4 cup chopped onion
1 clove garlic, minced
1 teaspoon Mexican oregano or regular oregano, crushed
1/2 teaspoon dried minced basil
3/4 cup cooked pasta, any small shape, or rice

VEGETABLES
Choose 1 cup each of 3 or 1/2 cup of 6
Beans—red, white, chili, black, your choice
Zucchini, yellow squash—cubed in small pieces
Corn—whole kernels, fresh, frozen, canned, or leftover
Potatoes—cubed into bite size
Peas—frozen, green, black-eyed, or crowder

In a fairly large Dutch oven or soup kettle, combine the liquid with the salsa, celery, onion, garlic, oregano, and basil. Bring to a boil, lower the heat to a nice strong simmer, and add the choice of vegetables. Add the raw ones first—they will take a little longer to cook than leftover cooked vegetables. Let raw veggies simmer about 15 minutes, then add the remaining vegetables and the pasta; continue to cook until the vegetables are hot and the soup is well blended, about 15 minutes.

Serve with Fiesta Corn Cakes (page 205) and a cool drink.

CHIMAYO CHICKEN SOUP

3 grams fat per serving

SERVES 4

PREPARATION	:25
COOK	:45
STAND	:00
TOTAL	1:10

This is a great soup to make the day ahead. The flavors blend and actually taste better than when served immediately. At least you might want to make it early in the day to serve for dinner.

4 boneless skinless chicken breast halves, cut into bite-size pieces
6 cups water
1/2 teaspoon Mexicano oregano or regular oregano, crushed
1/2 teaspoon ground Chimayo pepper (see Note)
4 fresh sweet banana peppers, chopped
4 small tomatoes, chopped (about 1 1/2 cups)
1 1/2 cups chopped onion
1 (10 3/4-ounce) can black-eyed peas
1 potato, cubed (about 1 1/2 cups)
1 cup corn kernels

Place the chicken in a medium to large stockpot. Cover with water, bring to a boil, lower the heat, and continue to cook for 15 to 20 minutes. During that time, prepare the remaining ingredients.

Add the seasonings and the chopped peppers, tomatoes, and onion; cook about 10 minutes longer. Add the black-eyed peas, cubed potatoes, and corn—plus more water if the soup seems too thick. Continue to simmer for 15 to 20 minutes longer, until the vegetables reach the desired tenderness.

Note: Chimayo chile powder is made from ground dried red chilies from Chimayo, New Mexico. It is mild to hot, with excellent flavor. Red chili powder may be used as a substitute.

CREAMY CABBAGE SOUP

Less than ½ gram fat per serving

SERVES 6

PREPARATION	:35
COOK	:25
STAND	:00
TOTAL	1:00

3/4 cup chopped frozen or fresh onion
3/4 cup thinly sliced celery
1/2 cup all-purpose flour
8 cups fat-free chicken broth
4 cups shredded cabbage
1/2 cup chopped green chilies
12 ounces fat-free smoked or Polish-type sausage, cooked and sliced into half-moon rounds
1 teaspoon snipped fresh parsley
1/4 teaspoon ground white pepper

Place a 4-quart Dutch oven over moderate heat and coat lightly with butter-flavored cooking spray. Sauté the onion and celery until tender but not browned.

Stir the flour into the onion mixture. Slowly stir in the chicken broth. Add the cabbage and chopped chilies; continue stirring and cooking until the soup is slightly thickened. Lower the heat to a steady simmer and cook for another 3 to 4 minutes, uncovered.

Stir the sliced sausage and parsley into the soup along with the pepper. Simmer the soup for 2 or 3 more minutes, until the sausage is heated through.

POTATO SOUP

Less than ¼ gram fat per serving

SERVES 6

PREPARATION	:15
COOK	:25
STAND	:00
TOTAL	:40

1 cup chopped frozen or fresh white onions
2 green onions, chopped fine (optional)
2 tablespoons chopped green chilies, canned or fresh
1/2 cup chopped celery
1 clove garlic, crushed
3 to 4 cups peeled and cubed potatoes
1 (16-ounce) can fat-free chicken broth
1 teaspoon Mexican oregano or regular oregano, crushed
Salt and pepper to taste
2 to 4 sprigs cilantro for garnish (optional)

In a nonstick medium to large saucepan, sauté the onions, white and green, the chilies, celery, and garlic in 2 tablespoons of water over medium heat until crisp-tender, stirring frequently. Add the potatoes, chicken broth, oregano, and salt and pepper to taste. Cover with 4 to 5 cups of water; you should have plenty of liquid over all. Bring to a boil; lower the heat to a simmer and let cook uncovered for 20 to 25 minutes, until the potatoes are soft.

When the potatoes are done, take a potato masher and mash them two or three times while still in the saucepan. Be careful not to remove all the small chunks, the soup needs a little texture.

Serve immediately in nice soup or chili bowls; garnish with a sprig of cilantro if available or desired, along with Mexican Spoon Bread, page 208.

POTATO CORN CHOWDER

1/2 cup chopped onion
1/2 cup chopped celery
4 tablespoons imitation bacon bits
1 1/4 pounds potatoes, peeled and cubed (about 3 cups)
1 (10-ounce) package frozen corn, thawed and drained
1 (13 1/2-ounce) can fat-free chicken broth
2 tablespoons flour
1/2 cup fat-free mayonnaise
2 cups skim milk

1 gram fat per serving

SERVES 6

PREPARATION	:15
COOK	:35
STAND	:00
TOTAL	:50

In a large saucepan, sauté the onions and celery along with the bacon bits in 2 tablespoons of water for about 2 minutes, or just until crisp-tender. Add the potatoes, corn, and chicken broth. Bring to a boil, lower the heat to medium high, and continue cooking uncovered until the potatoes are tender, about 15 to 20 minutes.

In a small bowl, mix the flour and mayonnaise. With a wire whisk, stir this into the milk until well combined. Add the milk mixture to the potato mixture. Continue cooking 3 to 5 minutes or until the chowder is thoroughly heated and starts to thicken.

Remember the chicken soup Grandma or Mom would make when you were sick with a cold? It has been proven that it does help your symptoms—why, no one knows. Keep that chicken soup low in fat and help in more than one way.

1.5 grams fat entire recipe

SERVES 2

PREPARATION :10

COOK :25

STAND :00

TOTAL :35

SPICY CORN CHOWDER

1 large potato, peeled and diced small
2 tablespoons chopped green chilies (canned or fresh)
3 cups fat-free chicken broth (or 3 teaspoons instant chicken bouillon dissolved in 3 cups water)
1/2 cup chopped onion
1 (8-ounce) can cream-style corn
1 (11-ounce) can Mexicorn (canned corn with red and green peppers) (see Note)
1 tablespoon imitation bacon bits
3/4 cup skim milk

In a large heavy saucepan, combine the potato, chilies, chicken broth, onion, creamed corn, Mexicorn, and bacon bits. Stir. Bring to a boil, lower the heat to a simmer, and continue to cook until the potatoes are soft.

Add the milk and continue to simmer for a short period, 5 minutes or so. If too thin, add about 1/4 cup of instant potato flakes, a small amount at a time, stirring after each addition to make sure you don't get your chowder too thick.

Note: Or use 2 cups of frozen corn if desired.

Healthy eating requires healthy thinking, shopping, and cooking of your food. Think about what you're doing to your health and body before you throw in those french fries.

CHILI BEAN SOUP

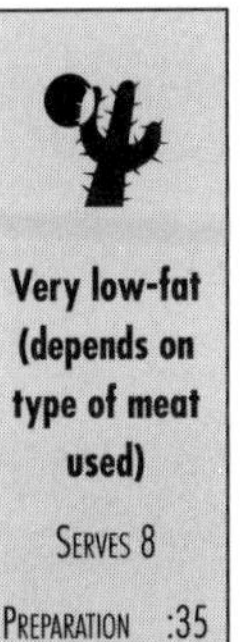

Very low-fat (depends on type of meat used)

SERVES 8

PREPARATION	:35
COOK	3:30
STAND	:10
TOTAL	4:15

This is a recipe for a snowy afternoon, a weekend, or a rainy day. It is the way I used to spend my days every day. Sometimes we do just like to putter in the kitchen and have the house smelling the way Grandma had it.

3 cups dried pinto or red beans
1 (1-ounce) package chili seasoning, such as McCormick
1 1/2 pounds leanest ground meat possible
1 cup chopped onion
3/4 cup chopped celery
1 1/4 teaspoons ground cumin
2 tablespoons chopped green chilies
1/2 teaspoon Mexican oregano or regular oregano, crushed
1 clove garlic, minced, or 1 teaspoon prepared garlic
Salt and pepper to taste
1 (11-ounce) can Mexican green tomatoes (tomatillos) (optional), drained
1 (14-ounce) can diced peeled tomatoes, juice and all

Put the beans on a flat surface and look at them carefully, discarding any pebbles and bits of dirt. Place the beans in a bowl and cover with very hot water. Wash and drain the beans several times. When the water is clear, leave them to soak, covered with very hot water, for 10 minutes or so. Drain, place them in a large stockpot or Dutch oven, and cover again with hot water. Place over high heat. When the water comes to a full boil, lower the heat to a steady rolling boil. At this time, empty the package of chili seasoning into the water and beans; stir to mix well. This will cook the chili seasoning into the beans. Cover partially and let boil until soft, up to 3 hours, stirring occasionally. Keep a check on your water level. Add more when needed; don't let them boil dry and burn.

Sometime during the bean cooking process, you might want to get your meat mixture cooked and have it ready. You could even do this the day before and refrigerate until it is time to use. In a medium-size nonstick skillet, break up the ground meat and brown, stirring often to break apart more. When the meat is almost done, but still not quite browned and crisp, transfer it to a colander and rinse it under the hottest water you have. Shake the colander to remove any water. Meanwhile, wash and dry the skillet and return it to the burner. Return the meat to the skillet and continue to cook, adding the onion, celery, cumin, green chilies, oregano, garlic, salt and pepper to taste, and green tomatoes if desired.

When the beans are soft, add the can of tomatoes, juice and all, to the meat mixture; stir to mix well. Add this mixture to the beans and continue to simmer for about another hour. The soup will be thinner than chili, because this is chili-flavored soup.

Chicken broth: If you do not have fat-free, place fresh-made broth in the refrigerator overnight. The next morning you can just lift the fat off and throw it away. You can also do this with canned regular chicken broth. Store it overnight in the refrigerator, open the top with a regular can opener, and away goes the fat. You will be able to lift 98% off and into the trash can. Sure looks a lot better on the trash can than on your hips, don't you think?

Fish

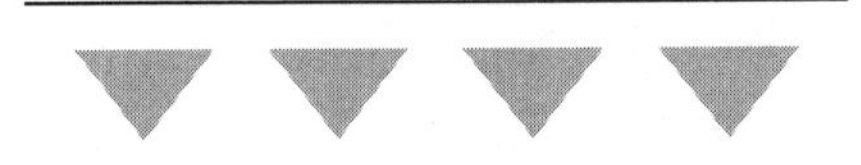

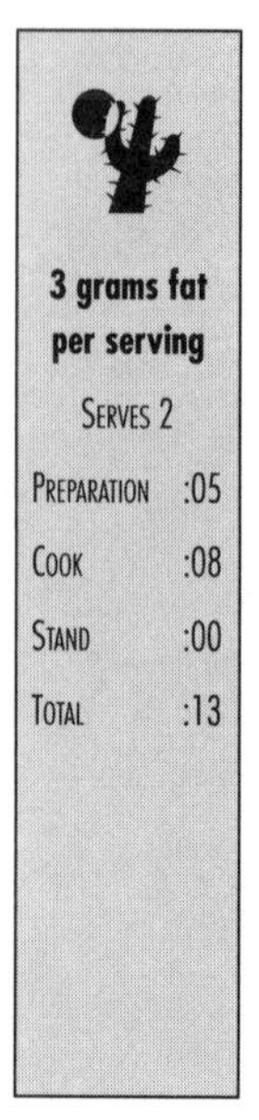

SOUTHWESTERN FISH FILLETS

2 fish fillets (catfish or your choice)
3/4 teaspoon dried basil
1/2 teaspoon dried thyme
1/2 teaspoon paprika
1/4 teaspoon salt
1/2 teaspoon ground black pepper
1/8 teaspoon ground red pepper (cayenne)

Coat the bottom of a heavy nonstick or cast iron skillet with a medium-heavy coating of vegetable oil cooking spray. Put the burner on your lowest heat to preheat the pan while you are preparing your fish.

In a small bowl, combine the basil, thyme, paprika, salt, black pepper, and cayenne. Lay the fillets flat and sprinkle with half the seasonings, rubbing with your hand to smooth and even them out. Turn the fillets over, sprinkle with the remaining half of the seasonings, and pat them in with your hand.

When your skillet is hot, put in the fillets, to virtually scorch the seasonings into the fish. Cook over medium-high heat for 6 to 8 minutes, turning once during cooking period.

Dad's Catfish System

I have mentioned my dad to you in previous stories many times. My dad was so special to me, and still is. I have mentioned to you about Dad being a farmer and all the gardens, vegetables, and so forth, but I don't think I have ever told you about his fish.

His dad was also a farmer. Dad had to quit school before graduating from high school to help in the fields, as so many of our older generation did. They were truly needed in the fields to help make a crop to feed the family during the coming winter. (And we think that having a two-year-old computer is roughing it. Please!)

Dad was a very proud man, and self-educated. He was always reading everything he could, and if he had an interest in something, needed to get more information, he was on top of it. Experience and print made him a very wise, very smart man.

When Bob and I were dating, thinking about getting married, I brought him to meet my parents. We were sitting in the kitchen, which faced the ponds at the end of the pasture. It was at that time a free-range pasture area; now it is mowed everywhere and looks like a golf course. Bob noticed some movement of a white object on a line stretched over the water. He asked Dad, "What is that white thing moving?" Dad smiled and answered, "That is so I will know if I have a fish on my line. Oh, I have a fish on my line now." Bob smiled back, with a question in his eyes. Being a connoisseur of fine fishing himself, he believed himself quite informed on the subject.

Dad had stocked the ponds with thousands of catfish a couple of years earlier. Now they were of some size—he saw to that by buying floating feed and feeding them one to two five-gallon buckets a day.

Dad could see the question and "Oh, yeah sure, old man" on Bob's face. Very wise man, my dad. Wise enough to tell me to marry Bob. But Dad always liked to win. "You don't believe me, do you?" he said. Bob, being the smart person he is, said, "Oh yes, I believe you, but could we go see?" Dad picked up a pair of binoculars: "Look for yourself." Bob did; the line was jumping up and down. He asked, "What do you use for bait?" Dad replied, "Nothing." The same smile came over Bob's face. Dad caught the gesture again. "You see, young man, the hooks are shiny. When the sun hits them, as I have them just under the water enough to cover the hooks, and the line is two to three feet over the water, the fish think it is a minnow swimming around reflected by the sun. They bite and they are mine."

"Well, could we just go see?" Bob said in utter fascination. "Sure, come on. I'll show you." I could tell when I heard the words "come on" to this thirty-four-year-old man that Dad was getting a little put out. Down the back yard and across the pasture they went, just stomping it out. Mom and I sat there laughing because we knew Bob was in for quite a surprise. When Bob became aware of the fact that he was not dressed for fishing, he was dressed for visiting the future hopeful in-laws, Dad assured him that he wouldn't even get wet because he had a "system." "A system, hum? What is your system—send Betty or Nola

(Mother) after them?" and Dad laughed. "No—come on." (*Oops*, there's that word again.)

Dad's system? He had a flat-bottomed boat, known to some as a John boat, plus a paddle, a net, and a pair of pliers. We would get in the boat, slip very quietly across the water using the paddle, go up to the line, reach down, and pick up the fish. Then, with the pliers, he would get the hook out of their mouth, plunk the fish into the boat, and back to the house we go. How's that for a system? Sure enough, there was no bait on any of the hooks, bare nothing. Bob has ever since that day, time, and moment had the utmost respect and belief in my dad. Bob loved Dad very much.

Dad finally confessed to Bob that when he would bait the hooks of the trot line to do some serious fishing, he would hook the hooks up in the top of the line when he was finished. One time the wind blew a couple of the hooks down, and that was the beginning of the baitless line.

Dad also had another "system," for when he wanted to catch a large mess (that is what you call a catch of fish in the South) of fish, for maybe a family gathering, lodge, or whatever. He had built a large net on a frame approximately 10 feet by 10 feet, and lowered it in and out of the water on a huge pivot pole mounted on a pylon.

He told Bob, "Wait a minute and I will call them." "What? Call them?" said Bob. He was sure thinking this old man is as crazy as a bedbug. Dad walked over and tapped with his pocket knife on the metal barrel that he kept the feed in. Then he threw the floating feed over the net. All of a sudden big waves were coming across the pond, then the water started boiling alive with fish, right over the net. Dad said, "Just wait a minute to let them settle down and see what happens." He pulled the net up just enough to trap the fish, yet they were still under water because the net was deep. Dad walked over and picked up this pole, about twelve to fifteen feet long, with a large dip net on the end, and started dipping out dozens and dozens of *big* fish. I could almost see the open-mouthed, bug-eyed look on my gentle giant's face. They came back toting a couple of five-gallon buckets full of fish.

Bob asked Dad what to do with the two very large fish they took off the net before the explanation of the second "system" started. Dad said, "Well, I have another system." By this time Bob asked no questions. "There is a box," Dad said, pointing to the water. "Put them in there." Bob said, "That doesn't look very big." "Yeah, but it's eight feet deep." Oh!" said Bob.

Dad had built a large box out of redwood slats, with a hinged top, where he could keep fish alive until he would catch enough to give to the preacher or to make a good mess. Then he would just walk down and take them out of his storage system. I suppose you could call it his fish pantry.

If you think that is all of the "systems" that Dad had, wrong! He had another for going to the pond and bringing the heavy buckets full of fish to the house, about 100 or 125 yards from the back gate. He would jump on his golf cart, throw on a couple of buckets full of fish, and away he could go. He would pour them out in the grass, then line them up like little soldiers and take their picture, almost every time he put his systems into action. He had a fish cleaning table in the lower part of the yard. He would then lay them up on the table and take a large claw hammer and whack them on the head. Man, that looked mean. "No, I'm just giving them a little 'claw hammer tea' to deaden their senses while I clean them." He put a large hook on one end of the cleaning table, to hook the fish onto while he skinned them. You also have to be very cautious of the catfish; they will spear you with their long wicked fins. They say they have poison on them, and that causes more pain. Bob believes this to be true because it really is painful to be speared by one.

Bob found out just how dangerous it could be by being

careless cleaning catfish. He had to have six stitches later on for letting a catfish slip while he was skinning it.

Dad's system was to stun the fish, then with a very sharp knife cut a ring in the skin around the head and dorsal fin, down to the tail under the belly meat. Then he would hang the fish on the hook at the skinning table and pull the skin off with downward pulls with the skinning pliers. Last of all, he would cut the fish into steaks with a large heavy knife. He later took to filleting the fish when the great-grandchildren started showing up. He was so afraid one would get a bone.

Nothing in the world was better than Daddy's deep-fried pond-fed channel catfish with home-grown locally ground yellow cornmeal coating them, turning them completely golden when the fish was done. Oh my goodness, I can smell and taste those babies now. Thousands of fat grams and cholesterol slithering off of each bite—no wonder I wound up at the doctor's with blood that had so much fat in it that he told me it looked like milk.

Those days are well remembered and gladly gone as far as the fried fish. Now I oven-fry my fish, without the oil, without the grams, without the cholesterol, without the milky-looking blood test. It's just as good, it looks crispy, and it looks fried. It also tastes fried, tastes crispy, and is good. *Yum!*

I do not in any way mean to lay the blame on Dad for my condition. He was always fussing at me and saying, "Girl, when are you going to lose some weight?" Gee, I miss Dad!

MEXICALI GRILLED FISH FILLETS

Very low in fat

SERVES 4

PREPARATION	:20
COOK	:30
STAND	:00
TOTAL	:50

The onion keeps the fish from sticking, and the fish will take on a wonderful flavor from the onion as does the onion from the fish. Very Heart Healthy. Serve the onions alongside the fish fillets.

1 large onion
4 frozen or fresh fish fillets
1 lemon
½ teaspoon lemon pepper seasoning
¼ teaspoon ground Chimayo pepper (or any ground red chili pepper, but be cautious)
½ teaspoon Mexican oregano or regular oregano, crushed
½ teaspoon ground dry barbecue seasoning

Preheat the oven to 400 degrees, or light a charcoal or gas-fired grill. Spray a flameproof baking pan lightly with vegetable oil cooking spray.

Place frozen fillets in a bowl of cold water to begin to thaw while you are peeling the onion. (I keep a bag of frozen fillets from a large wholesale supplier in the freezer at all times for a quick meal.)

Slice the onion about ¼ inch thick. Arrange the onion slices on the baking pan in a single layer, but touching so that you have a complete layer of onion.

Rinse each piece of fish in cold water and place flat side down on top of the onions.

Hold the lemon under running hot water or place in a bowl of hot water for about 5 minutes; this helps to release the juice. Roll the lemon on the counter with the palm of your hand a few times, then cut in half and squeeze the juice over the fish fillets.

Sprinkle all the seasonings evenly over the fish. Rub gently to smooth and blend the spices. (I use a disposable rubber glove to do this; it keeps the fish and peppers off your skin.)

Place the pan in the oven or on the hot grill and close the lid. Bake until the fish flakes and is tender. This depends on the type of fish, the size of fillets, and the thickness. You will need to be the judge on the amount of total time to cook. This also varies if the fish is frozen or fresh—fresh fish will take less time to cook. Generally about 12 to 15 minutes is sufficient if the grill is very hot.

Seafood is linked with lowering the risk of heart disease; it is low in saturated fat and most of it has very little cholesterol.

TEQUILA FISH

Very low in fat

SERVES 2

PREPARATION	:10
COOK	:15
STAND	:10
TOTAL	:35

1/4 cup tequila
1/4 cup lime juice
1/4 teaspoon paprika
1/2 teaspoon grated orange peel (optional)
2 fish steaks, such as tuna, swordfish, catfish, or your choice
1 large onion
3 tablespoons fat-free sour cream
Salt to taste if desired

Light a charcoal fire, or preheat the oven broiler or a gas-fired grill.

In a pie plate, combine the tequila, lime juice, paprika, and orange peel if using. Rinse the fish steaks under cold water and shake the excess water off. Place the fish in the tequila mixture, turning to coat evenly, and let stand in the marinade for about 5 to 10 minutes, depending on the thickness of the steaks. Have your grill heated to a fairly high heat. If you can hold your hand over the coals for about 3 or 4 seconds, it is just right.

Slice the onion thick. Arrange the slices on a flameproof cooking sheet such as an outdoor griddle or baking sheet. Remove the fish from the marinade; save the marinade liquid. Place the fish steaks on the onion slices and transfer the baking sheet to the grill or the oven; close the lid if using a grill. Bake, turning once, for 12 to 14 minutes or until the fish flakes when touched with a fork. While the fish is cooking, place the marinade liquid in a skillet and bring to a full boil. Keep boiling for 1 to 2 minutes, until the liquid is reduced to about 1/3 cup. Remove from the heat, whisk in the sour cream, and add salt to taste. Spoon the sauce over the fish and serve hot.

GRILLED CATFISH FILLETS

I have referred to the fish story many times, so I have told you the story of Dad's fish in this book. See "Dad's Catfish System" on page 65.

This can marinate for up to 2 hours if you want to do ahead for entertaining.

Very low in fat, depending on fish

SERVES 4

PREPARATION	:15
COOK	:16
STAND	:45
TOTAL	1:16

4 catfish fillets
1 teaspoon vegetable oil
1/4 cup lime juice
1/4 cup tequila
1/2 teaspoon crushed dried red chilies
1 teaspoon each Mexican oregano or regular oregano, sage, and tarragon, dried or fresh
1 large red onion, cut into 1/4-inch-thick slices

Wash the fish fillets and pat them dry. In a large zipper-lock plastic bag combine the oil, lime juice, tequila, chilies, oregano, sage, and tarragon. Mix the marinade well. Place the onion rings in the bag and lay the fish fillets on top. Turn the bag two or three times to cover the fish with marinade. Place the sealed bag in a dish or container (to be sure none leaks out) in your refrigerator. Let marinate for about 20 minutes; turn and continue to marinate for 20 minutes more.

Ten to fifteen minutes before cooking time, preheat a gas-fired grill. Prepare a baking pan by spraying it lightly with vegetable oil cooking spray.

Drain the fish and onions, discarding the marinade. Cover the prepared baking pan with an even layer of onion rings and arrange the fish fillets on top. Place the pan on the grill rack and close the grill top. Cook without turning for about 16 minutes or until the fish is opaque and flakes easily when touched with a fork.

Serve the fillets garnished with the onion rings.

MARINATED HALIBUT STEAKS

Very low-fat (halibut is the lowest in fat among fish)

SERVES 4

PREPARATION	:15
COOK	:16
STAND	:45
TOTAL	1:16

3 tablespoons lime or lemon juice
1 teaspoon minced garlic
1 teaspoon chili powder (Chimayo if available)
1/2 teaspoon ground cumin
1/4 teaspoon ground cinnamon
1/8 teaspoon ground cloves
4 halibut steaks (or any kind of fish steaks desired), about 1 inch thick

Combine in a zipper-lock plastic bag the lime or lemon juice, garlic, chili powder, cumin, cinnamon, and cloves. Knead until blended well.

Wash the fish steaks and pat them dry. Place the steaks in the bag and marinate in the refrigerator, turning to coat evenly a couple of times, for 30 to 45 minutes.

This can be cooked on the grill or in your oven. If cooking outside on a gas-fired grill, spray your grill while it's cold with vegetable oil cooking spray; heat the grill to medium high heat, and place the steaks on the grill for 7 to 8 minutes. Turn and continue to cook for another 7 minutes, or until the fish is opaque and flakes easily when tested with a fork. (Use caution when turning the steaks. Use a wide metal spatula, so they will not get torn up or fall apart.) I use a baking sheet even on the grill.

If cooking in the oven, preheat it to 400 degrees. Spray a baking sheet lightly with cooking spray and place the steaks on the sheet. Bake for approximately 7 minutes on each side. Turn halfway through the baking time, using a nice wide metal spatula so as not to tear the fish steaks up.

FILLETS OF ORANGE ROUGHY

1 gram fat per serving

SERVES 2

PREPARATION	:15
COOK	:16
STAND	:45
TOTAL	1:16

4 orange roughy fillets (frozen)
1 large onion
1/2 cup lime juice
1/2 teaspoon crushed dried basil
1/2 teaspoon fresh thyme, chopped fine
1/2 teaspoon paprika
1/2 teaspoon ground black pepper
1/4 teaspoon salt
1/8 teaspoon ground red pepper (cayenne)

Place the fillets in cold water to begin thawing. Spray a heavy rectangular baking pan with vegetable oil cooking spray. Slice the onion about 1/4 inch thick. Make four rows of onion slices across the pan for the orange roughy fillets. When the fillets are partially thawed, by the time you get the onions sliced and arranged on the baking sheet, remove them from the water and cover with the lime juice to marinate for about 40 minutes.

Meanwhile, mix the spices to be rubbed into the fillets. Preheat the oven to 350 degrees. When ready to bake, drain off the lime juice and rub the spices into the fish on both sides. Lay the fillets flat side down on the onion slices. Bake for about 12 to 16 minutes, depending on how large and thick the fillets are, or until flaky when touched with a fork. Serve with fat-free tartar sauce if desired, or with a wedge of lime or lemon.

QUICK & EASY FISH BAKE

Very low-fat (depends on fish)

SERVES 4

PREPARATION	:10
COOK	:20
STAND	:00
TOTAL	:30

You can use almost any type of fillets with this recipe. A nice dish to entertain with, except your house will smell a little like fish, but good.

1 large or 2 medium onions
3/4 cup picante sauce
4 fish fillets (about 1 pound)
1 cup corn flake crumbs, potato buds, or cornmeal
4 slices lemon or lime (optional)

Lightly spray a rectangular baking dish, large enough for the fillets to fit in one layer, with vegetable oil cooking spray. This will make the dish easier to clean. Preheat the oven to 350 degrees.

Slice the onion into 1/4-inch-thick slices. Do not separate the slices into rings. Place the slices in a single layer covering the bottom of the dish. You may need 2 onions, depending on the size.

Pour 1/4 cup of the picante sauce over the onions. Put the crumbs into a shallow dish, such as a pie plate, and coat the fillets evenly. Arrange the fillets without touching over the onion rings.

Pour the remaining picante over the fillets. Lay a slice of lemon or lime over each fillet. Bake uncovered and without turning for 15 to 20 minutes, until the fish flakes easily. Serve with Potato Spears (page 174) and Coleslaw (page 160) along with Corn Bread (page 206) or Fiesta Corn Muffins (page 205). Don't forget a nice before-dinner drink like Margaritas (page 242), and, for dessert, Apple Coffee Cake (page 237) or Praline Rice Pudding (page 230).

FISH FILLETS IN WINE SAUCE

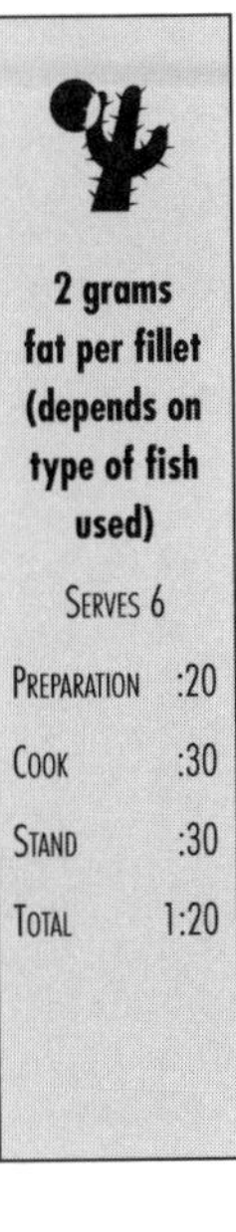

Use any type of fish fillets you prefer. I like to use catfish.

3/4 cup plus 1/2 cup white wine
4 tablespoons lime juice
6 small firm white fish fillets (about 2 pounds)
1 large or 2 medium-size fresh Anaheim chilies
3 sprigs fresh cilantro
3/4 cup very thin white onion rings
2 green onions, sliced thin
1 clove garlic, crushed in a press
1/4 teaspoon finely chopped fresh jalapeño pepper (optional)
1 1/2 cups quartered small mushroom caps
1 teaspoon minced fresh thyme
Salt and pepper to taste
1 to 2 teaspoons cornstarch
1/3 cup cold lemon juice or lime juice

Mix 3/4 cup of wine and 2 tablespoons of lime juice in a glass bowl large enough to dip the fish fillets in. Set aside.

Wash the fish fillets in cold water and drain them. With a fork, prick holes in both sides of the fillets. Dip the fillets in the marinade and rub with the marinade to coat each piece completely. Refrigerate the fish in the marinade for at least 30 minutes; turn the fish after about 15 minutes.

While the fish are marinating, roast the Anaheims according to the instructions on page 40. (While they are steaming, don't forget to turn the fish fillets over.) Carefully peel off the charred skin, as instructed; seed, rinse, and chop. Set aside.

Preheat the oven to 350 degrees.

Drain the fish fillets (reserve the marinade mixture) and arrange on a baking sheet lightly coated with vegetable oil cooking spray. Bake for approximately 20 minutes, or until the fish flakes apart when tested with a fork. Remove from the oven and cover with foil to keep warm.

Chop a couple of sprigs of cilantro into small pieces.

Combine in a skillet the roasted Anaheims, white and green onions, garlic, jalapeño pepper, mushrooms, thyme. Sauté in 2 tablespoons of water until the onions are tender, abut 4 minutes. Spoon into a separate container to keep warm.

Pour the marinade into the sauté skillet and bring to a boil, adding the additional ½ cup of white wine.

Combine the cornstarch and ⅓ cup lemon or lime juice in a cup and stir to dissolve. The amount of cornstarch will depend on how you like your sauce, thick, medium, or thin. When the marinade starts to boil, start adding a little of the lemon mixture, just about a teaspoonful at a time. Keep stirring with a whisk and keep adding until the right texture; stop just before it gets thicker than you like it. If you do get it too thick, add a little more wine.

Place the fish fillets on a serving platter. Spoon the onion and mushroom sauté down the centers of the fillets. Place the hot wine sauce in a gravy boat and serve alongside the fish so that each person may add as much or little as desired. Sprinkle the remaining 2 tablespoons of lime juice over the fish. Keep very hot and serve immediately.

You can have many of your all-time favorite dishes. Just train yourself to replace and rethink the recipe before you cook it. Replace items such as cheeses, milk, eggs, mayonnaise, and so forth with a nonfat version of the same. Check the labels and see how many fat grams you save just by doing this.

Chapter 4

Poultry

SPICY GRILLED CHICKEN

3 grams fat per serving

SERVES 4

PREPARATION	:20
COOK	:15
STAND	:10
TOTAL	:45

4 boneless skinless chicken breast halves
1/4 cup lemon juice
1 teaspoon Mexican oregano or regular oregano, crushed
1 teaspoon chili powder
1/2 teaspoon garlic powder

Light a charcoal fire, or preheat a gas-fired grill to medium high or the oven to 375 degrees.

Wash the chicken pieces and pat them dry. Place them in a shallow bowl or zipper-lock plastic bag and cover with lemon juice. Turn to coat; let marinate about 10 minutes. Drain the chicken and discard the lemon juice. While the chicken is draining, combine the oregano, chili powder, and garlic powder; stir to combine. Rub the chicken pieces with the mixture.

Place the chicken on an oiled grill rack or on a baking sheet lightly coated with vegetable oil cooking spray. Grill for about 7 minutes. (If chicken pieces are thinner, you may need to turn sooner and cook a little less time.) Turn and continue grilling for 5 minutes or until cooked through. Serve with a nice green salad.

Variation: Grilled Chicken Salad

Cut the chicken into strips or slices while still hot and serve atop a green salad.

Many kinds of mustard add zesty flavors to your foods; watch for the fat-free. Mix a little mustard and honey and spread on meats and poultry for a pick-me-up flavor.

LEMON CHICKEN

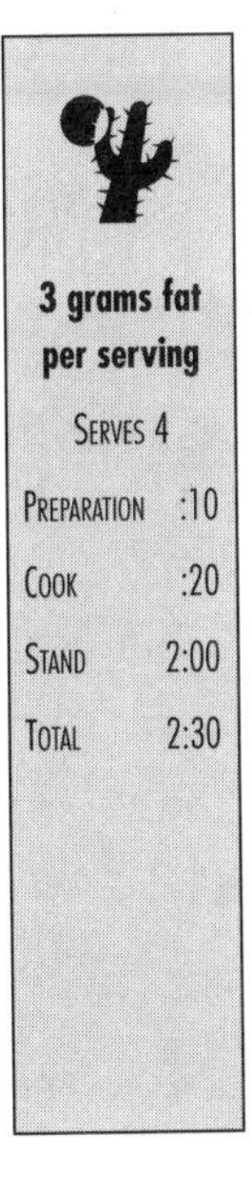

1/2 cup lemon juice
1/2 cup orange juice
3 cloves garlic, chopped fine
1 teaspoon Mexican oregano or regular oregano, crushed
1 teaspoon ground ginger
4 boneless skinless chicken breast halves

Combine in a small mixing bowl, or a zipper-lock plastic bag, the lemon and orange juice, garlic, oregano, and ginger. Place the chicken in the marinade and refrigerate for at least two hours. Turn a couple of times to be sure all the chicken is evenly coated.

Drain off the marinade and discard. Grill or broil the chicken, or cook in a nonstick skillet, as desired. Cook about 7 to 10 minutes on each side, depending on the thickness of the chicken breasts.

CORNMEAL-CRUSTED CHICKEN

4 grams fat per serving

Serves 4

Preparation	:35
Cook	:15
Stand	:00
Total	:50

4 boneless skinless chicken breast halves
1/2 cup egg substitute
3/4 cup yellow cornmeal
1/2 teaspoon lemon pepper
1/4 teaspoon ground red pepper (cayenne)
Dash of salt if desired
1/4 cup grated fat-free Parmesan cheese (packaged is fine)
2 tablespoons lime juice

Rinse and drain the chicken breasts. Place one at a time in a large zipper-lock plastic bag. Leaving the bag unzipped, use a meat mallet to pound the chicken to 1/3 to 1/4 inch thick. Repeat with each remaining breast. This can be done ahead of time and the chicken stored in the refrigerator in the sealed bag.

Set two shallow bowls or pie plates on the counter. Place the egg substitute in one bowl, the cornmeal mixed with the lemon pepper, red pepper, salt, and cheese in the other bowl. Rub the chicken with the lime juice. Dip one piece of chicken at a time in the egg substitute and then coat evenly with the cornmeal mixture. If you have time, place on a wire rack to dry out a little.

These can be grilled or baked in a 400 degree oven. If grilling, make sure the grill is very hot, spray the grate fairly heavily with vegetable oil cooking spray, then place the chicken on the grill and spray the top of each piece lightly. Cook for 5 to 7 minutes, turn carefully with spatula, and continue to cook about 5 minutes on the other side, or until the chicken is tender and lightly browned.

The same procedure can be used if baking in the oven. Spray the pan and top of the chicken, and turn halfway through cooking time. Serve with salsa if desired.

COLA CHICKEN

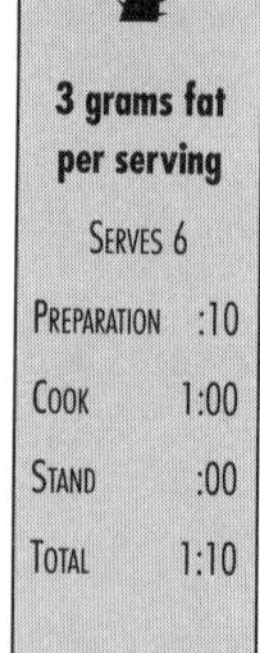

6 boneless skinless chicken breast halves
1 small bottle mild or medium picante sauce
1 (6-ounce) can Coca-Cola (no substitutes)

Preheat the oven to 350 degrees. Arrange the chicken in a single layer in a 7 x 11-inch baking dish. (You might want to spray the dish with vegetable oil cooking spray to help with the cleanup.)

Pour the picante sauce over the chicken. Pour the Coca-Cola over all. Bake for 1 hour, turning the chicken after the first ½ hour.

CCC STIR-FRY ONE-DISH MEAL

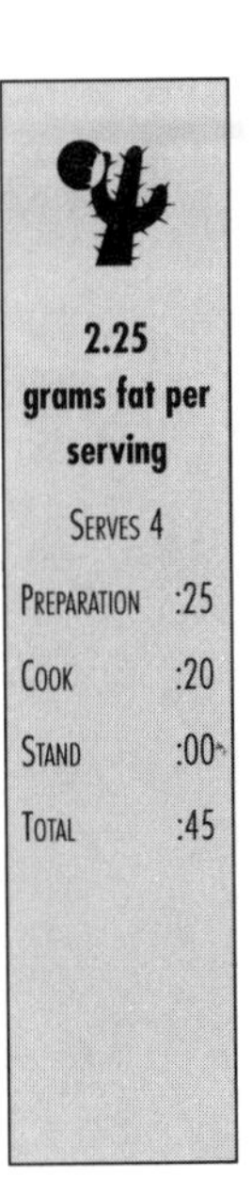

3 cups cubed cooked chicken white meat (or cubed fresh boneless chicken breasts)
1/2 teaspoon Mexican seasoning
1 cup finely chopped celery
3/4 cup chopped frozen or fresh onion
3/4 cup chopped frozen or fresh green peppers
1 teaspoon chopped green chilies
1 1/2 to 2 cups chopped cabbage
1 cup frozen or canned whole-kernel corn
1/8 teaspoon ground cumin

Preheat a nonstick wok or skillet for about 3 minutes on high heat. Add the chicken and let it brown for just about a minute. Stir, lower the heat to medium high, and continue to brown while adding the remaining ingredients:

Sprinkle Mexican seasoning over the chicken, stirring to distribute evenly. Continue browning; add the celery, onion, and green peppers, stirring after each addition. Add the green chilies and cumin and let cook about 2 more minutes, or until the chicken is done. If using fresh chicken this will take a little longer, if using frozen or leftover cooked chicken, it will be according to this recipe.

Add the cabbage and stir about 1 minute. Add the corn (if frozen, turn the heat up just a little for 1 minute, then adjust back to medium high). Continue cooking until all is hot and the cabbage wilted and crisp-tender.

CHICKEN POTATO STIR-FRY

5 grams fat entire dish

SERVES 2

PREPARATION	:04
COOK	:20
STAND	:00
TOTAL	:24

This is a very fast dish.

2 cups diced frozen chicken white meat (see Note)
1/2 cup diced green peppers
1/2 cup chopped onions
1 large potato, peeled and cut into very small thin pieces (here you could use frozen small-cut hash browns or a leftover baked potato)
1 teaspoon Mexican oregano or regular oregano, crushed
1/4 teaspoon or more chili powder (put in a pinch and taste)
1/4 cup juice from Ro-Tel (10-ounce can) tomatoes

Spray a nonstick skillet very lightly with vegetable oil cooking spray and place over high heat until your skillet gets hot. Pay attention to what you are doing—don't leave the skillet unattended.

Pour the frozen chicken or leftover chicken cut into small pieces into the hot skillet. Stir for a minute; add the peppers, onions, and potato. Stir to mix; keep watching and stir occasionally as the mixture cooks. The potatoes will start to brown along with the rest; stir to scrape the nice brown up from the bottom. After about 10 minutes, add the oregano, chili powder, and tomato juice. Lower the heat and continue to cook as well as stir for about 10 more minutes. If everything looks done and is soft except the potatoes, you may want to add 1/4 cup hot water to soften the potatoes, cooking about 1 more minute.

Note: I find mine in a large wholesale-type store such as Sam's; great to keep on hand for quick-fix meals or casseroles. The diced green pepper and onion are also available, and I also keep bags of each on hand in the freezer.

LIME CHICKEN

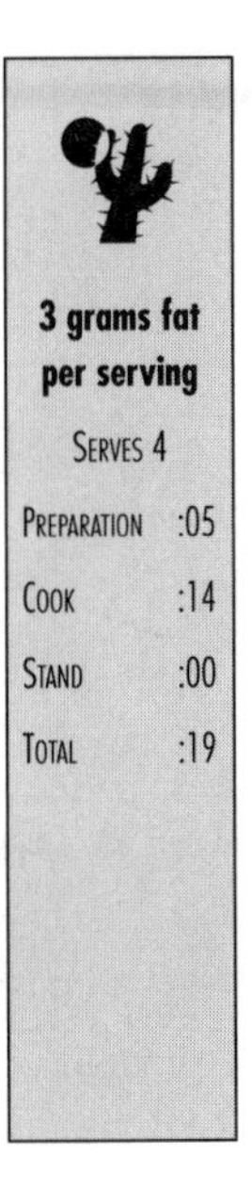

4 boneless skinless chicken breast halves
1 medium lime
1 cup apple juice or apple cider
2 tablespoons cornstarch
3/4 teaspoon instant chicken bouillon granules

Place the chicken breasts in a hot nonstick skillet and cook until browned on each side and no longer pink. You may need to lower the heat just a bit before you are finished, so as not to burn the chicken, but do have the heat up enough to brown the meat nicely, then finish cooking at a lower heat, about 8 to 10 minutes.

While the chicken is cooking, remove the peel from the fresh lime, cut it into thin strips, and place half the strips in a small bowl. (Reserve the rest for garnish.) Squeeze 1 tablespoon of fresh juice from the lime; add to the bowl along with the apple juice, cornstarch, and chicken bouillon granules. Stir well to blend the juices and cornstarch.

Remove the chicken pieces from the skillet and cover loosely with foil to keep warm. Very carefully add the lime juice mixture to the skillet, stirring with a wire whisk. Cook and stir until thick and bubbly. Continue to cook and stir for an additional 2 minutes.

To serve, slice each breast into medallions or rounds about 1 inch thick. Place on a plate or serving dish; spoon some of the sauce over each serving. Pass the remaining sauce in a gravy boat.

Garnish with the remaining lime peel strips and/or a slice of lime, twisted and standing up on the side of the plate. Serve with steamed carrots, Fried Rice (page 187) or Garlic Mashed Potatoes (page 176) and Marilyn's Santa Fe Roasted Corn (page 163).

CHICKEN BREASTS IN WHITE WINE SAUCE

3 grams fat per serving

SERVES 4

PREPARATION :30

COOK :35

STAND :00

TOTAL 1:05

This is a very nice little wine sauce to dress up chicken or other meats—good enough to serve to any guests any day. Add a touch of Mexican flavor if desired: half a teaspoon of Mexican seasoning or ground red pepper will make the chicken sing ¡Olé, José!

3/4 cup sliced fresh mushrooms
2 green onions, sliced thin
1 teaspoon crushed dried basil
1 clove garlic, crushed, or 1/2 teaspoon prepared garlic
1/2 cup fat-free chicken broth
1/2 cup dry white wine, or as needed
Dash of salt (optional)
Dash of pepper
1/2 teaspoon Mexican seasoning (optional) or 1/2 teaspoon ground red pepper (cayenne) (optional)
4 nice-size skinless chicken breast halves, bone in
1 tablespoon cornstarch

Spray a large nonstick skillet with vegetable oil cooking spray. Sauté the mushrooms, onions, basil, and garlic over medium heat for 4 minutes or until the onion is tender. With a wire whisk, stir in the chicken broth, wine, salt, black pepper, and Mexican seasoning or red pepper if desired. Arrange the chicken breasts evenly spaced in the skillet. Bring to a boil over high heat, then lower the heat, cover, and simmer for 30 minutes or until the chicken is no longer pink.

Transfer the chicken pieces to a serving platter and tent with foil to keep warm while you finish the sauce. Mix 1 tablespoon of cold water and the tablespoon of cornstarch in a small dish or custard cup, with a very small wire whisk if available. Strain the liquid out of the skillet into a glass measuring cup, reserving the solids. If there is not enough liquid to make 1 cup, add enough wine to finish filling. Pour back into the skillet. Add the cornstarch mixture slowly, stirring with a wire whisk to prevent any lumps. Continue to cook until thickened, about 2 additional minutes. Return the mushrooms and onions to the pan and stir. Spoon the sauce over the chicken pieces and serve.

CHICKEN ROLL-UPS

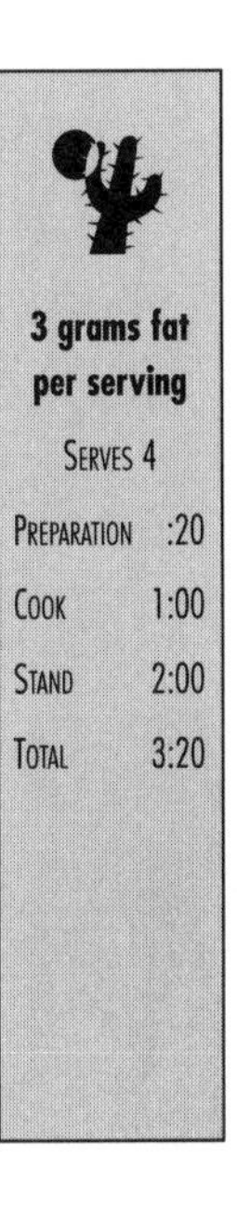

A very nice day-ahead dish to make for entertaining or just for the family.

3/4 cup sliced celery
1/2 cup sliced fresh mushrooms
3/4 cup chopped onion
1 clove garlic, minced
1/2 cup canned chopped green chilies
1/2 cup minced green bell pepper
1 (8-ounce) can diced Just for Chili brand (spicy) canned tomatoes
1 (8-ounce) can tomato sauce
1/4 teaspoon sugar
4 boneless skinless chicken breast halves
1/2 cup fat-free ricotta or cottage cheese, drained
4 tablespoons shredded fat-free Cheddar cheese
1 tablespoon snipped fresh parsley
1/2 cup shredded fat-free mozzarella cheese

First make the sauce: Spray a large nonstick saucepan or skillet with vegetable oil cooking spray while the pan is cold. Place over moderate heat. Add the celery, mushrooms, onion, garlic, green chilies, and green pepper. Cook until the onion is crisp-tender. Add the tomatoes, tomato sauce, and sugar to the mixture. Bring up to boiling; lower the heat to a simmer. Cook uncovered for 20 minutes or until the mixture is reduced to about 2 cups. Remove from the heat and let cool.

While the sauce is cooling, prepare the chicken: Place one piece at a time between two pieces of waxed paper or plastic wrap; pound with a meat mallet until about ¼ inch thick.

In a small bowl, combine the ricotta, Cheddar cheese, and parsley. Stir to mix together. Place the chicken pieces flat on a work surface and spoon about ¼ of this cheese mixture down the center of each. Fold the long sides in to lap over, then roll up from the short end.

Place the chicken rolls seam side down in an 8-inch square baking dish, sprayed with vegetable oil cooking spray for easy cleanup. Pour the cooled sauce mixture over the chicken rolls. Cover with foil, sealing around all sides well. Refrigerate from 2 to 24 hours.

When ready to serve, take the baking dish out of the refrigerator about 10 minute before placing in the oven. Bake covered at 350 degrees for 35 to 40 minutes or until chicken is no longer pink. Remove the foil, sprinkle mozzarella cheese evenly over the top, and bake an additional 3 to 4 minutes, or until the cheese is melted.

Serve with a nice side of rice and a green vegetable such as green beans.

In an average day, many of us—an estimated one out of ten—have no fruit. I used to have none. Three things I hated: fruit, fish, and exercise. I still hate exercise, but I try to make myself walk, time permitting. I have learned to love fresh fruit (canned I am still working on). I also have learned how much vitamin B and C and fiber we gain from eating fruit. I am working on the fish side. I have trained myself to eat a little, not too much. Still working on it.

HEALTHY HAPPY CHICKEN ENCHILADAS

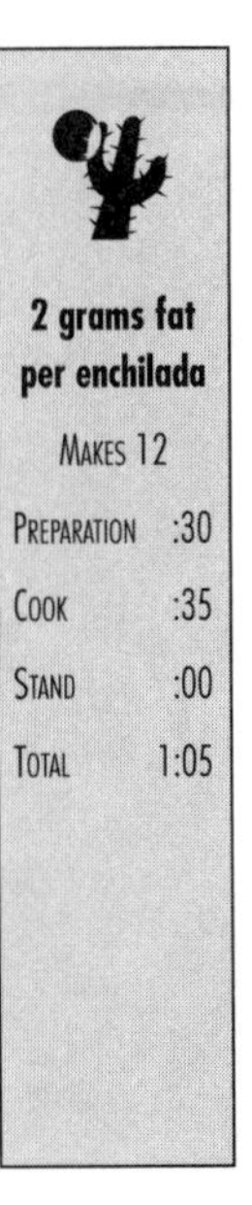

Don't tell me you can't have your enchiladas and eat them too.

1 (8-ounce) container fat-free sour cream
1 (10¾-ounce) can 99% fat-free cream of chicken soup
1 (4-ounce) can chopped green chilies, drained
12 (7-inch) fat-free flour tortillas
1 cup shredded fat-free Cheddar cheese
1½ cups finely chopped cooked chicken breast
2 to 3 green onions, sliced thin

Preheat the oven to 350 degrees. Lightly coat a 9 x 13-inch baking dish with vegetable oil cooking spray.

In a medium-size mixing bowl, combine the sour cream, soup, and chilies; mix well.

Place the tortillas on a work surface. Spoon about 3 tablespoons of the sour cream mixture down the center of each tortilla. Reserving ¼ cup of the shredded cheese, sprinkle each tortilla with some of the remaining cheese, the chicken, and onions. Roll up the tortillas (you may need to stab them with a toothpick to keep together temporarily) and fit them seam side down and touching in the prepared baking dish. Spoon the remaining sour cream mixture over the tortillas. Cover with foil.

Place in the oven and bake for 25 to 30 minutes or until bubbly and hot. Remove the foil, sprinkle with reserved shredded cheese, and bake uncovered for an additional 5 minutes or until the cheese is melted. If desired, garnish with shredded lettuce and chopped fresh tomatoes.

PEPPER-JELLY BAG CHICKEN

3 grams fat per serving

SERVES 4

PREPARATION	:20
COOK	:45
STAND	:00
TOTAL	1:05

This makes a very nice thick sweet and sour sauce.

1 cup red pepper jelly
1 envelope onion soup mix
3/4 cup honey
4 skinless boneless chicken breast halves, or 2 skinned split whole breasts
1 tablespoon all-purpose flour

Preheat the oven to 350 degrees.

In a small mixing bowl, combine the pepper jelly, onion soup mix, and honey; stir to mix well. Let stand while you are washing and preparing the chicken. Rinse the chicken and trim away any visible fat.

Prepare a large (14 x 20-inch) oven baking bag according to the manufacturer's directions. Put the flour in the bag and shake to coat it. Place the bag inside a large baking dish at least 2 inches deep. Put the chicken pieces in the bag, arranging them evenly spaced. Pour the pepper jelly mixture over the chicken, turning a couple of times to coat evenly. Close the bag with the provided tie; punch holes in the top as directed to let the steam escape.

Bake for 45 to 50 minutes, turning the chicken pieces over about halfway through baking time. Serve with rice.

Variation: Place 3 to 4 cups of cooked rice in the bag, place chicken on top, pour sauce over all, and bake.

AFTER THE HOLIDAYS TURKEY ENCHILADAS WITH TOMATILLO–GREEN CHILE SAUCE

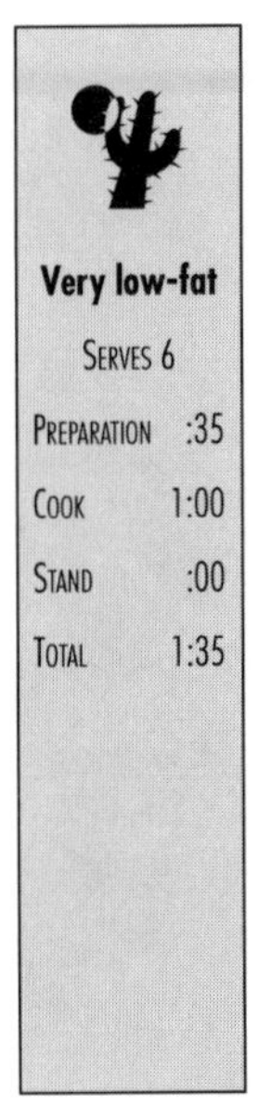

3/4 cup chopped onion
1 teaspoon minced garlic
1 large (about 1 pound) zucchini, quartered lengthwise and sliced thin crosswise (quarter-moon shapes)
1 1/2 teaspoons ground cumin
1/2 teaspoon Mexican oregano or regular oregano, crushed
1 pound chopped cooked turkey (2 cups)
3/4 cup shredded fat-free Monterey Jack cheese
12 (6-inch) corn tortillas
Tomatillo–Green Chile Sauce, homemade (page 202) or commercial
Fat-free sour cream for garnish

Preheat the oven to 350 degrees. Coat the bottom of a 13 x 9-inch baking pan with vegetable oil cooking spray.

In a large nonstick skillet, cook and stir the onion over medium-high heat for 3 to 4 minutes or until crisp-tender. Reduce the heat to medium and add the garlic. Cook and stir 3 to 4 more minutes or until the onion is light golden brown. Add the zucchini, 2 tablespoons of water, the cumin, and oregano. Cover and cook over medium heat for 8 to 10 minutes, just until the zucchini is tender. Stir a couple of times during cooking. Add the turkey and stir in the cheese. Remove from the heat; set aside.

Heat a nonstick griddle over medium-high heat. Dip one of the tortillas in hot water, just in and out; shake off the excess water and lay the tortilla flat on the hot griddle. Heat for 10 to 15 seconds on each side, or until limp and flexible. Repeat with remaining tortillas, stacking them as they are warmed.

Put about 1/4 cup of filling down the center of each tortilla and fold the sides over to enclose. Place seam side down in the prepared baking dish. Spread the top of each with some of the tomatillo sauce. If you are using a commercial sauce, be careful it is not too hot to bear.

Cover tightly with foil; bake for 30 to 40 minutes or until heated through. Serve garnished with the remaining tomatillo sauce along with a dollop of fat-free sour cream.

6.25 grams fat per serving

SERVES 8

PREPARATION	:40
COOK	:55
STAND	:00
TOTAL	1:35

TURKEY TORTILLA CASSEROLE

2 pounds extra-lean ground turkey
1 cup chopped onion
1 clove garlic, chopped
1 (15-ounce) can tomato sauce
1 (4-ounce) can chopped green chilies, drained
1 package taco seasoning
1 teaspoon chili powder
12 (6-inch) corn tortillas
1 (10¾-ounce) can Healthy Request cream of chicken soup
¾ cup skim milk
2 cups shredded fat-free Cheddar or Mexican cheese

Preheat the oven to 350 degrees. Lightly spray a 13 x 9-inch baking dish with vegetable oil cooking spray.

Brown the turkey, onion, and garlic in a nonstick skillet over medium-high heat, stirring, for about 10 minutes. Place in a colander and rinse under very hot water to remove any fat. Shake excess water off. Place the meat mixture in a bowl; add the tomato sauce, chilies, and spices. Mix well.

Arrange 6 of the tortillas in the bottom of the prepared baking dish. Pour the turkey mixture over the tortillas. Arrange the remaining 6 tortillas over the turkey. Spread the undiluted soup over the tortillas, pour the milk over the soup. Sprinkle evenly with shredded cheese.

Bake uncovered for 45 minutes, until hot and bubbly.

STIR-FRY CHICKEN TACOS

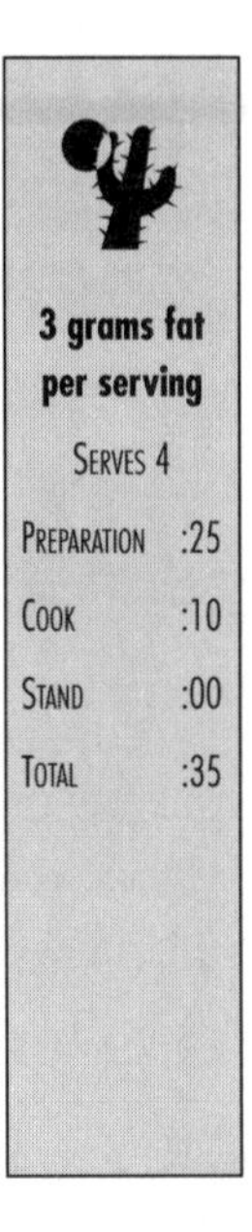

2 medium red or green bell peppers
2 fresh New Mexico or Anaheim green chilies
2 fresh jalapeño chilies (1 ounce prepared)
1 pound boneless skinless chicken breasts
2 cloves garlic, minced
1 teaspoon ground cumin, or to taste
1/4 cup chopped fresh cilantro
Salt and pepper to taste
12 warm (6- or 7-inch) fat-free flour tortillas (see Note)
Lime wedges and fat-free sour cream for garnish

Stem and seed the bell peppers, green chilies, and jalapeños (be sure to use rubber gloves). Cut all the peppers into thin slivers.

Cut the chicken crosswise into thin slices about 3 inches long.

Place a nonstick skillet over high heat until fairly hot. Add the chicken and stir-fry until the chicken is opaque throughout, 4 or 5 minutes. Remove the chicken to a serving dish. Return the pan to the heat, add the garlic and cumin; stir-fry for about 1 minute, being careful not to let the garlic burn. Add the bell pepper and chilies. Stir-fry until they begin to wilt, about 2 more minutes. Return the chicken to the pan; add chopped cilantro, and salt and pepper to taste. Stir to mix evenly and transfer to a serving dish.

Serve with warm tortillas. To assemble a taco, fill a tortilla with chicken mixture, squeeze a lime wedge over the filling, and add a bit of sour cream. Enjoy!

Note: To warm tortillas, stack them on top of each other and wrap tightly in aluminum foil. Heat for 10 to 12 minutes in a 350 degree oven. Or wrap loosely in waxed paper and microwave; a stack of 6 tortillas will take 45 to 60 seconds at full power.

CHICKEN TAMALE PIE

2.5 grams fat per serving

SERVES 4

PREPARATION	:30
COOK	:45
STAND	:00
TOTAL	1:15

Make ahead, make with leftover chicken, make with frozen chicken, or use canned low-fat chicken, drained. You may also use turkey, left from the holidays.

1 medium-size onion, chopped (about 2/3 cup)
1 1/2 cups cubed skinless boneless chicken white meat
1 tablespoon chopped green chilies
1 tablespoon chili powder, or to taste
1 (14 1/2-ounce) can low-sodium tomatoes
1 cup corn kernels
1 cup chopped green bell pepper
1 (16-ounce) can chili hot beans, drained
1 teaspoon Mexican oregano or regular oregano, crushed

TOPPING:

1/2 cup cornmeal
1/2 cup all-purpose flour
1 1/2 teaspoons baking powder
1/3 cup skim milk
1/4 cup egg substitute

Preheat the oven to 400 degrees. Coat a medium-size casserole with vegetable oil cooking spray.

Heat a nonstick skillet to medium hot; add the onion, chicken, green chilies, and chili powder. Cook and stir over medium heat until the chicken is browned. (If using left-over cooked or frozen cooked chicken, cook until it is heated and lightly browned, and the onions are tender.) Add the tomatoes, juice and all, corn, bell pepper, beans and oregano.

Continue stirring until all is heated and well mixed. Spoon into the prepared casserole and place in the oven for about 10 minutes while you prepare the cornbread topping.

Combine the cornmeal, flour, and baking powder in a zipper-lock plastic bag; shake to mix. (Don't forget to zip the bag!) When mixed, open the bag; add the milk and egg substitute. Close and knead to mix the ingredients. Cut one corner off the bag and squeeze the batter over the casserole. Reduce the oven heat to 375 degrees. Continue to bake for about 20 to 25 more minutes or until a toothpick inserted near the center of the cornbread comes out clean. Serve a bowl of spicy salsa on the side.

CHICKEN OLÉ (MEAL-IN-ONE CASSEROLE)

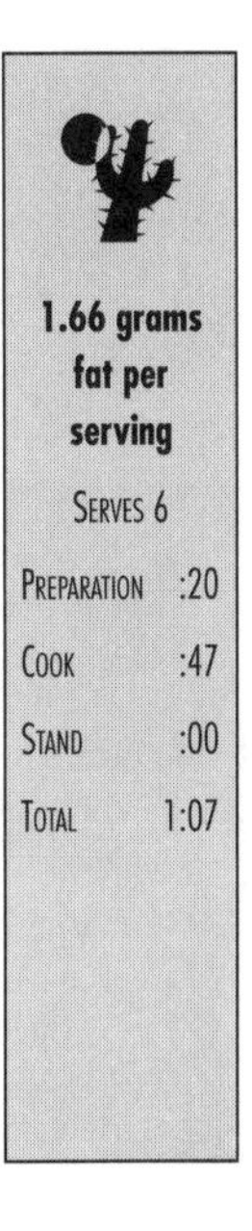

1 1/2 pounds raw white-meat chicken, cut into tiny pieces or ground
1 cup finely chopped onion
1 cup thick and chunky salsa
1/4 cup water
1 (1 1/4-ounce) package taco seasoning
1 cup whole-kernel corn
1/2 teaspoon jalapeño juice (from jar of canned jalapeños)
1 (8 1/2-ounce) package corn muffin mix, plus egg substitute and skim milk
1 cup shredded fat-free Cheddar cheese
1 (4-ounce) can chopped green chilies

Preheat the oven to 350 degrees. Lightly coat an 8-inch square baking dish with vegetable oil cooking spray.

Heat a large nonstick skillet and cook the chicken along with the onion, stirring and browning until no pink is left. Place in a colander and rinse with your hottest water to remove all traces of fat. Shake slightly to get rid of any excess water. Wash the skillet; return to the heat. Pour the meat mixture into the skillet, adding the salsa, water, and taco seasoning. Bring to a boil, stir, reduce the heat, and continue to cook for 5 to 6 minutes or until the mixture begins to thicken.

Stir in the corn and jalapeño juice. Pour into the prepared baking dish.

Prepare the muffin mix according to package directions *except* substitute egg substitute for the eggs, leave out the oil, and use skim milk. Don't let any mean old grams slip in on you. Stir in the cheese and green chilies until smooth. Pour over the meat mixture, spreading to distribute evenly, to within about 1/4 inch of the edge of the baking dish.

Bake for 25 to 30 minutes, or until the top is golden brown and done to the touch.

Serve with extra salsa on the side. A little fat-free sour cream is also nice with this dish.

Variation: This can become Turkey Olé if you substitute an equal amount of fresh ground turkey for the chicken. Or for Beef Olé, use very lean ground round.

CHICKEN ENCHILADA BAKE

Fat from chicken: 3.5 grams per 3 ounces

SERVES 4

PREPARATION	:25
COOK	:40
STAND	:05
TOTAL	1:10

This recipe is great for leftover chicken.

30 low-fat, baked white or yellow tortilla chips
1 medium onion, chopped
1 medium green bell pepper, chopped
2 to 3 teaspoons chili powder, or to taste
2 cups diced fresh tomatoes, or diced canned tomatoes, drained
1 1/2 cups diced cooked chicken white meat
1 cup low-fat or fat-free (if available) onion and garlic gravy, or 1 cup mild salsa
1/2 cup shredded fat-free Cheddar cheese

Lightly coat a 9-inch square baking dish with vegetable oil cooking spray. Preheat the oven to 375 degrees.

Reserve 6 chips; crush the remainder into bite-size pieces. Spread the broken chips over the bottom of the prepared baking dish.

Spray a nonstick skillet lightly with cooking spray. Sauté the onion, pepper, and chili powder for 2 to 3 minutes, stirring often. Remove from the heat. Stir in the tomatoes, chicken, and the gravy or salsa. Spoon this mixture over the chips. Cover with foil and bake for 30 minutes.

Remove the foil, crush the reserved chips, and sprinkle over the casserole. Cover the chips with the shredded cheese. Return to the oven and bake uncovered for 8 to 10 minutes or until the cheese is melted.

Serve immediately, or this is a good make-ahead dish. Prepare the casserole, cover with foil, and refrigerate or freeze. Bake for 45 to 50 minutes, until heated through; remove the foil, add crushed chips and cheese, and return to bake an additional 10 minutes.

Tortillas: To make them limp and flexible, dip them in hot fat-free broth. Chicken or vegetable broth instead of hot fat will also give a creamy texture to refried beans.

Very low-fat

SERVES 6

PREPARATION	:45
COOK	:45
STAND	:05
TOTAL	1:35

ENCHILADA CASSEROLE

3 cups Spicy Tomato Sauce (page 199) or 3 (8-ounce) cans tomato sauce plus spices of your choice
1 (10-ounce) package frozen whole-kernel corn, thawed and drained
2 cups finely chopped cooked chicken white meat
1 1/4 cups shredded fat-free Monterey Jack cheese
1 (4-ounce) can diced green chilies
12 (6-inch) corn tortillas
1 lime, cut into 6 wedges, and fat-free sour cream (optional) for garnish

Lightly spray a 13 x 9-inch baking dish with vegetable oil cooking spray. Preheat the oven to 375 degrees.

Combine 2 cups of tomato sauce, the corn, chicken, 1 cup of the cheese, and the green chilies in a mixing bowl and stir well.

Cut each tortilla into 4 wedges. Place one-third of the tortilla wedges in the bottom of the prepared baking dish, overlapping to make a solid layer. Spread half the meat mixture on top. Repeat with another layer of tortilla wedges, the remaining meat mixture, and the remaining tortillas. Spread the remaining cup of tomato sauce over the top. Cover with foil.

Bake 30 to 40 minutes or until heated through. Remove the foil and sprinkle the remaining 1/4 cup of cheese evenly over the casserole. Return to the oven and continue to bake an additional 5 minutes or until the cheese melts.

Serve with wedges of lime, to be squeezed over individual servings. Place a dollop of fat-free sour cream atop each serving after the lime juice is squeezed on.

Variation: Instead of chicken you could use 2 cups of chopped cooked pork loin (see Pork Loin Ablaze page 110) or 10 to 12 ounces of fresh crabmeat or surumi flakes.

CHICKEN CHILI CASSEROLE

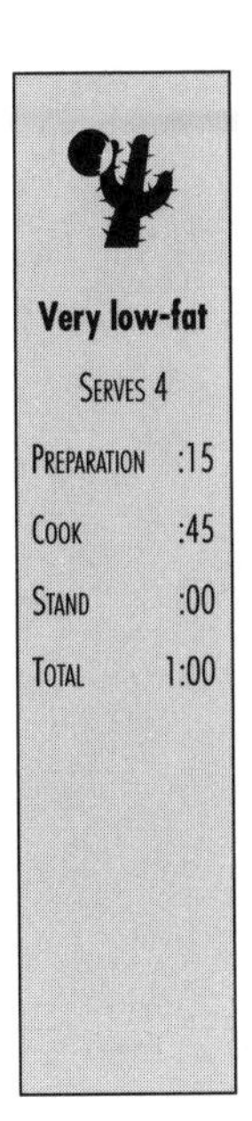

This is a good use for leftover chicken—or try it with turkey left over at the holidays.

6 to 8 tortillas
1 (10¾-ounce) can Healthy Request cream of mushroom soup
1 (10¾-ounce) can Healthy Request cream of chicken soup
½ cup skim milk
1 cup chopped onion
4 cups diced cooked chicken
1 (7-ounce) can chopped green chilies
Salt and pepper to taste
1½ cups shredded fat-free cheese (such as Cheddar)

Preheat the oven to 325 degrees. Spray a medium-large casserole with vegetable oil cooking spray.

Cut the tortillas into 1-inch strips; set aside.

In a mixing bowl, combine the soups, milk, and onion and salt and pepper to taste. Cover the bottom of the prepared casserole with a layer of the soups, using about ¼ of the mixture. Add a layer of half the tortilla strips. Add all the chicken, then spread the chilies evenly over the chicken. Layer on the remaining tortillas. Add the remainder of the soup mixture and top with grated cheese.

Bake uncovered for 45 minutes, until hot and bubbly.

SOUTH OF THE BORDER CHICKEN AND RICE

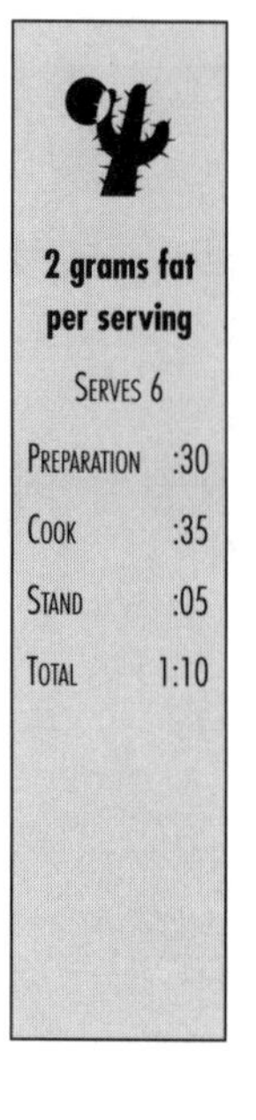

2 cups raw rice
2 boneless skinless chicken breast halves
1 teaspoon ground cumin
1 (14-ounce) can black beans, drained
1 (8-ounce) can Mexicorn (canned corn with red and green peppers), drained
1 (16-ounce) jar picante sauce, mild or spicy—your preference
1 cup shredded fat-free Cheddar cheese

Preheat the oven to 350 degrees. Coat a 13 x 9-inch baking dish lightly with vegetable oil cooking spray.

Cook the rice according to package directions, leaving out any margarine or butter called for. Set aside.

Brown the chicken breast, sprinkled with cumin, in a nonstick skillet until tender. Cut the chicken into small cubes. Set aside.

Spoon the rice into the prepared baking dish. Layer the remaining ingredients in this order: beans, corn, chicken, picante sauce, and cheese.

Bake uncovered for 25 to 35 minutes or until heated through. Cool 5 minutes before serving.

MEXICALI QUICK FIX (CHICKEN AND RICE)

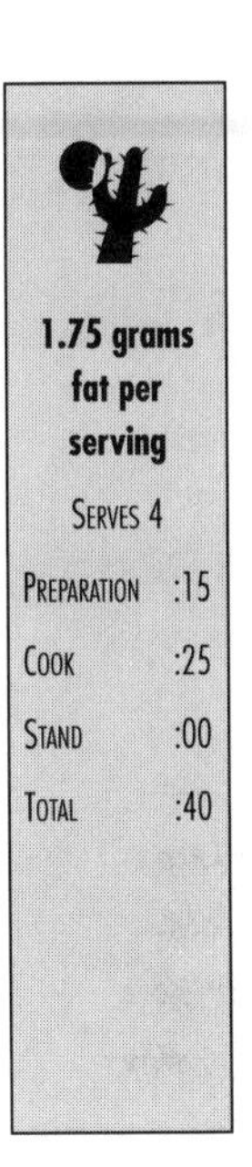

1 (4-ounce) package quick-cooking Spanish rice, such as Rice-A-Roni
1/2 cup chopped onion
1 small green bell pepper, chopped (about 3/4 cup)
1 small zucchini, peeled and chopped (about 1 1/2 cups)
1/2 cup water
3/4 teaspoon Mexican oregano or regular oregano, crushed
1/4 teaspoon ground green chilies or 2 teaspoons canned chopped chilies
1/4 teaspoon chili powder
Pinch of crushed dried red chilies (chile Caribe if available)
3 cups diced cooked chicken white meat

Prepare the rice according to package directions, leaving out any margarine called for. While that is cooking, prepare your vegetables; now you are ready to start.

In a nonstick skillet over medium heat, sauté the onion, pepper, and zucchini, adding water when the mixture starts to look dry. Add the oregano, green chilies, chili powder, and crushed chilies. Continue to sauté for a couple of minutes, stirring to blend the spices. Add the chicken (if frozen, you will need to let it sauté a few minutes longer than fresh or leftover). Stir well to heat the chicken through.

When the chicken is hot, add the rice. Stir to blend evenly, and serve. Or if you prefer, you can serve the chicken and vegetable mixture over the rice instead of mixing them together.

TORTILLA ROLL-UPS

Less than 1 gram fat each (depends on the filling)

SERVES 1

PREPARATION	:10
COOK	:00
STAND	:30
TOTAL	:40

These are quick, easy, low-fat or fat-free, great for last-minute company, plan-ahead company, maybe just an after-school treat, or a side with nice hot bowl of soup.

FOR EACH SERVING:

1 (6-inch) fat-free flour tortilla
1 tablespoon fat-free cream cheese, softened
1/4 teaspoon Mexican seasoning
Pinch of Mexican oregano or regular oregano, crushed (optional)
1 slice fat-free turkey sandwich meat
2 tablespoons alfalfa sprouts (optional)
1 spear of dill pickle, drained (optional)
1 tablespoon thinly sliced green onion (optional)
1 tablespoon finely chopped ripe tomato (optional)
1 tablespoon shredded fat-free Cheddar cheese (optional)
1 teaspoon salsa (optional)

Lay the tortilla flat on a work surface and spread it with softened cream cheese. Sprinkle the Mexican seasoning and oregano, if using, evenly over the cream cheese. Add the slice of turkey. Choose the additional items you want to use and place them down the center, lengthwise.

After you have added the items you want, roll the tortilla up, using a toothpick to secure. Wrap in plastic wrap; keep chilled until ready to serve, for at least 30 minutes. You may slice it into rounds or serve whole, cut in half or in fourths.

Repeat as many times as needed.

BAKED CHICKEN SANDWICHES

2.25 grams fat per serving

Serves 6

Preparation	:30
Cook	:30
Stand	:00
Total	1:00

This is a dish you can prepare the night before or the morning before you go to work. It's an easy and delicious dinner.

1/2 cup chopped onions, frozen or fresh
1 small green bell pepper, chopped
1/2 cup egg substitute
3 cups 98% fat-free canned chicken white meat, drained and chopped, or use leftover cooked chicken (see Note)
1 teaspoon Mexican seasoning
1/2 cup canned sliced mushrooms, drained (optional)
1 (8-ounce) can sliced water chestnuts, drained
1/2 cup fat-free mayonnaise
12 very thin slices white bread, crusts removed
1 (10 3/4-ounce) can low-fat cream of chicken soup
1/2 cup canned chopped chile peppers
1 cup fat-free sour cream
1/2 teaspoon ground red pepper (cayenne)
1 cup shredded fat-free Cheddar cheese

Spray a 9 x 13-inch baking dish lightly with vegetable oil cooking spray.

In a small nonstick skillet, sauté the onions and green pepper until soft and almost dry. Pour the egg substitute in and scramble until the eggs are fairly dry.

In a medium to large mixing bowl, chop the scrambled eggs into small pieces; add the chicken, Mexican seasoning, mushrooms, water chestnuts, and mayonnaise. Mix well.

Lay 6 pieces of bread on a work surface. Spread the chicken mixture on the 6 slices and top with the remaining slices of bread, thus making your sandwiches. Place in a single layer in the baking dish.

In a small bowl, combine the chicken soup, chopped chilies, and sour cream; stir to mix. Spread over the sandwiches. Sprinkle the red pepper scantily over the soup mixture. Cover with foil or plastic wrap and refrigerate overnight, or during the day while you're at work.

Before cooking, set the casserole out for 10 or 15 minutes to get the chill off. Preheat the oven to 325 degrees. Bake uncovered for 20 to 25 minutes. Top with the cheese the last 5 minutes of baking time and continue to bake until the cheese is melted.

Garnish with wedges of tomato or with salsa. Serve with a nice green salad and offer fruit for dessert. What could be easier? No excuses for not entertaining—call those friends and enjoy.

Note: If you're using leftover cooked chicken, be careful of the dark meat: it has twice as much fat content as the white.

CHICKEN BURGERS

3 grams fat per serving

SERVES 4

PREPARATION	:16
COOK	:10
STAND	:00
TOTAL	:26

1 pound ground lean chicken white meat
1/4 cup diced onion
1 teaspoon dry mustard (or prepared)
1/2 teaspoon ground cumin
1/2 teaspoon chili powder
1/4 cup egg substitute
1/4 cup fine dry bread crumbs

In a large mixing bowl, combine all ingredients. Mix thoroughly with your hands or a large heavy spoon. Shape into 4 patties. Grill on hot grill or in the broiler for about 4 to 5 minutes on each side.

These can also be prepared in a nonstick skillet. When cooked, blot on a paper towel to soak up any excess fat that has cooked out.

CHICKEN CHILE VERDE

2 grams fat per serving

SERVES 8

PREPARATION	:35
COOK	1:00
STAND	:00
TOTAL	1:35

4 whole chicken breasts, bone in
1 teaspoon cumin seed
1 cup frozen or canned corn
1 (28-ounce) can green chile enchilada sauce
1 (15-ounce) can black beans, drained
1 cup chopped onion
2 cloves garlic, minced
1 teaspoon chopped fresh cilantro
Salt and pepper to taste

Remove all skin and visible fat from the chicken; leave the bone in. Place the chicken breasts in a large stockpot or Dutch oven and cover with water. Bring to a rapid boil. Add the cumin seed, lower the heat to medium, and continue cooking uncovered for about 20 minutes.

When the chicken is tender, remove it from the stock with tongs; let cool long enough to handle. Remove the chicken from the bones; chop into small bite-size pieces. Remove half the stock and reserve.

In the remaining stock combine the corn, enchilada sauce, beans, onion, garlic, and seasonings. Continue simmering for 35 to 40 minutes, or until all ingredients are tender and the chili has thickened. If it starts to get a little too dry, add a small amount at a time of the extra stock.

RED CHICKEN CHILI

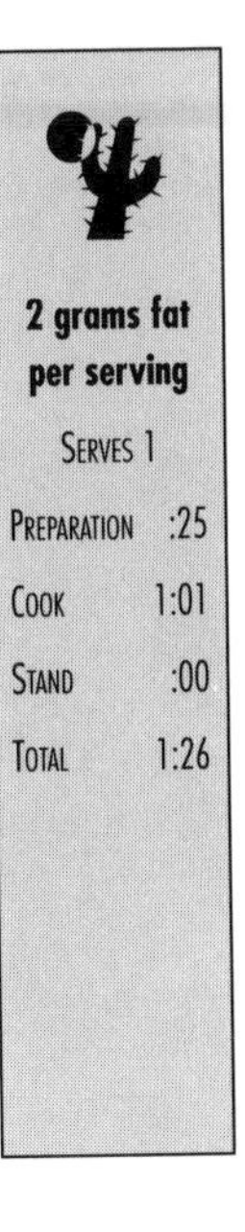

This recipe may be halved or doubled, depending on the occasion. Using a lower-fat-count cut of chicken will take some of the grams away. Chicken tenders have only .5 grams each. I use frozen cubed chicken for convenience and time.

1½ cups chopped onion
1½ cups chopped green bell pepper
4 cups cubed chicken, frozen or leftover
2 cups chopped zucchini
1 teaspoon Mexican oregano or regular oregano, crushed
½ teaspoon ground cumin
1 (4-ounce) can chopped green chilies
½ teaspoon minced garlic
1 (15-ounce) can kidney beans, drained
1 (15-ounce) can black beans, drained
1 (15-ounce) can tomato sauce
1 (15-ounce) can stewed tomatoes, juice and all
1½ (1.25-ounce) packages chili seasoning (such as McCormick), or to taste
½ cup Coca-Cola
1 (16-ounce) can fat-free plain or spicy refried beans

Place a large nonstick Dutch oven over medium heat and sauté the onion, green pepper, chicken, and zucchini for about 12 minutes. Lower the heat; add the oregano, cumin, chilies, and garlic. Cook for 10 to 12 minutes. Stir in the kidney beans, black beans, tomato sauce, stewed tomatoes, chili seasoning, and Coca-Cola. Simmer on low heat for 25 to 30 minutes longer, stirring occasionally. Add the refried beans; stir well to heat and distribute the refried beans. Simmer 5 to 6 minutes longer and serve.

TURKEY CHILI

Very low-fat

SERVES 4

PREPARATION	:10
COOK	:35
STAND	:00
TOTAL	:45

3/4 cup chopped onion
1 pound lean ground turkey
2 cloves garlic, minced
1 (8-ounce) can tomato sauce
1 (14-ounce) can stewed tomatoes
1 (15-ounce) can pinto beans or kidney beans, drained
4 or 5 drops of liquid hot pepper seasoning
1 tablespoon unsweetened cocoa powder
1 teaspoon ground cumin
1/2 teaspoon Mexican oregano or regular oregano, crushed
1/4 teaspoon crushed dried basil leaves
1 (16-ounce) can fat-free refried beans

In a 6-quart saucepan, sauté the onion in about 1/4 cup of water over medium heat until lightly browned, 5 to 6 minutes. Add a couple tablespoons of water if necessary to loosen browned onion bits from the pan bottom; add the turkey and garlic. Stir and crumble the meat until it is no longer pink and the juices have cooked away, 4 or 5 minutes.

Add the tomato sauce, tomatoes, pinto beans, hot pepper seasoning, cocoa, cumin, oregano, and basil. Bring to a boil, reduce the heat, cover, and simmer for 15 to 20 minutes, letting the flavors blend. Add the refried beans, stirring until blended; let simmer an additional 5 minutes. Serve in chili bowls with fat-free tortilla chips if desired.

Meats

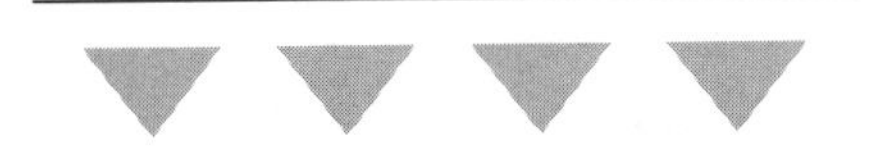

PORK

PORK LOIN ABLAZE

Very low-fat

SERVES 8

PREPARATION :20

COOK 2:00

STAND :00

TOTAL 2:20

You'll need a large oven baking bag to make this. Pick a rainy or winter afternoon; the house will smell great and you will be prepared for any occasion with this meat as a base for many recipes. All you have to do is keep it in the freezer and measure out what you need.

1 tablespoon all-purpose flour
2 pounds boneless pork loin
2 tablespoons Chimayo chili powder (see Note)
1 teaspoon Mexican oregano or regular oregano, crushed
1 (16-ounce) can chunky mixed fruit, light syrup

Preheat the oven to 350 degrees. Prepare a large (14 x 20-inch) oven baking bag according to the manufacturer's directions. Put the flour in the bag and shake to coat it.

Prepare the roast by trimming off all visible fat. Wash the meat with cold water and pat dry with paper towels. With disposable rubber gloves, rub the chili powder over and into the roast. Do the same with the oregano.

Place the roast in the cooking bag, which you have fitted into a 9 x 13-inch cooking pan. Pour the fruit and its syrup evenly over the roast. Tie the bag with the provided tie. Punch 5 or 6 holes in the top of the bag as instructed. Bake for about 2 to 2½ hours, or until tender when pierced with a sharp knife.

When the roast is done, immediately take it out of the bag with wide tongs. Rinse briefly under cold running water to wash off any excess chili powder. Dispose of bag and fruit sauce used to cook roast.

When the meat cools, chop it into bite-size pieces and store it in a zipperlock plastic bag in the freezer for further use. Or use a portion at cooking time and store the remaining portion.

Note: If you cannot find Chimayo chili powder or Mexican oregano, you may use regular chili powder and regular crushed oregano. The taste difference is slight. Be careful with the regular chili powder; use a little less than called for. It's a hotter-type pepper than Chimayo.

CARNE ADOVADA (PORK STEW CHILI)

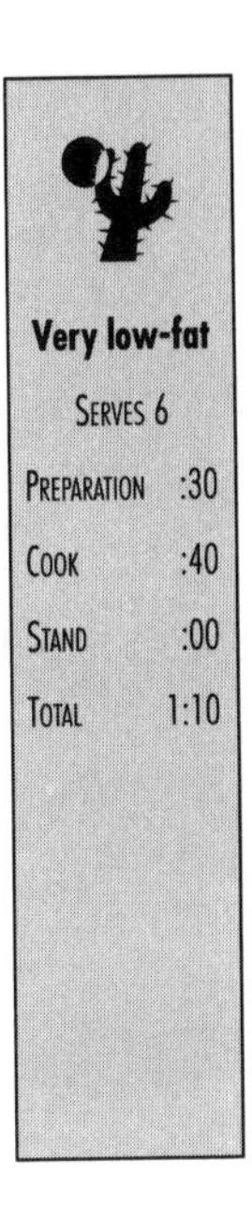

1 large onion, chopped
1 medium green bell pepper, chopped
2 fresh sweet banana peppers, chopped
1/2 cup chopped carrots
2 cups chopped Pork Loin Ablaze (recipe page 110)
1 (14-ounce) can fat-free chicken broth
1 (11-ounce) can shoepeg corn
1 (15-ounce) can pinto beans, drained
1 (16-ounce) can fat-free refried beans
1 (16-ounce) can red kidney beans, drained
1 (4-ounce) can chopped green chilies
1/4 teaspoon ground green chilies (if available) (see Note)
1/2 teaspoon ground cumin
Salt and pepper to taste (be careful with the pepper)

In a deep heavy stockpot, sauté the chopped onion, bell pepper, and banana pepper along with the carrots. You will want to keep a watch on the heat and stir often; you won't even need to add any water to sauté these; they will cook in their own juices.

When the vegetables are crisp-tender, add the meat; cook long enough to heat through. If frozen, you may just dump it in as is—it only takes a few minutes to be heated. So you can do this at the last minute if desired, although it is better to be made ahead so the flavors will blend nicely.

Add the chicken broth, a broth can of water, the shoepeg corn (I use these small crisp kernels to give my recipes a little body; you may use frozen if desired), pinto beans, refried beans, kidney beans, green chilies, and seasonings. Simmer uncovered for 30 to 40 minutes. Serve with cornbread or baked tortilla chips. Dollop on a little fat-free sour cream and sprinkle with some fat-free shredded Cheddar cheese and a bit of minced raw onion for an attractive serving complement.

Note: If you do not have the ground green chilies or cannot find them in your local grocery store, you may substitute additional ground cumin. There is just a slight difference in taste.

The ground green chilies are one of the spices I found in New Mexico while doing research for this book. I did not find this in Gore, America. Please do not feel that you cannot make changes and substitutions. Don't skip a recipe just because you don't have one item. Make a reasonable substitution. My recipes are easy recipes and can be altered if necessary, as any recipe can. I love it when ladies tell me they like my books because the ingredients are easy to find. For the recipes that call for the spices found in New Mexico and not in my local grocery store, I will suggest a reasonable substitution.

Variation: If you do not have Pork Loin Ablaze prepared or in the freezer, you may make this recipe with fresh pork. Use about ¾ pound of a very lean cut, such as loin chops, all fat removed. Chop the meat into small bite-size pieces; cook in a nonstick skillet until tender and browned. Stir often. When done, place in a colander and rinse with hot water to remove any excess fat. Shake the water off and continue with recipe. You may brown the meat while you are preparing the onions, etc.

For Carne Adovado (chili) even lower in fat, try turkey or chicken in place of the pork.

GREEN CHILE AND PORK STEW

On a cold winter's day this will certainly open your sinuses and bring out the perspiration on your forehead. What a treat when the wind howls in January!

1½ pounds extra-lean pork tenderloin, all fat trimmed
1 scant tablespoon ground red chile, or to taste
2 teaspoons ground cumin
1 tablespoon Mexican oregano or regular oregano, crushed
1 cup chopped onion
1 clove garlic, minced
2 (14-ounce) cans fat-free chicken broth
4 Anaheim green chilies, charred, peeled, seeded, and chopped (or an 8-ounce can of green chilies, chopped)
1 jalapeño chile, seeded and minced (see Note)
4 red potatoes, peeled and cut into fourths
½ cup coarsely chopped celery
1 cup sliced carrot rounds

Choose the leanest pork you can find. You can tell by looking at it if there is entirely too much fat or if it passes your inspection. Wash the meat and cut away any visible fat, then cut the meat into 2½- or 3-inch chunks.

Blend the ground red chile, cumin, and oregano. Wearing rubber gloves, rub the meat with the mixed spices. Brown the meat over medium heat in a large nonstick saucepan or stockpot sprayed with vegetable oil cooking spray. You may want to do this in two or three batches. Remove the meat to a platter as it browns. After the meat is all browned, sauté the onion in the same pot until softened. Stir in the garlic, then pour in the chicken broth. Return the meat to the pot at this time. Bring to a steady simmer. Meanwhile, assemble the chilies that you choose to use. Stir the Anaheim chilies into the simmering meat mixture, along with the minced jalapeño. While this is cooking, prepare the potatoes, celery, and carrots. Add the vegetables to the pot, and continue to simmer for 20 to 25 minutes longer or until the vegetables are tender.

Serve with corn muffins or a cornbread of your choice. I would not serve a spicy bread like jalapeño cornbread at this time; you will have plenty of fire already.

Note: When preparing any type of chilies, wear rubber gloves and use eye protection such as safety glasses. Read the "Jalapeño Pepper Jelly" story, page 46.

POSOLE

Very low-fat

SERVES 6

PREPARATION	:25
COOK	3:00
STAND	:00
TOTAL	3:25

This recipe was originally made with pig's feet, pork neck bones, spareribs, etc. As you know, those cuts are very high in fat, but the natives of the land used every part possible of the animal. I can remember seeing Grandma cook pig's feet, the tail, the head . . . and she used to pickle them also. I think I will pass, thank you very much!

2 pounds very lean pork loin
1 medium-size onion, quartered
3 cloves garlic, coarsely chopped
1 teaspoon Mexican oregano or regular oregano, crushed
Salt to taste
1 (14-ounce) can hominy, drained
1/4 cup mild red chili sauce

Trim all visible fat from the pork and cut the meat into small bite-size pieces. Sauté in a nonstick skillet just until lightly browned, adding the onion and garlic at the last minute. Stir and sauté about 1 minute longer. Pour into a colander and rinse under very hot water to remove excess fat.

Place the meat, onion, and garlic in a large stockpot; cover with 4 to 5 quarts of water. Bring to a boil, lower the heat, and add the oregano, and salt if desired. Continue to cook, partially covered, for about 2 hours or until the pork is done to the desired tenderness. Add the hominy and chili sauce; continue to cook for an additional 30 minutes, stirring occasionally.

Ladle into bowls and serve with warm tortillas.

CHILE VERDE

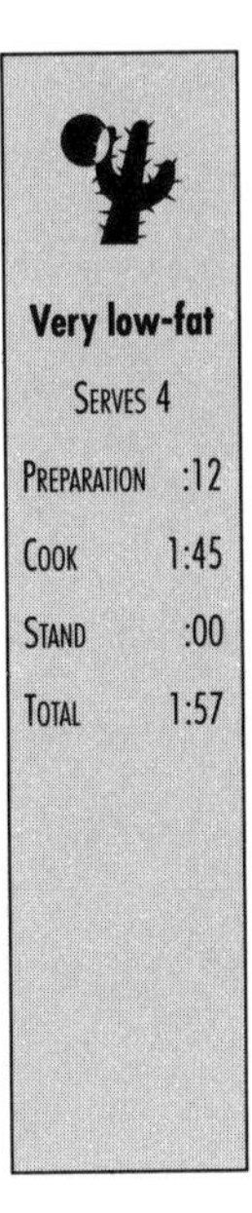

¾ pound very lean pork loin
1¼ cups chopped onion
3 cloves garlic, minced
2 cups (1 pound) fresh tomatillos (or a 10-ounce can, drained)
1 (14½-ounce) can fat-free chicken broth
1 (4-ounce) can diced mild green chilies
1 teaspoon ground cumin
1 (15-ounce) can Great Northern beans, drained and rinsed
2 tablespoons chopped fresh cilantro
Fat-free sour cream (optional) for garnish

Choose the leanest pork loin you can find, and trim any and all visible fat away. Cut the meat into very small cubes, about ½ inch or so. Place the pork, onion, garlic, and ½ cup of water in a large saucepan. Cover and simmer for about 30 minutes, stirring occasionally. You may need to add a little water along the way; check when you're stirring. Uncover when tender, and continue to cook, stirring, until the liquid evaporates and the meat browns.

Remove the husks from the tomatillos; boil them in water to cover for 5 minutes or until softened. Add them to the meat, along with the broth. Cover; simmer over medium heat for 20 minutes or until the tomatillos are tender and fall apart. Add the chilies and cumin. Cover and simmer another 45 minutes over low heat. You may need to add a little water or broth to keep the liquid level the same. Cook until meat is tear-apart tender. Add the beans; simmer for another 10 minutes or until heated through. Stir in the cilantro. Serve with fat-free sour cream if desired.

Variation: Use turkey or chicken in the place of pork. Choose very lean white meat.

Very low-fat

Serves 6

Preparation	:24
Cook	:40
Stand	:05
Total	1:09

SAUSAGE CASSEROLE

1 1/2 cups chopped onion
1 small green bell pepper, chopped (about 1 cup)
3 fresh sweet banana peppers, cut into rings
1/2 package (2-pound package) frozen hash browns or country chunk-style potatoes
1 (7-ounce) stick fat-free smoked sausage
1 (16-ounce) package frozen stir-fry vegetables
1 (19-ounce) can vegetarian chili
1/2 cup water
1/4 cup fine dry bread crumbs
1 cup shredded fat-free Cheddar cheese (Mexican flavor)

Preheat the oven to 350 degrees. Spray an 11 x 7-inch baking dish with vegetable oil cooking spray.

In a nonstick skillet, sauté the onions with both peppers and the hash browns over medium-high heat. Stir often to brown evenly.

Pour the potato mixture into the baking dish and spread evenly. Slice the sausage the long way into 4 or 5 thin slices. Lay the slices lengthwise in the baking dish over the potato mixture.

Pour the frozen vegetables over the meat. Mix the chili with the water and pour over the vegetables. Sprinkle bread crumbs over the top. Bake uncovered for 25 to 30 minutes or until the vegetables are tender. Remove from the oven, cover with cheese, return to the oven, and continue to bake for another 10 minutes or until the cheese is melted. Let stand for 5 minutes before serving.

TAMALE CASSEROLE

1 cup chopped onion
1 cup chopped green bell pepper
2 rings jalapeño pepper, finely chopped (about 1 tablespoon)
8 ounces lean ground pork or lean fresh ground turkey
1 teaspoon minced garlic (commercially prepared or 1 clove fresh)
1 1/4 cups tomato sauce
3/4 cup fresh corn kernels (from 1 ear of corn)
Salt
1/2 teaspoon chili powder
1/2 cup yellow cornmeal
3/4 cup shredded fat-free Monterey Jack cheese

Very low-fat (depends on type of meat used)

SERVES 4

PREPARATION	:20
COOK	1:00
STAND	:10
TOTAL	1:30

Preheat the oven to 350 degrees. Lightly coat an 8-inch square baking dish with vegetable oil cooking spray.

In a large nonstick skillet, sauté the onion, bell pepper, and jalapeño pepper until crisp-tender, stirring frequently, about 5 minutes. Add the pork or turkey and cook, stirring to break up the meat, for 3 to 4 minutes or until no longer pink. If using pork, at this time remove the meat mixture to a colander and run the hottest water possible over it, shaking to remove any excess fat. If your turkey looks as if it has a little fat, do the same with it. Shake the colander to remove any excess water. Wash the skillet, dry, return to the heat, and return the meat mixture to the skillet. Add the garlic, tomato sauce, corn, salt if desired, and chili powder. Bring to a boil, stirring occasionally, lower the heat and simmer for about 15 minutes.

Transfer the meat mixture to the prepared baking dish and set aside.

In a medium saucepan, combine 1 cup of water with 1/4 teaspoon of salt; bring to a boil. Meanwhile, in a small mixing bowl, combine the cornmeal and 1 cup of water. Start pouring the cornmeal mixture into the boiling water, stirring constantly, and pouring in a very thin steady stream.

Continue stirring until the mixture returns to a boil. Reduce the heat to low; simmer, stirring constantly, about 4 or 5 minutes, until the mixture thickens and forms large bubbles.

Top the meat mixture with the cornmeal mush, spreading evenly. Bake uncovered for 25 to 30 minutes. Sprinkle the cornmeal topping mixture with the cheese; bake 5 minutes longer or until the cheese melts. Remove from oven and let stand for 10 minutes before cutting.

Our new society of low-fat and no-fat cooking, eating, and living has created many new spice and/or seasoning blends in the spice aisles. Stop and take a few minutes to read some of the labels. You will more than likely come away with a couple of new blends that are fat-free and low in sodium. They are an excellent way to lower the fat and add the flavor. Read labels very closely, and check to make sure you're not getting too much sodium and/or sugar. This is the most important thing you need to watch out for in the fat-free items, even spices. They sometimes have an abundance of sodium.

SPINACH PIE

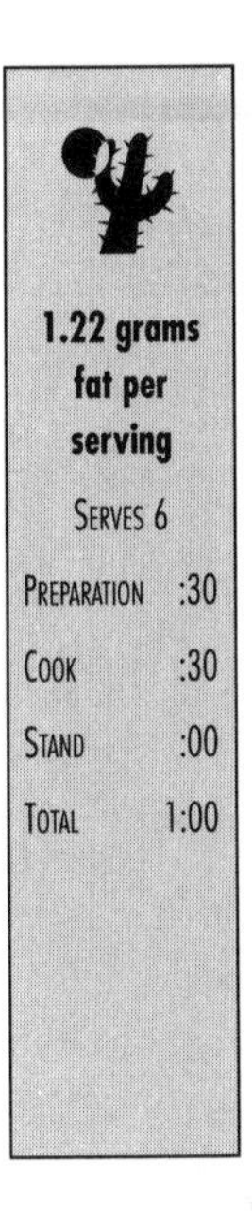

1 (10-ounce) package frozen chopped spinach, thawed and well drained
1 cup shredded fat-free Cheddar cheese
3/4 cup diced 99% fat-free ham
1/3 cup chopped onion
3/4 cup cracker meal, such as Nabisco
2 tablespoons baking powder
1/4 cup pourable fat-free margarine, such as Fleischmann's
3/4 cup egg substitute
1 1/4 cups skim milk
Salsa for garnish

Spray the bottom of a 9-inch pie plate with vegetable oil cooking spray. Preheat the oven to 400 degrees.

Squeeze the spinach to remove as much liquid as possible. Combine the spinach, cheese, ham, and onion in a bowl and mix thoroughly. Press lightly in the bottom of the pie plate.

In another mixing bowl, combine the cracker meal and baking powder. Mix well. Pour in the margarine and mix with a fork until crumbly. Add the egg substitute and milk; beat until blended. Pour over the spinach mixture, spreading evenly.

Bake for about 30 minutes or until puffed and golden. Serve in wedges with salsa on the side.

Very low-fat

SERVES 6

PREPARATION :40

COOK 1:20

STAND :00

TOTAL 2:00

BEEF

CHILI CON CARNE

2½ pounds eye of the round beef, trimmed of all fat, ground
1½ cups chopped onion
1 clove garlic, chopped fine
½ cup chopped green bell pepper
3 cups finely chopped zucchini
2 teaspoons Mexican oregano or regular oregano, crushed
1 tablespoon crushed dried celery flakes
1 teaspoon Mexican seasoning
⅛ teaspoon hot red pepper flakes
2 (1¼-ounce) packages chili seasoning, such as McCormick
2 (14-ounce) cans chili-flavored diced tomatoes,
  juice and all
1½ (14-ounce) cans water
2 (15-ounce) cans chili beans, sauce and all
1 (15-ounce) can tomato sauce
1 (4½-ounce) can chopped green chilies

Choose a Dutch oven or a large heavy saucepan; if it's not nonstick, spray it very lightly with vegetable oil cooking spray. Heat the pan to slightly hot and start adding the ground meat. Crumble the meat as much as possible as you add it; as it starts to brown, stir and break clumps apart with a large spoon or spatula. Continue browning, stirring occasionally. While the meat is browning, peel and chop the onion; add it to the meat along with the garlic. Stir in the chopped green pepper and add a few of the seeds to the chili; this adds a great flavor.

Continue to cook and brown while you peel the zucchini and chop it into small pieces, about ¼ inch cubes. Stir the meat mixture, adding the zucchini. Add the oregano, celery flakes, Mexican seasoning, and red pepper flakes, and stir to combine all.

Open the packages of chili seasoning and sprinkle over all evenly; stir, continue simmering, and add the tomatoes, water, beans, tomato sauce, and green chilies. Stir to mix evenly; let simmer uncovered at the lowest heat for an additional 20 to 25 minutes.

Serve with shredded fat-free cheese sprinkled over the top of each bowl if desired.

TACO PIE

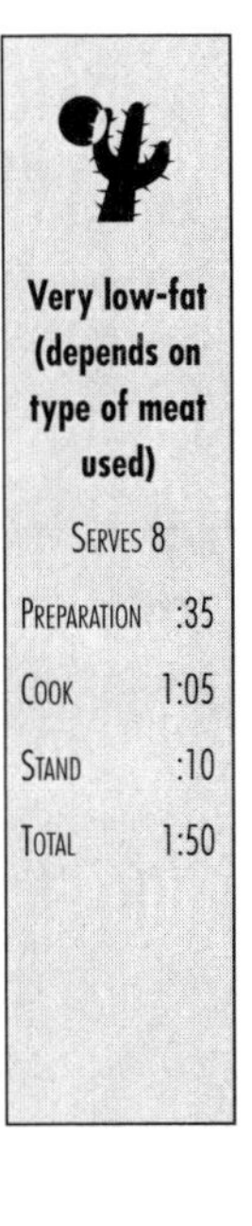

You may make this recipe with ground eye of round beef, or a very, very lean cut of ground turkey, very lean ground pork, or ground chicken.

1/2 (16-ounce) package Spanish-flavor yellow rice, such as Vigo
2 1/2 cups water
1 1/2 pounds extra-lean ground beef
1 cup chopped green bell pepper
1 cup chopped onion
1 cup whole kernel corn, frozen or canned
3/4 teaspoon Mexican oregano or regular oregano, crushed
2 tablespoons canned chopped green chilies
1 (1-ounce) package taco seasoning
1/2 teaspoon Tabasco jalapeño sauce (add gradually and taste—don't add too much)
1 (14-ounce) can diced tomatoes, juice and all
1 (16-ounce) can chili beans, not drained
1 (16-ounce) can pinto beans, drained and rinsed
1/3 cup shredded Mexican mix fat-free cheese, such as Healthy Choice
1 1/2 cups crushed low-fat tortilla chips

Preheat the oven to 375 degrees. Spray a 13 x 9-inch baking pan with vegetable oil cooking spray.

First: Make the rice. Combine rice and water and start boiling; lower the heat, cover, and cook for 10 to 15 minutes, until tender. Watch it—just because it is covered, you might forget it. When done, set aside off the heat but keep covered.

Second: While the rice is cooking, make the meat mixture. In a large nonstick skillet or saucepan, start the meat to browning. Stir to break up lumps as it browns. When the meat is about halfway done, add the pepper, onion, corn, oregano, green chilies, taco seasoning, and Tabasco. Continue cooking on medium-high to high heat, to brown or sear quickly. Turn with a flat spatula, to brown both sides. (We are sort of roasting this mixture.) When browned and/or roasted, set aside.

Third: Prepare the beans. Mix the tomatoes and their juice with the chili beans and pinto beans in a medium bowl.

Fourth: Start assembling the pie. Put the rice in the bottom of the baking dish. Wet your hands slightly with cold water and pat the rice into a crustlike layer that goes halfway up the sides. Retouch your fingers into the water as needed. Layer the bean mixture over the crust and spread to make the surface even. Layer the meat mixture over the beans, spreading to make it even.

Place the pan in the preheated oven and bake uncovered for 15 minutes. Mix the cheese and crushed chips; sprinkle evenly over the meat layer. Spray the entire layer of chips lightly with butter-flavored cooking spray. Return to the oven and continue to bake for another 15 minutes, or until heated through. Let stand for 5 to 10 minutes before serving with a green salad and hot chips or cornbread.

CORNMEAL MUSH "TAMALE PIE"

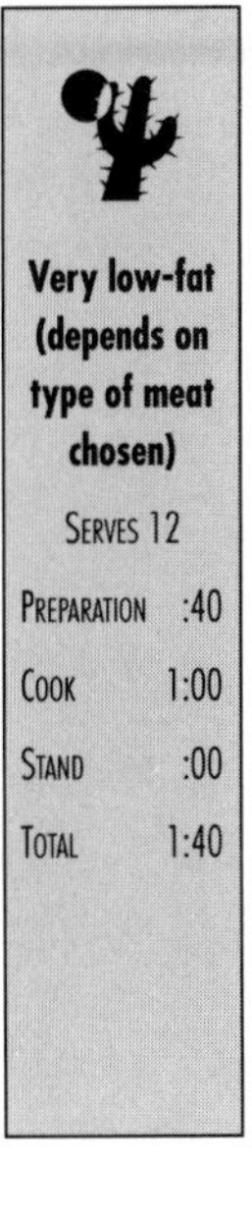

This is great for family night or potluck supper at church or any gathering.

FILLING:

1½ pounds very lean ground beef
1 cup chopped green bell pepper
1¼ cups chopped fresh or frozen onion
1½ teaspoons prepared minced garlic
½ cup tomato paste mixed with 1 cup water
1 (11-ounce) can Mexicorn (canned corn with red and green peppers), drained
1 teaspoon ground dried red chilies

CORNMEAL TOPPING:

1⅛ cups skim milk
Small touch of salt
1 teaspoon fat-free pourable margarine, such as Fleischmann's
¼ cup cornmeal
⅓ cup grated fat-free Parmesan cheese
⅓ cup grated fat-free Cheddar cheese
¼ cup egg substitute
1 (4-ounce) can green chilies, chopped and drained
2 large egg whites
Salsa and fat-free sour cream for garnish (optional)

Preheat the oven to 350 degrees. Coat the bottom and sides of a 2½-quart baking dish with vegetable oil cooking spray.

First prepare the filling: In a nonstick skillet, brown the ground meat, while stirring to break up lumps, until no pink is showing. If any fat has cooked out, transfer the browned meat to a colander and rinse under the hottest water available. Shake the excess water off, wash the skillet, and return the meat to the skillet. Continue to sauté while adding the pepper, onion, garlic, and green chilies. Cook until the meat is completely done and the peppers and onions are crisp-tender. Combine the tomato paste with the meat mixture, the water, the corn, and the ground chilies. Bring to a boil, reduce the heat, and simmer uncovered for about 20 minutes. Pour the filling into the prepared baking dish. Set aside.

Prepare the cornmeal topping: In a small saucepan, heat the milk with the salt and margarine until it simmers. With a wire whisk, slowly stir in the cornmeal; continue to whisk to blend well. Cook for about 2 minutes or until thickened. Stir in the two cheeses, the egg substitute, and the drained chopped chilies. In a separate clean, grease-free glass bowl, beat the egg whites until soft peaks form. Fold gently into the cornmeal mush. Very carefully spread the batter over the meat mixture.

Bake for 30 minutes or until the top is lightly golden and feels done to the touch. Serve with salsa and, if desired, a dollop of fat-free sour cream on each serving.

If you want to use beef instead of turkey for hamburgers, chili, spaghetti sauces, etc., buy the eye of the round roast and have your butcher remove any visible fat. Ask him to grind it for you and separate it into one-pound packages. Freeze for convenience. You can barely see any fat when it's cooked. Bob thought I had pork, it was so lean and white the first time he grilled a hamburger. Bring up your spices.

SOUTH OF THE BORDER CASSEROLE

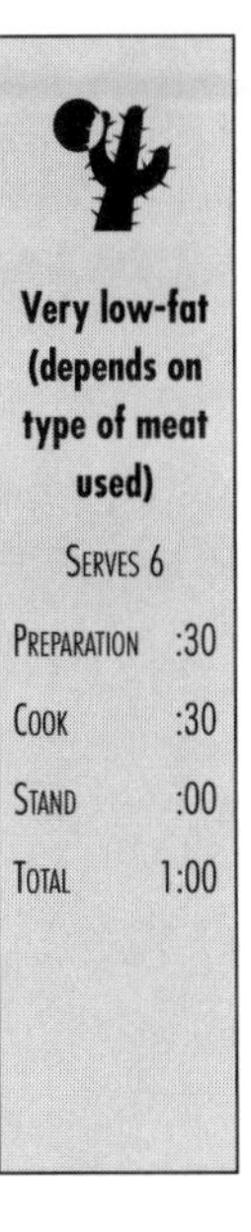

Served with the suggested garnish, this makes a meal in one.

1 pound very lean ground beef or lean ground turkey
1 (16-ounce) can chili-type beans, sauce and all
1 cup tomato sauce
3 tablespoons picante sauce
3 tablespoons chili powder (if you like milder, just use 1 to 2 tablespoons; or if you like spicier, use 4)
1 clove garlic, minced
2 cups baked tortilla chips, broken into small pieces (if you bake your own, you will save several grams)
1 cup fat-free sour cream
4 green onions, sliced
/4 cup chopped tomato
1 1/2 cups shredded fat-free Cheddar cheese
Lettuce leaves and tomato wedges for garnish

Preheat the oven to 350 degrees. Have ready an ungreased 2-quart baking dish.

In a nonstick skillet (about 10-inch) sauté the meat over medium heat, stirring to break up lumps. When the meat is browned and done, place it in a colander and rinse under the hottest running water possible. Shake to dispose of any excess water. Wipe the skillet with paper towels or wash to remove any grease left from the meat.

Return the browned meat to the skillet. Add the beans, tomato sauce, picante sauce, chili powder, and garlic. Stir to blend. Bring to a boil and remove from the heat.

Place the tortilla chips in the baking dish and cover with the meat mixture. Spread the sour cream over as evenly as possible. Sprinkle with the onions, tomato, and cheese.

Bake uncovered for 20 to 30 minutes or until hot and bubbly. Garnish with additional chips, lettuce, and tomato wedges.

FAMILY NIGHT SUPPER

Less than 4 grams per serving

SERVES 12

PREPARATION	:40
COOK	:40
STAND	:00
TOTAL	1:20

This is a big 13 x 9-inch casserole that serves 12 to 15 people. I created this for our Family Night supper at church.

MEAT MIXTURE:

1 pound extra-lean ground beef
1 teaspoon Mexican oregano or regular oregano, crushed
1/2 teaspoon minced garlic
1/4 teaspoon red chili powder
1/2 cup chopped onion
1/2 cup chopped green pepper
1 (14-ounce) can Just for Chili brand diced tomatoes

CRUST OR BOTTOM LAYER:

1 (6-ounce) envelope stovetop-type stuffing with spices
1 cup boiling water
1/2 cup tomato sauce
1/2 cup shredded fat-free Mexican Cheddar cheese

LAYERS 3, 4, 5, 6

1 (16-ounce) can pinto beans, drained
1 (11-ounce) can Mexicorn (canned corn with red and green peppers), drained
2 tablespoons chopped green chilies
1 cup tomato sauce
1 cup thick and chunky salsa
1/2 teaspoon Mexican seasoning

TOPPING:

26 low-fat ranch-flavored Doritos
1 cup shredded fat-free Mexican Cheddar cheese

Preheat the oven to 350 degrees. Lightly coat a 13 x 9-inch baking dish with vegetable oil cooking spray.

Prepare the meat mixture: Heat a heavy nonstick skillet over medium heat and brown the ground beef, stirring to break up any lumps. When the meat is about halfway done, or ready to turn over, add the oregano, garlic, chili powder, onion, and green pepper. Continue to cook until the meat is done and the vegetables are tender. Add the can of diced tomatoes, juice and all. Simmer a couple of minutes longer. Remove from the heat; set aside.

Prepare the bottom crust: In a mixing bowl, combine the stuffing mix, the packet of seasoning included in the box, the boiling water, tomato sauce, and the half-cup of shredded cheese. Toss to mix well; let stand until nice and moist. Place the stuffing mix in the prepared baking dish and pat it down with your hands to form the bottom crust, making sure there are no holes in it.

Pour the meat mixture over the crust.

Add layers 3, 4, 5, and 6 over the meat mixture: First spread the pinto beans over the meat, then the Mexicorn, then the chopped green chilies. Stir and push these ingredients around to make them nice and evenly spread. Mix together the tomato sauce, salsa, and the Mexican seasoning. Pour evenly over the top of the dish.

Bake uncovered for about 30 minutes. Remember that all your layers are already cooked; you just need to get everything nice and bubbly hot.

In the meantime, in your processor, crush the chips and cheese together to make the topping. It should be a nice fine mixture. Scatter the crumbs evenly over the top, return to the oven, and bake for another 10 minutes. Serve with additional red or green salsa.

"FRIED" CHIMICHANGAS

Slight trace of fat

SERVES 4

PREPARATION	:25
COOK	:30
STAND	:00
TOTAL	:55

These will look and taste like fried chimichangas, so why subject yourself to all those grams? Eat healthy and live stronger, healthier, happier, and longer.

4 (8-inch) fat-free flour tortillas
1 (11-ounce) can fat-free refried beans, plain or spicy
½ cup chopped onion
½ cup shredded fat-free Monterey Jack
½ cup shredded fat-free Cheddar cheese
1 cup fat-free chili, canned or leftover

Stack the tortillas, wrap them in foil, and heat them in a 350-degree oven for 10 minutes or so while you are preparing your filling ingredients.

Warm the beans in a saucepan; this makes them spread easier. Chop the onions, and mix the two cheeses. Coat a baking sheet lightly with vegetable oil cooking spray. After removing the warmed tortillas, turn the oven heat up to 400 degrees.

Place a warm tortilla flat on your work surface. Spread a strip of warm beans down the center; top with a couple tablespoons of the chili (it can be cold or warm). Add a layer of onion over the chili, and sprinkle the mixed cheese over all. Fold in the ends of the tortilla about ⅓ or so on each end; fold the sides over to make a rectangle, and secure by sticking a toothpick straight up and down but not all the way through the bottom. Repeat with the rest of the tortillas and filling.

Arrange the chimichangas well apart from each other on the prepared baking sheet. Spray the tops very lightly with cooking spray. Place in the oven for 10 minutes, or until lightly browned. Take the toothpicks out and carefully turn the chimichangas with a wide spatula. Continue to bake 10 minutes longer or until nicely browned. Serve with salsa alongside and a dollop of fat-free sour cream on top.

You may add a circle of chopped lettuce around the edge of your serving plate with some chopped fresh tomatoes and green onions scattered nicely to make the dish prettier. Or turn the vegetables into a salad, serving some of the lettuce, onion, and tomatoes along with the chimichanga and sour cream. This becomes a meal in one—so easy and so good as well as good for you. What time is dinner? I'll be there!

When you sauté, use water instead of oil. If baking tortillas, or something like chimichangas, brush them very lightly with water or mist them with a misting spray, then bake; this will give them the same crispness as oil.

MEAT LOAF

About 5 grams fat per serving (depends on type of meat used)

SERVES 6

PREPARATION	:15
COOK	1:00
STAND	:06
TOTAL	1:21

You may choose to use very lean ground eye of the round, ground turkey, ground pork (just the lean part), or ground chicken. You will probably need to grind the chicken at home or ask your butcher if he will grind it for you. Maybe someday we will be able to find lean ground chicken in the meat markets.

3/4 cup tomato sauce
1 teaspoon brown sugar
1 teaspoon prepared mustard
3/4 teaspoon Mexican seasoning (more if you prefer spicier)
1 1/2 pounds very lean ground meat, your choice
1/4 cup egg substitute
1/3 cup fine dry bread crumbs
1 clove garlic, minced
1 teaspoon or more minced fresh or canned jalapeño chile (optional) (be sure to use rubber gloves)
1 teaspoon Mexican oregano or regular oregano, crushed
2 sprigs fresh cilantro, minced (optional)
3/4 cup finely chopped white onion
1/4 cup thinly sliced green onions
Salt and pepper to taste if desired

Preheat the oven to 350 degrees. Have ready an 8 x 4 x 3-inch loaf pan—preferably a meat loaf pan, which has a liner with holes in the bottom to let excess grease drain off the loaf and into the bottom pan.

In a small bowl, combine the tomato sauce, brown sugar, mustard, and Mexican seasoning. Whisk to blend well. Set the sauce mixture aside.

In a large mixing bowl, combine the meat, egg substitute, bread crumbs, garlic, minced jalapeño, oregano, cilantro, white onion, and all but 1/4 cup of the sauce mixture. Reserve the remaining 1/4 cup of sauce mixed with the green onions for topping. Add salt and pepper if desired.

Mix well. (I use my hands for meat loaf—it's the first tools God gave us. Use them, but don't forget to wash before, during, and after handling any meat.)

Pack the meat loaf mixture into the pan and use a spoon to spread the tomato sauce mixture evenly over the top of the loaf. Bake for about 1 hour. If you do not have a meat loaf pan, drain any excess fat cooked out of the meat at this time. Let the loaf stand for 6 minutes or so before serving. Garnish with a sprig of rosemary or cilantro if you have on hand. A slice of lemon on the side of the plate also adds a touch of color if desired.

Variation: Have you ever had a meat loaf sandwich? This makes a great leftover to do just that, so you can have two meals in one. Serve with a fruit salad, roasted corn, potatoes or rice, and hot bread or chips. Yum!

Very low-fat: 0 grams without meat

Serves 6

Preparation	:30
Cook	:45
Stand	:10
Total	1:25

LAYERED MEAT PIE

Meal in one. Serve with green salad.

7 (8-inch) fat-free flour tortillas
3/4 pound, very lean beef, fresh ground turkey breast, or chicken white meat
1 1/2 cups finely chopped green and red bell peppers, fresh or frozen
1/2 cup finely chopped onion, fresh or frozen
1 (4-ounce) can chopped green chilies
1 teaspoon minced fresh cilantro
1 teaspoon Mexican oregano or regular oregano, crushed
1 1/2 teaspoons chili powder
1/2 teaspoon ground cumin
2 (10-ounce) cans V-8 juice (may substitute tomato juice)
2 (15-ounce) cans hot chili beans, drained
2 (15-ounce) cans white beans, drained
1 1/2 cups shredded fat-free Cheddar cheese, sharp if available
3/4 cup shredded fat-free white cheese, such as Monterey Jack
1 green onion, sliced thin for garnish (optional)

Prepare a 9-inch pie plate or quiche pan: Tear off two lengths of foil about 24 inches long. Lay them crosswise across the pan, centering them with about 6 inches overhang on each side. Preheat the oven to 325 degrees.

Prepare the layers before you start assembling them:

Heat a large nonstick skillet and spray it lightly with vegetable oil cooking spray. Sauté the meat until half done. Then add the bell peppers, onion, chilies, cilantro, oregano, chili powder, and cumin, stirring several times to distribute the spices, for about 5 minutes.

Pour half the V-8 juice into each of two separate bowls. Add the chili beans to one and the white beans to the other, mashing the beans a little to soak up some of the liquid.

Combine the Cheddar and white cheeses, mix well, and set aside.

Assembly:

Spray the foil well with cooking spray. Place one tortilla on top of the foil in the bottom of the dish. Spread about 1 cup of the white bean mixture over the first tortilla; sprinkle ¼ cup of the cheeses over the bean mixture. Place the second tortilla over the cheeses. Gently press down.

Spread about 1 cup of the chili bean mixture over the second tortilla. Sprinkle ¼ cup of cheese over the bean layer. Place the third tortilla over the cheese layer. Gently press down.

Spread half the sautéed vegetable mixture over the third tortilla. Top with half the remaining cheese. Gently press down.

Repeat layers, ending with the remaining white bean and chili mixtures and the cheese on top of the seventh tortilla.

Bring the edges of the foil to the center; fold to seal all around. Bake in the preheated oven for 35 to 40 minutes. Remove from the oven and let stand for about 10 minutes.

Carefully slide the foil package from the dish with a wide spatula or pancake turner. Open the foil and use a spatula to gently slide the layered pie onto a serving dish. Garnish with sliced green onions if desired. Cut into wedges and serve with a green salad. You may like to serve salsa alongside.

FIESTA DINNER

1.5 grams fat per serving

SERVES 4

PREPARATION	:40
COOK	:06
STAND	:00
TOTAL	:46

This is a great entertaining dinner. It can be served plated or the ingredients can be set out buffet style for your guests to serve themselves. This idea came from my friend Shirley.

4 cups shredded lettuce
1 cup chopped green onions
1 1/2 cups chopped fresh tomatoes
2 cups shredded fat-free cheese, Cheddar or your choice
2 cups chunked fat-free processed cheese, such as Healthy Choice (comes in 1- or 2-pound packages in a long green box—looks like Velveeta)
1/4 cup skim milk
2 cups Minute rice
2 (15-ounce) cans fat-free chili (with or without beans)
3 to 4 cups crushed low-fat tortilla chips

Shred the lettuce and chop the onions and tomatoes if you are serving buffet style. Place the vegetables and the shredded cheese in separate serving dishes.

Put the chunked processed cheese in a microwave-safe bowl along with the skim milk. Cover with a loose sheet of plastic wrap; microwave for 2 minutes. Stir; microwave for 2 more minutes, repeating until heated and smooth.

Prepare the rice according to package directions, leaving out any butter or margarine; keep warm. Meanwhile, heat the chili in a saucepan over low heat (be careful not to scorch) and keep warm.

Line the dishes up if serving buffet style in the following order, or if you are serving the plates, layer in this order:

1. 3 to 4 cups crushed low-fat tortilla chips (1 cup reserved)
2. Shredded lettuce
3. Rice
4. Chili
5. Shredded cheese
6. Chopped onion
7. Chopped tomatoes
8. Melted cheese over all
9. Reserved crushed tortilla chips

Serve with low-fat tortilla chips, warmed if desired.

Chapter 6

Meatless Entrees

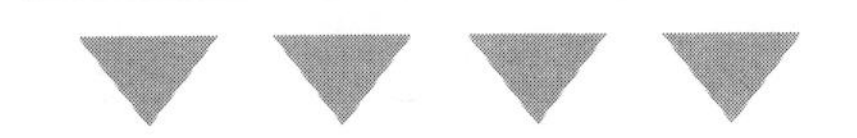

CRUSTLESS SPINACH QUICHE

This is nice for a brunch or ladies' club meeting.

0 grams fat

SERVES 6

PREPARATION	:35
COOK	:35
STAND:	:05
TOTAL	1:15

1 (10-ounce) package frozen spinach, thawed
1 (8-ounce) container egg substitute
1/3 cup all-purpose flour
2 green onions, chopped
1 cup fat-free cottage cheese
Pinch each of salt and pepper
3 tablespoons chopped green chilies
1/8 teaspoon ground cumin
1/3 cup fat-free shredded Mexican-flavor Cheddar cheese
Salsa and fat-free sour cream for garnish

Preheat the oven to 350 degrees. Spray a 9-inch pie plate or quiche baking dish with vegetable oil cooking spray.

Bring a saucepan of water to a boil, drop in the spinach, and cook for about 2 minutes. Drain, cool, squeeze all the water out, and chop fine.

Combine the egg substitute, flour, green onions, cottage cheese, salt, pepper, green chilies, and cumin in a blender or food processor. Blend about 30 seconds; add the spinach and continue to blend until the spinach is puréed.

Pour the batter into the prepared dish. Bake for 25 to 30 minutes, until a knife inserted near the center comes out clean. Remove from the oven and let stand about 5 minutes. Cut into wedges and serve with a spoonful of salsa on top and a small dollop of sour cream for garnish.

GREEN TOMATO PIE

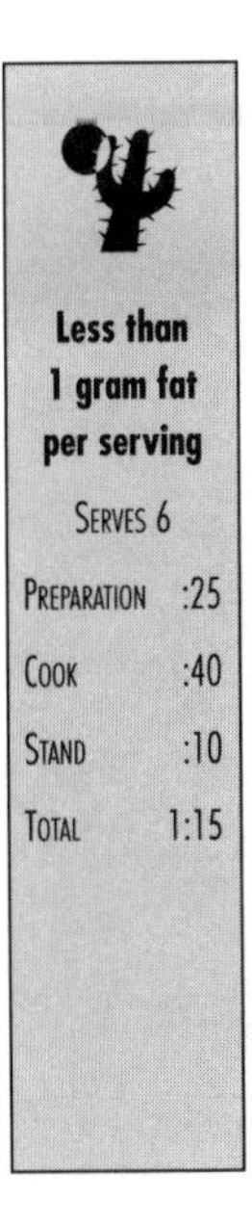

This is a great vegetarian meal in one.

1 (16-ounce) can fat-free refried beans
2 medium-size green tomatoes, sliced about 1/4 inch thick
1/2 cup chopped onion
1 (14-ounce) can diced tomatoes, juice and all
1/4 cup water

CORNBREAD TOPPING:

1 1/2 cups cornmeal mix
1/4 cup egg substitute
1/2 cup skim milk
1/2 cup water
1/4 cup salsa
1 1/2 tablespoons chopped green chilies
1/2 cup shredded fat-free Cheddar cheese

Preheat the oven to 350 degrees. Spray an 11 x 7-inch baking dish with vegetable oil cooking spray.

Spread the refried beans evenly over the bottom of the dish. Arrange the green tomato slices on top of the beans and scatter the chopped onion over the tomatoes. Pour the canned tomatoes and 1/4 cup of water over all.

Make the cornbread topping: Put the cornmeal mix in a medium-size mixing bowl. In another bowl, combine the egg substitute, skim milk, water, and salsa. Add to the dry ingredients and stir just until they are moistened—don't overmix. Fold in the chopped chilies and cheese.

Bake uncovered for about 40 minutes, or until the cornbread topping is set and lightly browned. Let stand about 10 minutes before serving.

½ gram fat per serving

SERVES 9

PREPARATION	:25
COOK	:55
STAND	:05
TOTAL	1:25

TA-MOLLY PIE

1 (6-ounce) package Santa Fe rice with seasonings (such as Lowry's)
1 (15-ounce) can chunky or diced tomatoes, undrained
1 cup water
2 (10-12-inch) fat-free flour tortillas
1 (15-ounce) can black beans, drained and rinsed
1 (4-ounce) can chopped green chilies
1 cup chopped onion
1 (19-ounce) can fat-free vegetarian chili
1 (8-ounce) package shredded fat-free Mexican cheese

Preheat the oven to 350 degrees. Spray a 13 x 9-inch baking dish lightly with vegetable oil cooking spray.

In a medium saucepan, combine the rice with the tomatoes and water. Cook according to package directions for 20 to 25 minutes.

Meanwhile, prepare the remaining ingredients. Cut the tortillas into 1-inch-wide strips. Layer the casserole, starting with the rice mixture, spreading evenly over the baking dish. Make a layer of tortilla strips, cutting to fit. Cover with the black beans, then with the green chilies and chopped onion. Top with the vegetarian chili and smooth the surface.

Bake for 25 to 35 minutes. Remove from the oven, cover with shredded cheese, and bake for an additional 10 or 12 minutes. Serve with salsa on the side and a dollop of fat-free sour cream on top of each serving, accompanied by low-fat tortilla chips.

CORN PONE PIE

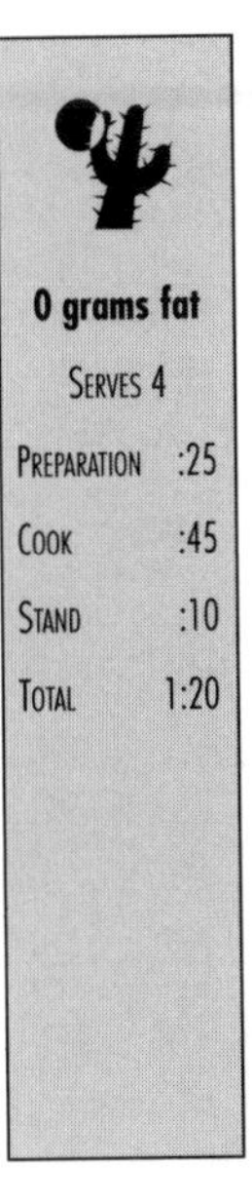

1 cup self-rising yellow cornmeal mix
1 (16-ounce) carton fat-free cottage cheese
2 cups canned or frozen shoepeg corn, drained
3 green onions, chopped
4 egg whites, room temperature
2 (14-ounce) cans Mexican-style stewed tomatoes

Preheat the oven to 350 degrees. Spray an 8-inch square glass baking dish with vegetable oil cooking spray.

In a large bowl, combine the cornmeal mix with the cottage cheese, stirring to blend. Add the corn and green onions. When well blended, set aside.

In a smaller bowl, beat the egg whites until stiff but not dry. Fold the egg whites into the cornmeal mixture in two additions.

Transfer the batter to the prepared dish. Bake until the top of the pone is golden and feels firm in the center, about 35 to 45 minutes. Let stand 10 minutes.

While the pone part is baking, make a tomato sauce: Boil the stewed tomatoes uncovered in a heavy saucepan until reduced to sauce consistency, about 10 minutes. Stir frequently to prevent scorching.

Cut the pone pie into squares and leave in the baking dish. Spoon the tomato sauce over and serve.

Garnishing idea: Sprinkle fat-free shredded cheese over the tomato sauce; top with a little finely chopped green onion.

VEGETARIAN CHILI PIE

4 grams fat entire dish

SERVES 4

PREPARATION	:06
COOK	:37
STAND	:05
TOTAL	:48

3½ slices low-fat white bread
2 cups frozen vegetables, such as gumbo mix
1 teaspoon vinegar
1 (19-ounce) can fat-free vegetarian chili
½ cup water
2 cups shredded nonfat Cheddar cheese
1 teaspoon crushed red pepper flakes
1 cup crushed low-fat potato chips
¾ cup chopped onion

Preheat the oven to 350 degrees. Lightly coat an 11 x 7-inch baking dish with vegetable oil cooking spray. Line the bottom of the dish with bread slices, cutting them as necessary to fit. Set aside.

Place the frozen vegetables in water to cover, add the vinegar, and bring to a boil. Cook for 2 minutes; drain and rinse in a colander. Make an even layer of the vegetables over the bread slices.

Mix the chili with ½ cup of water and pour this over the vegetable layer. Layer chopped onions over vegetables. Cover with the cheese. Sprinkle pepper flakes over the cheese layer.

Scatter crushed potato chips over the casserole and bake uncovered for about 10 minutes. When the chips are lightly browned, place a piece of foil over and continue to bake for 20 to 25 more minutes. Let stand 5 minutes before serving.

VEGETABLE CHILI

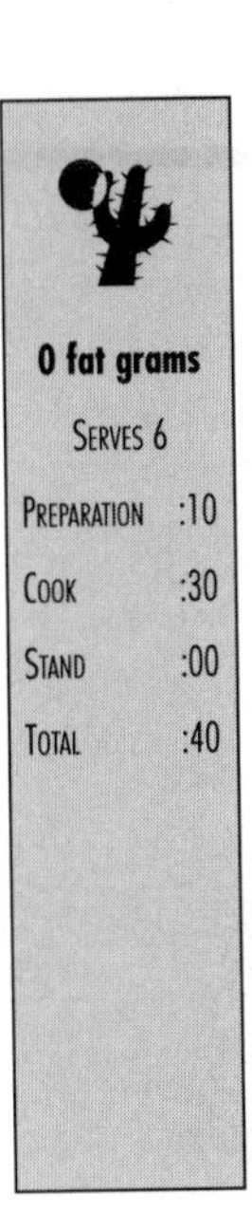

0 fat grams

SERVES 6

PREPARATION	:10
COOK	:30
STAND	:00
TOTAL	:40

1 large onion, chopped
2 carrots, peeled and chopped small
1 (28-ounce) can tomatoes
1 (16-ounce) can black beans
1 (16-ounce) can pinto beans
1 (16-ounce) can kidney beans
1 (16-ounce) can fat-free refried beans
2 to 3 tablespoons chili powder, or to taste
Fat-free sour cream
Dried hot chili flakes

In a medium-large nonstick saucepan or skillet, combine the onion, carrots, and ½ cup of water. Sauté until crisp-tender. Be careful not to let all the water evaporate; if needed, add a little more.

Add the tomatoes (I cut mine up a little with a knife before pouring out of the can), juice and all. Add all the beans and their liquid; stir in the chili powder. Bring to a boil, reduce the heat, and simmer for about 15 minutes, uncovered. Stir often, because the refried beans will thicken your chili; don't let it scorch.

Serve in nice chili bowls with a dollop of sour cream on top and pepper flakes sprinkled over.

Cumin: You can find this spice in three colors in larger spice shops: amber (most commonly found), white, and black. It comes both ground and in seed form. It is mostly used in making chili powder, curry, and some liqueurs. Used very widely in Mexican cooking.

BEAN/TORTILLA PIZZAS

Less than ½ gram fat per serving

SERVES 4

PREPARATION	:10
COOK	:10
STAND	:00
TOTAL	:20

This is a great child pleaser.

It is also a great way to get children interested in the kitchen and healthy cooking. They can even make these themselves after school if they're old enough to use the oven or a toaster oven. Let them help you shop for the ingredients in the recipe; teach them to always read the label and look for fat-free items.

4 (6- or 8-inch) fat-free flour tortillas
1 cup spicy (medium-hot) salsa (you may want to use mild)
½ cup canned black beans, drained
½ cup hot chili beans, drained
⅓ cup chopped canned green chili peppers (see Note)
1 cup shredded fat-free Monterey Jack or Cheddar cheese
2 tablespoons minced fresh cilantro
Fresh ground black pepper if desired

Preheat the oven to 375 degrees. Place tortillas on a baking sheet; spray them lightly with vegetable oil cooking spray.

Spread each tortilla evenly with ¼ of the salsa. Mix the black beans and the hot chili beans together; top each tortilla with ¼ of the beans. Scatter the chili peppers over the beans; top with cheese, cilantro, and black pepper if desired. Bake in the oven for 10 to 15 minutes, or until the cheese has melted.

Variation: You may care to add some ingredients of your own: onion, green peppers, mushrooms, green onions, mixed cheeses, jalapeños, olives (watch out for Mr. Fat Gram hiding in those olives).

Variation: Here's another idea: top with shredded lettuce, and turn it into a tostada, like pizza and salad all in one. Sprinkle with fat-free shredded cheese and serve hot sauce alongside.

Note: Remember, it is cheaper to buy larger cans of chopped green chilies and then keep what you don't use in a plastic container in the refrigerator. "A spoonful of chilies makes the medicine go down, medicine go down, in the most delightful way."

Herbs are an important way to create wonderful flavor in low-fat, no-fat cooking. When you take out the fat, you take out the flavor, so remember to add spices and herbs to pick up the flavors. In Mexican cooking, cilantro, oregano, cumin, red pepper, garlic, onion, hot and mild peppers are all very important. Always taste and add just a little extra if needed to bring up the flavor even more. In low-fat baking you sometimes need to add more spices. Always taste-test first—too many can ruin your efforts.

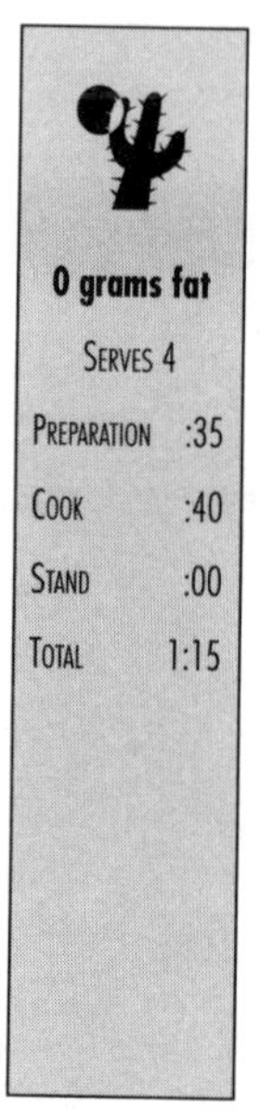

VEGETABLE BEAN BURRITOS

1 cup chopped onion
3/4 cup chopped bell pepper
1 tablespoon chopped jalapeño pepper (optional)
1 tablespoon chili powder
2 cloves garlic, minced (about 1 teaspoon prepared)
2 teaspoons Mexican oregano or regular oregano, crushed
1 teaspoon ground cumin
1 large baking potato, baked, cooled, peeled, and diced (see Note)
1 (15-ounce) can Mexican-style pinto beans, drained and rinsed
1 cup frozen whole corn kernels, thawed and drained
2 tablespoons lime juice
4 (10-inch) fat-free flour tortillas
3/4 cup shredded fat-free Monterey Jack cheese
Fat-free sour cream for garnish

Preheat the oven to 375 degrees.

Place a Dutch oven or large saucepan over medium-low heat and spray very lightly with vegetable oil cooking spray, or use a nonstick pan. Sauté the onion and bell pepper in 2 tablespoons of water, stirring until soft, about 6 to 7 minutes. Add the jalapeño, chili powder, garlic, oregano, and cumin. Cook a minute or so longer, add 1 tablespoon of water, and stir. Remove from heat, stir in the potato, beans, corn, and lime juice.

Lay the tortillas flat on a work surface and spoon about 2 tablespoons cheese down the center of each. Spoon about 1 cup of the filling down the center of each tortilla. Fold the ends in about 1½ inches, then roll up the sides to make a burrito. Place the burritos seam side down on a baking sheet. Cover with foil and bake for 25 to 30 minutes or until heated through.

Serve with a dollop of sour cream atop each.

Variation: Salsa alongside is also nice. Hot sauce may be served on the side for those who like a little more fire.

Note: When you're baking potatoes for dinner, make an extra one; dice it and freeze it for this recipe.

Studies show that in Mexico, people who eat chile peppers at almost every meal lower their risk of stomach cancer.

LAYERED RICE AND BEANS

Less than 2 grams fat per serving

SERVES 6

PREPARATION	:35
COOK	:45
STAND	:00
TOTAL	1:20

2 cups water
1 cup raw rice
4 (8-inch) nonfat corn tortillas
2/3 cup skim milk
2 tablespoons all-purpose flour
1 cup nonfat sour cream
1 (15-ounce) can tomatoes, juice and all
1 cup salsa
2 (15-ounce) cans Mexican-flavored or pinto beans
1 cup shredded nonfat Cheddar cheese
Sliced jalapeño for garnish

Preheat the oven to 350 degrees. Spray a medium-size baking dish with vegetable oil cooking spray.

Bring the water to a boil in a medium saucepan; add the rice, stir, cover, and let simmer for 20 minutes or until the rice is tender and the water absorbed.

Stack the tortillas, wrap them in foil, and place them in the oven to heat for approximately 10 minutes.

In a small mixing bowl, combine the milk, flour, and sour cream. Blend well.

Combine the tomatoes and salsa in a medium-size bowl. Drain the beans slightly and stir them into the pan of cooked rice.

Cut the softened tortillas into fourths; arrange half the tortillas in the bottom of the prepared baking dish.

Layer half the beans and rice mixture over the tortillas.

Layer half the tomato mixture over the bean layer.

Layer half the sour cream mixture over the tomato mixture.

Repeat layers, ending with cheese.

Bake uncovered for 25 to 30 minutes or until heated through. Sprinkle cheese over before serving. Garnish with rings of jalapeño.

ALMOST VEGETARIAN BEAN BAKE

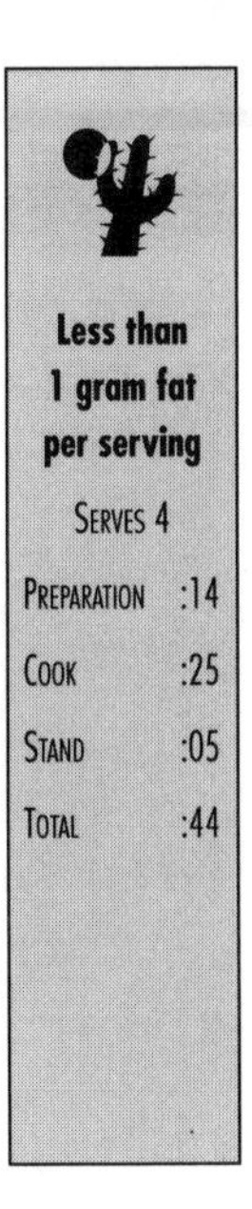

Keep packages of frozen chopped onions in your freezer for quick and easy dishes such as this. They may be used in almost any casserole or dish when in a hurry. I keep frozen chopped green peppers, as well as many other products that can save time for the cook. Women of this day and time do not have the luxury of spending four or five hours a day in the kitchen, nor do they want to. This means we need many tips and hints on quick and convenient ways to have dinner ready to serve in 30 or 45 minutes or less, watching the amount of fat as we go. Anyone can fry-cook dinner in a flash of light, but you and I know that we can't eat that way anymore.

CRUST:

1 2/3 cups plus 1/4 cup canned fat-free chicken broth
  or water
Package of vegetable seasoning enclosed with stuffing mix
1/3 cup chopped onion, frozen or fresh
1/2 tablespoon Mexican oregano or regular oregano, crushed
1/8 teaspoon ground Chimayo red pepper or plain ground red
  pepper (cayenne)
1 small box of stuffing mix, such as Stove Top for pork

FILLING:

1/4 cup chopped onion
1 (16-ounce) can hot chili beans, partially drained
3/4 cup plus 1/2 cup shredded fat-free Cheddar cheese
1 tablespoon canned chopped green chilies
1 cup crumbled low-fat baked tortillas
1 (15-ounce) can vegetarian chili with black beans, or leftover
  Vegetable Chili, page 141
2 tablespoons red enchilada sauce, mild, such as Old
  El Paso

Preheat the oven to 350 degrees. Prepare an 8-inch baking dish by spraying with vegetable oil cooking spray.

Make the crust: In a large saucepan, combine the 1⅔ cups of broth with the packet of seasoning, the ⅓ cup of onion, the oregano, and the ground red pepper. Bring to a boil and stir in the stuffing. Remove from the heat and continue to stir, adding the additional ¼ cup of broth if necessary. Continue to mix until all the stuffing is moist. Pour the stuffing into the prepared baking dish. Dip your fingers in water (I use a thin plastic glove) and press the mixture into a crust shape, halfway up the side and over the bottom of the dish. Set aside.

For the filling: Spread the ¼ cup of onion evenly over the crust. Add the hot chili beans, spreading them evenly. Layer ¾ cup of the shredded cheese over the beans. Sprinkle the green chilies over the cheese; spread the crushed tortillas on top. Pour the vegetarian chili over all.

Drizzle enchilada sauce over evenly—not too much; it is hot—or you may add an additional amount according to your heat level. Bake uncovered for 20 to 25 minutes, or until bubbly. The last 5 minutes, spread the additional ½ cup of shredded cheese over and continue to bake until the cheese is melted.

You may serve this with heated salsa (it keeps the casserole hot longer when served hot). I serve mine in a gravy boat; it's easier to pour without drips on the tablecloth.

ROASTED CORN AND ZUCCHINI CASSEROLE

This is a very nice dish to use some of the many zucchini we grow. It seems like it all comes at the same time. My dad use to have so many zukes in the summer, I had to invent ways to use them. That is how and why the vegetarian chili in my first book was created. Try it: in book number one, So Fat, Low Fat, No Fat.

Less than 1 gram fat per serving

SERVES 6

PREPARATION	:35
COOK	:20
STAND	:00
TOTAL	:55

3/4 cup long-grain rice
1 cup fresh corn kernels, roasted
3/4 cup chopped white onion
1/3 cup finely sliced green onions
2 fresh Anaheim chilies, seeded, washed, and chopped fine, or chopped canned chilies
2 slices jalapeño pepper, chopped fine, fresh if available (remember to use rubber gloves)
1 1/4 cups finely chopped zucchini
1 cup halved and sliced fresh mushrooms
1 (11-ounce) can tomato sauce
1 teaspoon Mexican seasoning
1/2 teaspoon thyme, crushed
1/2 teaspoon Mexican oregano or regular oregano, crushed
Salt and pepper to taste
1/2 cup shredded fat-free Monterey Jack cheese

Preheat the oven to 350 degrees. Spray a medium-size casserole lightly with vegetable oil cooking spray.

Put the rice on to cook according to package directions.

Meanwhile, roast your corn. One ear is usually enough. Shuck the corn, clean the silk away, wash, and shake dry. Cut the kernels off the cob. (Use a sharp knife and cut away from you, from top to bottom, holding the corn cob with one hand and cutting into a bowl. Take the edge of your knife—the dull side—and scrape from top to bottom, retrieving all the corn juice, or milk.) Heat a nonstick skillet to very hot; dump the corn all at once into the hot skillet. It will start to roast, which turns the corn just lightly brown. Stir occasionally, turning the roasted corn up and getting all the uncooked kernels to the bottom. When your corn is all roasted, pour it into a dish and set aside for a few minutes.

In the same nonstick skillet, sauté the white and green onions, Anaheim peppers, jalapeños, and zucchini in about 2 tablespoons of water. When these vegetables are crisp-tender add the mushrooms and corn; continue to cook another 2 minutes over medium-high heat, stirring frequently.

At this time stir in the tomato sauce, Mexican seasoning, thyme, oregano, and salt and pepper if desired, stirring to mix well. Remove from the heat.

Spread the cooked rice evenly over the bottom of the prepared baking dish. Pour the corn and zucchini mixture over the rice and smooth the surface.

Sprinkle the shredded cheese evenly over the casserole. Cover and bake in a 350 degree oven for 10 minutes, or until the cheese melts. (The vegetables are still warm and so is the rice, so this only needs to get nice and hot.)

Serve immediately with a tray of raw vegetables or a green salad. You have a nice meal in a hurry, with no meat, low-fat. Hey, let's do it! Get some of that fat off!

Chapter 7

Vegetables and Side Dishes

GREEN BEANS OLÉ

½ gram fat per serving

SERVES 4

PREPARATION :10

COOK :05

STAND :00

TOTAL :15

2 slices turkey bacon

1 clove garlic, minced

1 teaspoon fresh rosemary leaves or 1/2 teaspoon dried

1 pound french or slender green beans, or 1 (16-ounce) can, drained

Salt and pepper to taste

Cook the bacon on paper toweling in the microwave until crisp. Crumble; set aside.

In a wok or nonstick skillet, combine the garlic and rosemary with about 2 tablespoons of water. Sauté just until the garlic is fragrant, about 30 seconds. (Watch out; remember about burned garlic—terrible!!)

Add the beans and another ⅓ cup of water, cover and simmer for 10 minutes (3 minutes for canned beans). Uncover and stir-fry until the liquid has evaporated. Season to taste with salt and pepper.

Turn the beans into a serving dish and sprinkle with crumbled bacon.

BASIC POT OF BROWN OR PINTO BEANS

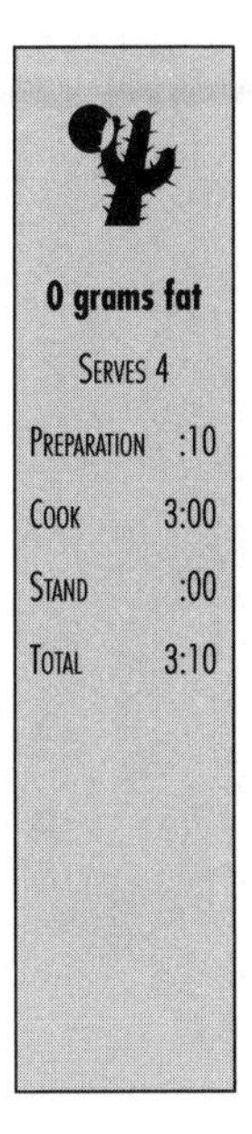

There are different opinions about soaking beans. What is yours? I have tried it both ways, but I understand that presoaking is unnecessary. They say if you do soak, you get rid of some of the gas effects. They say if you don't soak, you get rid of some of the gas. Which is it?

My theory is just to sort the beans, wash four or five times, and put them on to cook in a large stockpot or other cooking container. Add your garlic and onion at this time.

I have my favorite old bean pot. I bet you do also if you cook very many beans. If you are a first-timer, you are in for quite a treat.

2 cups dried pinto or brown beans
2 cloves garlic, minced
1 small onion, minced
Salt to taste—about 2 teaspoons

Bring the beans, garlic, and onion to a rapid boil and lower the heat to a steady medium-high boil. Don't cover the pot. Watch out that you don't boil them over or you will have a terrible mess. You also need to stir occasionally. Make sure your water is not boiling away—the beans should be floating freely and the water level should remain about 2 inches above the beans.

Don't add the salt until about the last 30 minutes; it will make the skins tough. When your beans are tender, the broth will start to thicken just a bit and the beans will be immersed but no longer floating. Stirring frequently as suggested seems to thicken them also.

I always cook my beans a day ahead; it seems to make them tastier. You may season to taste if desired, and heat over low heat until bubbly hot.

RO-TEL REFRIED BEANS

0 grams fat

SERVES 2

PREPARATION	:03
COOK	:05
STAND	:00
TOTAL	:08

This quick bean dish is excellent to serve with many, many dishes. You may also decide to add a few onions and green bell peppers for a little more body to your dish. If so, use about ¼ cup of each and sauté them in a nonstick skillet with ¼ cup of water until crisp-tender, then add to your beans.

1 (15-ounce) can fat-free refried beans (use the spicy ones if you like really spicy dishes)
1 (10-ounce) can Ro-Tel diced tomatoes with green chilies

Place the beans in a nonstick saucepan over low heat. Open the Ro-Tel and drain the liquid off, reserving it for another use, such as the Chicken Potato Stir-Fry on page 84.

Add the tomatoes to the beans, stir to blend, and continue to heat until steaming hot. Stir often so as not to scorch the beans or allow them to stick on the bottom.

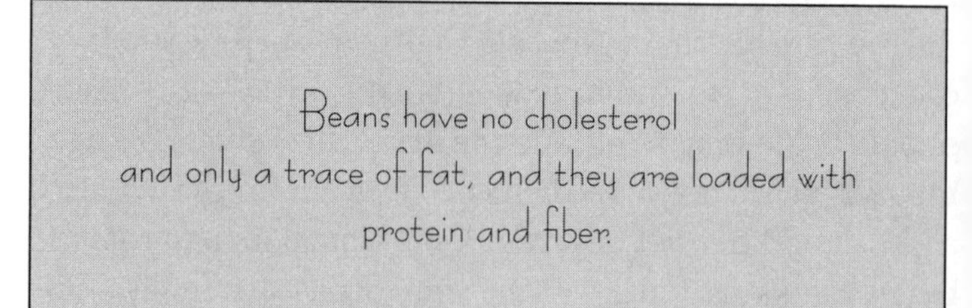

CHILI GANG BAKED BEANS

1 gram fat per serving

SERVES 8

PREPARATION	:30
COOK	2:30
STAND	:00
TOTAL	3:00

6 slices turkey bacon
4 (15-ounce) cans ranch or barbecue-style beans
1 tablespoon chopped green chilies
1 cup salsa
1/2 cup barbecue sauce
3/4 cup chopped onion
1/4 cup chopped sweet banana pepper
1 teaspoon prepared mustard
1/2 teaspoon garlic powder
Chili powder to taste (Chimayo if available)
Mexican oregano or regular oregano, crushed, to taste
1/2 cup coconut amaretto

Preheat the oven to 375 degrees. Spray a medium-large casserole with vegetable oil cooking spray.

Cook the turkey bacon in the microwave between thicknesses of paper towels—this will help to blot any excess fat cooked out. When crisp, pat with additional paper towels; crumble and reserve.

Pour the undrained beans into the casserole and add the chilies, salsa, barbecue sauce, onion, banana pepper, and seasonings. Stir in the amaretto and mix well. Cover and bake for 2 to 2½ hours. Remove from the oven and stir about three times during the baking period to keep the beans from getting too dry around the edges. Bake longer if your preference is drier, thicker baked beans.

PASTA BEAN SALAD

3.5 grams fat entire dish

SERVES 6

PREPARATION	:25
COOK	:20
STAND	:15
TOTAL	1:00

1 (7-ounce) package ditalini, orzo, or any very small pasta
1 (15-ounce) can ranch-style beans, drained and rinsed
1 (15-ounce) can green peas, drained
1/2 cup chopped onion
1/2 cup chopped green bell pepper
2 tablespoons fat-free mayonnaise, such as Miracle Whip
1 tablespoon fat-free sour cream
1/4 teaspoon lemon pepper
1/4 teaspoon Mexican seasoning
1 tablespoon red wine vinegar

In a medium size saucepan, cook macaroni according to package directions. Drain and rinse with cold water.

While the pasta is cooking, prepare the other ingredients. Assemble the beans, peas, onion, and bell pepper in a medium-large salad bowl. Add the cooled pasta.

In a small bowl, combine the mayonnaise, sour cream, lemon pepper, Mexican seasoning, and vinegar. Blend. Pour over the salad and toss gently to cover all. Chill about 15 minutes before serving if possible.

Pasta is a wonderful low-fat healthy way of adding to many, many recipes. I cook extra when I have the time to cook for one. I double the recipe, cool, place the extra in a zipper-lock plastic bag, and take out just as much as I need to add a little color and/or stretch the recipe for extra servngs.

LAYERED MEXICAN SALAD

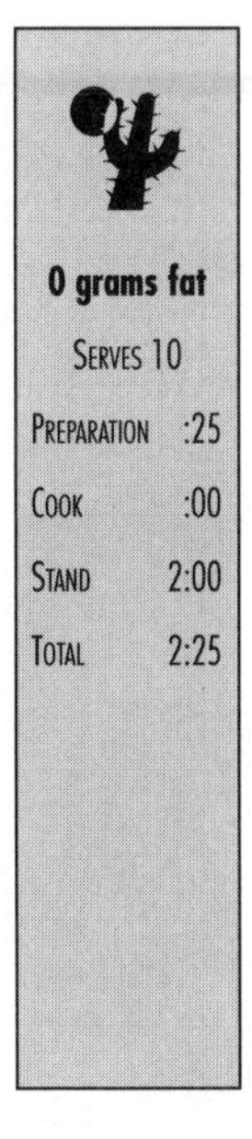

This is a great make-ahead salad for entertaining. You can very easily make it larger.

1 small head romaine lettuce, washed, cored, and drained
Fresh Salsa (page 192) or 2½ cups commercially prepared salsa
1 (15-ounce) can black beans or Mexican-flavored pinto beans, drained and rinsed
1 (8-ounce) can shoepeg corn (or use frozen if desired—about 1 cup)
1 medium cucumber, peeled
¾ cup shredded fat-free Cheddar cheese (optional)
1 green onion, sliced into thin rounds for garnish

DRESSING:

1 large lemon (or bottled juice—about ¼ cup)
1 cup fat-free mayonnaise, such as Miracle Whip
¼ cup fat-free yogurt
1 clove garlic, minced (optional)

Stack the lettuce leaves on top of each other and slice crosswise into ½-inch strips. Place half the lettuce in a large clear-glass serving bowl. (The reason for the clear glass is strictly for appearance; it can be made in any bowl, but it is so pretty in a clear bowl.)

Spread the salsa over the lettuce. Layer the beans over the salsa and layer the corn over the beans.

Cut the cucumber in half lengthwise and scoop out the seeds; slice the cucumber thin and layer over the corn. Top with the remaining lettuce.

Make the dressing: Grate the lemon peel and measure out 1 teaspoon. Combine with the mayonnaise and yogurt in a small bowl. Add 3 to 4 tablespoons of lemon juice and the garlic, if using. Mix well with a wire whisk.

Spread the dressing over the lettuce layer, making sure you touch the edges of the bowl all the way around. This seals the salad in and the air out. Sprinkle with cheese (if desired) and green onion.

Cover and refrigerate at least 2 hours before serving and as long as 1 day ahead. Dip straight up and down when serving; this ensures that each person gets all the vegetables in the salad.

CORN AND BEAN SALAD

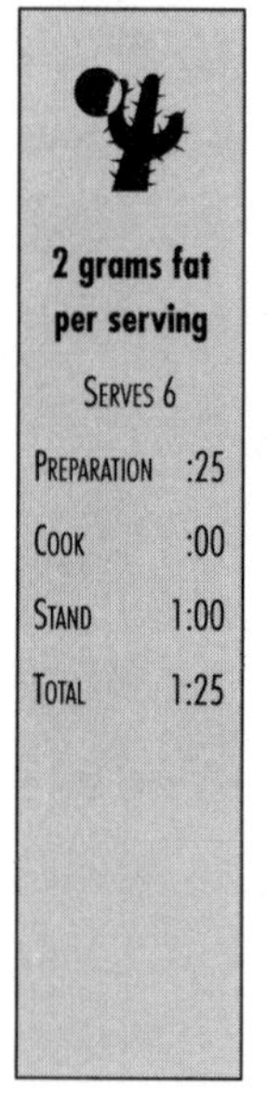

2 grams fat per serving

SERVES 6

PREPARATION	:25
COOK	:00
STAND	1:00
TOTAL	1:25

1 (15-ounce) can black turtle beans (regular black beans may be substituted)
1 (15-ounce) can garbanzo beans (chick-peas)
1 (15-ounce) can pinto beans
1 cup frozen yellow or shoepeg corn
2 green onions, chopped
1 1/4 cup red or green bell pepper strips (roasted according to instructions, page 40)
1 recipe Cumin Dressing (page 159)

Rinse and drain the beans well. Place in a medium-large bowl; add the corn, green onion, and bell pepper. Pour cumin dressing over and toss gently to coat evenly. Let stand 1 hour.

CUMIN DRESSING

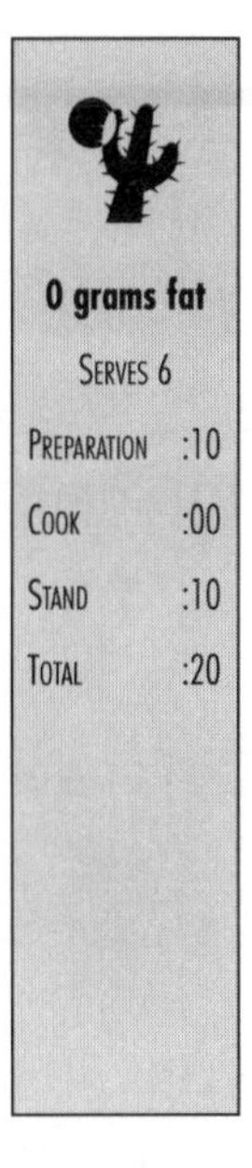

This is great for a vegetable salad or green salad.

2 tablespoons white wine vinegar
2 tablespoons fresh lemon juice
1 teaspoon grated lemon peel
1 clove garlic, minced
1/2 teaspoon ground cumin

Mix all the ingredients in a small bowl and let stand about 10 minutes.

FRIED CABBAGE

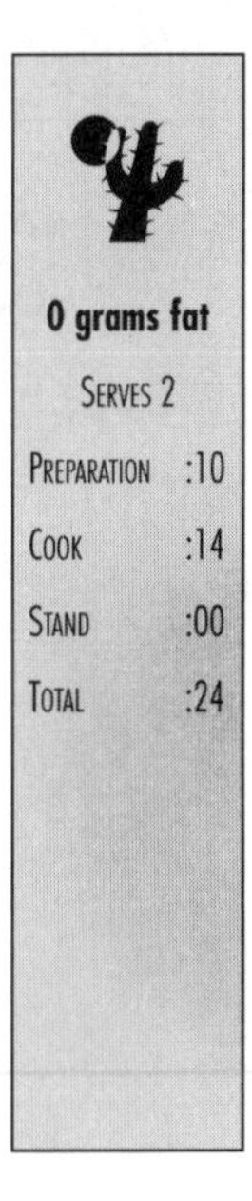

1 medium-size head of cabbage
1 medium-size onion
1 (10-ounce) can Ro-Tel tomatoes with chilies, partially drained
1/2 teaspoon Mexican oregano or regular oregano, crushed
Salt and pepper if desired
2 tablespoons cider vinegar (optional)

Clean and chop the cabbage; slice the onion thin.

Spray a large nonstick skillet with vegetable oil cooking spray; preheat the pan to medium hot. Put the cabbage and onions in the skillet to quickly brown over medium-high heat. Stir and turn with a spatula to brown all areas possible. After the cabbage has started to wilt, lower the heat to medium. Pour in the tomatoes with chilies, add the oregano, salt, and pepper, and sprinkle with vinegar.

Cover and simmer for 5 minutes; stir and continue to simmer for about 5 minutes longer, until the cabbage is done to your liking.

COLESLAW

0 grams fat

SERVES 6

PREPARATION	:30
COOK	:10
STAND	:00
TOTAL	:40

5 cups shredded white cabbage
1 small onion, sliced thin and separated into rings
2 cups prepared barbecue sauce (check label for fat-free)
Ground black pepper to taste
4 drops green Tabasco sauce, or to taste
1 teaspoon chopped green chilies
1 teaspoon prepared mustard
Pinch of Mexican seasoning

Combine the cabbage and onion in a medium to large mixing bowl; set aside.

In a smaller mixing bowl, combine the remaining ingredients to make the dressing. Stir to mix well. If too thick, add water, a teaspoon at a time; if too thin, add fat-free mayonnaise, a tablespoon at a time, until you have the desired consistency. Pour just enough dressing over the vegetables to coat them. Toss well and serve immediately.

For make ahead, store the cabbage and onion in cold water to cover and the dressing in a covered container. Drain the cabbage well, pour out on a towel to blot the excess water, dry the bowl, and continue as instructed.

OKLAHOMA TEX-MEX COLESLAW

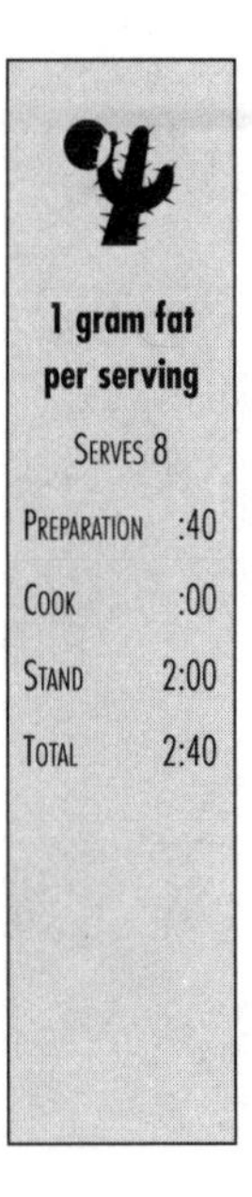

DRESSING:

1/3 cup picante sauce, temperature of your choice
1 tablespoon sugar
4 teaspoons white vinegar
1 teaspoon vegetable oil, such as canola

SLAW INGREDIENTS:

4 to 5 cups finely shredded cabbage
2 cups peeled and shredded jicama (see page 24)
1 cup shredded carrots
1/4 cup chopped red or green bell pepper
3 to 4 green onions, sliced thin

In a large glass mixing bowl, mix dressing ingredients; set aside. Prepare the remaining slaw ingredients and add to the dressing; toss well to blend all. Cover and refrigerate for at least 2 hours and up to 24 hours.

COOKOUT COLESLAW

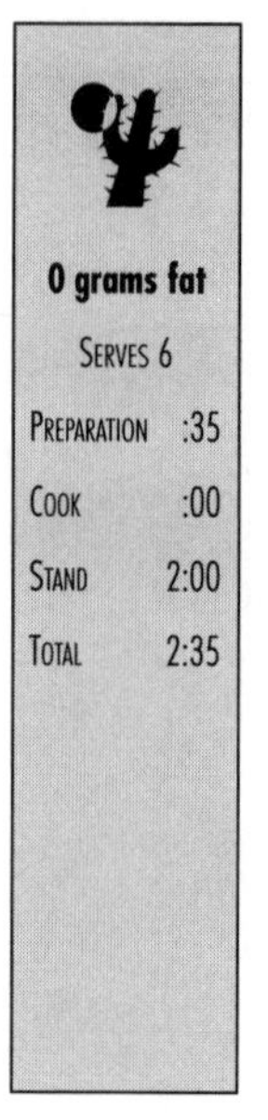

SLAW:

3 cups finely shredded green cabbage
1/2 cup finely shredded red cabbage (see Note)
1 small onion, sliced very thin, cut in half, and separated into half rings
1/4 cup finely chopped fresh cilantro
1 small red bell pepper, diced

DRESSING:

1 cup fat-free mayonnaise
2 tablespoons honey
1 teaspoon Dijon mustard
Salt and pepper to taste
1/4 teaspoon ground cumin
1 teaspoon minced jalapeño
2 tablespoons lime juice

In a large salad bowl with a cover, combine the red and green cabbage, the onion, cilantro, and bell pepper. Toss to mix well. Set aside.

Mix the dressing: Combine in a smaller bowl the mayonnaise, honey, mustard, salt, pepper, cumin, jalapeño, and lime juice. Blend with a wire whisk. Pour half the dressing over the slaw mixture. Refrigerate at least 2 hours before serving; stir again before serving.

If you like a creamier or wetter type of slaw, add more dressing until you reach the desired texture. Otherwise, keep the leftover dressing; it is also good on green salad, or you can use it for a dip (add a little more mayonnaise for the right consistency).

Note: The red cabbage is just for color; if you do not have red, use all green. There are several different cabbages in the markets; you can mix types as well.

MARILYN'S SANTA FE ROASTED CORN

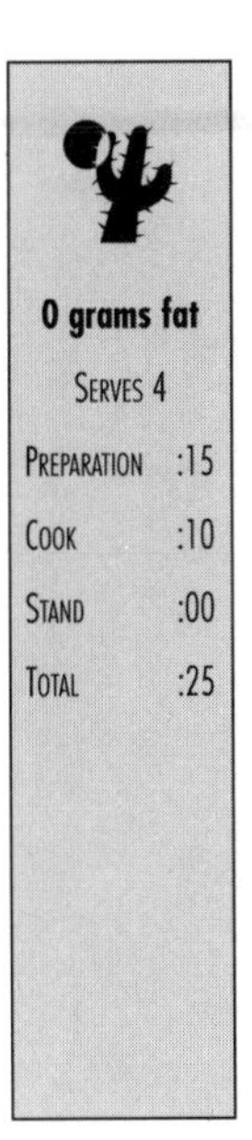

4 ears fresh corn
1/2 cup chopped red bell pepper
1/2 cup chopped green onion
1/4 cup chopped fresh cilantro
1 teaspoon ground cumin
Salt and pepper to taste

Using a sharp knife, cut the kernels of corn off the cobs and into a large bowl (see page 149 for further instructions). Heat a nonstick skillet until fairly hot. Pour in the corn kernels all at once. They will start to brown in the very hot dry skillet, thus roasting the corn.

Stir occasionally to roast the corn evenly. When about half the kernels have taken on color, add the bell pepper and green onion. Cook for another 4 minutes and add the cilantro and cumin. Continue to stir and cook until the vegetables are crisp-tender. Season with salt and pepper if desired.

One red bell pepper has 16 times the beta carotene and twice the vitamin C of an orange.

MEXICAN CORN

0 grams fat

SERVES 6

PREPARATION	:15
COOK	1:00
STAND	:00
TOTAL	1:15

3/4 cup chopped onion
2 cups tomato sauce
1 1/2 tablespoons chili powder
Salt and pepper to taste
3 cups corn kernels (fresh or frozen)
2 tablespoons fat-free margarine

Preheat the oven to 350 degrees. Lightly spray an 11 x 7-inch baking dish with vegetable oil cooking spray.

In a nonstick skillet, sauté the onion in 2 tablespoons of water until crisp-tender. Remove and set aside.

In a large mixing bowl, combine the tomato sauce, chili powder, salt and pepper, corn, margarine, and onions. Mix well. Pour into the prepared baking dish. Cover and bake for 1 hour.

SEASONED CORN

0 grams fat

SERVES 6

PREPARATION	:08
COOK	:10
STAND	:30
TOTAL	:48

You would know that I would have to have corn dishes in my book if you had read the stories in my previous books, *So Fat, Low Fat, No Fat*, *More So Fat, Low Fat, No Fat*, and *Italian So Fat, Low Fat, No Fat.*

6 ears fresh corn (6 cups corn kernels)
1/2 cup white vinegar
1/4 cup lime juice
1 medium onion, chopped
2 tablespoons sugar
1 (2-ounce) jar diced pimientos
1 teaspoon mustard seed
1/4 teaspoon or less hot chile flakes
Salt and pepper to taste

Place the corn in a large saucepan and cover with water; bring to a boil and cook for 4 to 5 minutes. Drain the corn and, when cool enough to handle, cut the kernels off the cobs and place in a heatproof serving dish.

In a nonreactive saucepan, combine the vinegar, lime juice, onion, sugar, pimientos, mustard seed, and chile flakes. Bring to a boil over high heat, stirring to dissolve the sugar. Lower the heat and boil for 3 to 4 minutes.

Pour the marinade over the corn; let stand, stirring occasionally, for 30 to 45 minutes. Season to taste with salt and pepper. This can be served cold as a salad or hot as a side dish.

QUICK SKILLET CORN

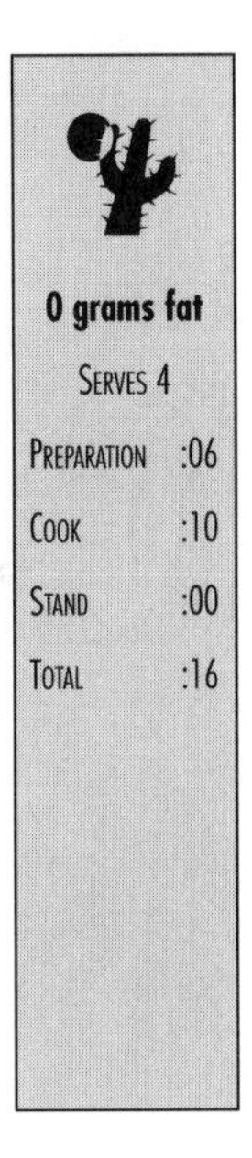

1 (10-ounce) package frozen whole-kernel corn
1/2 cup water
1/2 cup chopped green bell pepper
1/2 cup chopped red bell pepper (if not available, use chopped canned pimiento for color)
1/4 cup thinly sliced celery
1/2 cup fat-free cream cheese
1/4 cup canned diced green chilies
1 tablespoon skim milk
Salt and pepper to taste

In a nonstick skillet combine the corn, water, green pepper, red pepper or pimiento, and celery. Bring to a boil, lower the heat, and cook for about 5 minutes or until the corn is tender. Drain in a colander.

Return the vegetables to the skillet; add the cream cheese, diced chilies, milk, and salt and pepper if desired. Heat through, stirring to melt the cheese and mix evenly. Serve hot.

SOUTH OF THE BORDER HOMINY CASSEROLE

Less than 1 gram fat entire dish

SERVES 4

PREPARATION	:10
COOK	:30
STAND	:05
TOTAL	:45

1/4 cup fresh or frozen chopped onion
1/4 cup fresh or frozen chopped green bell pepper
1 (4-ounce) can chopped green chilies
2 tablespoons drained chopped pimiento (optional)
1 (30-ounce) can whole white or yellow hominy
1 (8-ounce) carton fat-free sour cream
1/2 teaspoon Mexican oregano or regular oregano, crushed
Pinch of Mexican seasoning or ground red pepper (cayenne)
1/4 cup shredded fat-free cheese, or as needed
3/4 cup fine dry bread crumbs

Preheat the oven to 350 degrees. Lightly coat a medium-large casserole with vegetable oil cooking spray.

In a nonstick skillet, sauté the onion and green pepper in 2 tablespoons of water until crisp-tender, about 5 minutes. Add the green chilies and pimiento and continue to sauté for 1 minute.

Drain the hominy and pour into a medium-size mixing bowl. Add the sour cream and stir to mix well. Add the sautéed chile mixture, oregano, Mexican seasoning, and cheese. Mix well.

Pour the mixture into the prepared casserole and sprinkle bread crumbs over the top. Spray lightly with butter-flavored cooking spray (or plain will do if you do not have butter-flavored). Be careful—spray from a distance and lightly, or you will blow the crumbs all over the kitchen.

Cover and bake for 25 to 35 minutes or until bubbly. You may desire to remove the cover and sprinkle an additional ¼ cup of cheese over the top about 5 minutes before removing the casserole from the oven.

HOMINY WITH A TOUCH OF THE BORDER

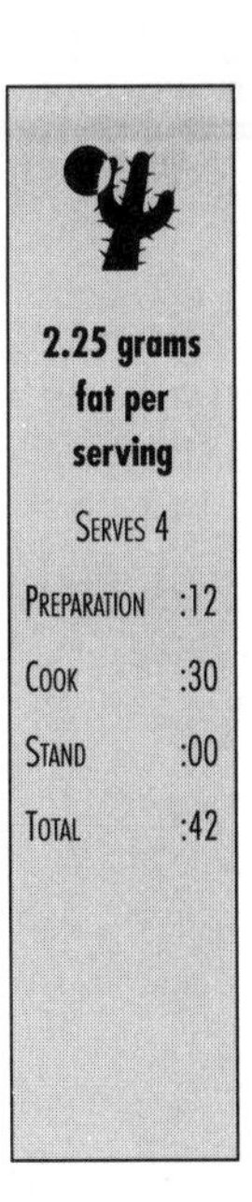

1 (15½-ounce) can whole hominy, yellow or white, drained
2 tablespoons fat-free pourable margarine, such as Fleischmann's
1 (10¾-ounce) can low-fat cream of mushroom soup
1 teaspoon garlic salt
1 teaspoon chili powder
¼ cup canned chopped green chilies
Ground black pepper to taste (optional)
1 cup crushed low-fat baked tortillas
½ cup shredded fat-free Cheddar cheese

Preheat the oven to 350 degrees.

Combine the drained hominy and margarine in a medium-large saucepan; stir to mix. Add the soup, garlic salt, chili powder, green chilies, pepper if desired, and ½ cup of crushed tortillas. Stir well to blend and heat until heated through.

Pour the mixture into a medium-size baking dish. Mix the cheese and the remaining tortilla chips. Sprinkle over the top.

Bake uncovered for 20 to 25 minutes, until hot and bubbly.

Processed cheese: This can be bought in a form that is fat-free, usually made by a company like Healthy Choice. It can be found in the refrigerated section of your supermarket, usually in a long green one- or two-pound box; it looks a lot like Velveeta and can be used very much like Velveeta. Remember it is fat-free. Those are the two words you look for.

MOM'S GREEN CHILE HOMINY CASSEROLE

Less than 1 gram fat in entire casserole

SERVES 8

PREPARATION :10

COOK :40

STAND :00

TOTAL :50

2 (15½-ounce) cans whole hominy, white or yellow, drained
¼ cup finely chopped onion
1½ cups fat-free sour cream
1½ cups shredded fat-free Monterey Jack or Cheddar cheese
1 (4-ounce) can chopped green chilies, drained
¼ teaspoon salt
½ cup fine dry bread crumbs

Preheat the oven to 350 degrees.

Combine the hominy, onion, sour cream, cheese, green chilies, and salt in a mixing bowl. Stir to mix well. Pour into a medium-size baking dish. Bake uncovered for 35 minutes, sprinkle with crumbs and brown for 5 minutes longer.

This also can be made ahead, covered, and stored in refrigerator. Leave the bread crumbs off, cook for 35 to 40 minutes, let cool, cover, and store. When ready to serve, set out of refrigerator about 30 minutes before baking, heat about 10 to 12 minutes, or until hot and bubbly, add bread crumbs, and brown.

CHEESY HOMINY BAKE

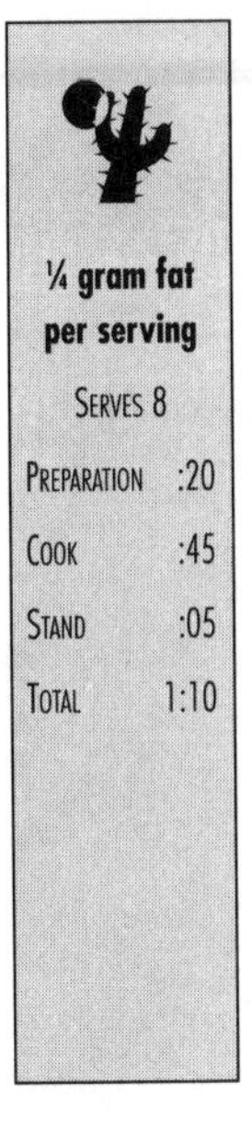

1/4 cup egg substitute
2 (16-ounce) cans whole hominy, yellow or white, rinsed and drained
12 ounces cubed fat-free processed cheese, such as Healthy Choice (comes in 1- or 2-pound packages in a long green box—looks like Velveeta)
3/4 cup skim milk
1/2 cup finely chopped onion
2 tablespoons bacon bits (1 gram fat per tablespoon)
1 tablespoon fat-free margarine
Dash of ground black pepper
Parsley for garnish (optional)

Preheat the oven to 350 degrees. Lightly coat an 11 x 7-inch baking dish with vegetable oil cooking spray; set aside.

In a large mixing bowl, beat the egg substitute slightly; add the hominy, cheese, milk, onion, bacon bits, margarine, and pepper. Mix well. Spoon into the prepared baking dish.

Bake uncovered for about 45 minutes or until bubbly and slightly browned. Let stand about 5 minutes before serving. Garnish with parsley if desired.

BORDER GRITS

0 grams fat

SERVES 6

PREPARATION :20

COOK :52

STAND :00

TOTAL 1:12

This is another dish you can make ahead, cover, and refrigerate until time to use. It can even be frozen.

1 cup uncooked hominy grits
1/2 cup chopped green chilies, or 2 to 4 rings of jalapeño, chopped
2 1/4 cups fat-free sour cream
2 cups shredded fat-free Monterey Jack cheese
1/2 cup fat-free shredded Cheddar cheese

Preheat the oven to 350 degrees. Lightly coat a medium-size casserole with vegetable oil cooking spray.

Bring 4 cups of water to a boil; stir in the grits slowly and mix well. Lower the heat to medium low, cover, and continue to cook for 5 to 7 minutes. If the grits are a tad too dry, add a touch of hot water and stir.

Spread half the cooked grits in the bottom of the casserole. Sprinkle with half the chilies, spread with half the sour cream, and top with half the Jack cheese. Repeat to make a second layer. Top this layer with half the Cheddar cheese. Cover and bake for 35 minutes. Add the rest of the Cheddar cheese and continue baking uncovered for 10 minutes or until well melted.

CHEESY CHILE GRITS

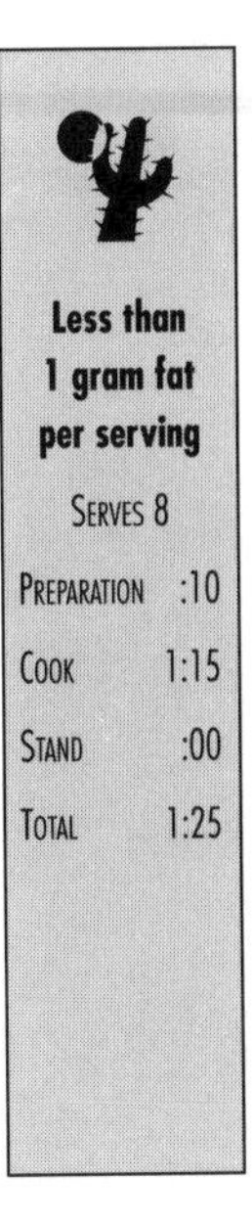

1 1/2 cups hominy grits
1 teaspoon salt
3/4 cup fat-free pourable margarine, such as Fleischmann's
1 1/4 cups diced fat-free processed cheese, such as Healthy Choice (comes in 1- or 2-pound packages in a long green box—looks like Velveeta), or shredded fat-free Cheddar cheese
3/4 cup egg substitute
1/2 (4-ounce) can pimientos, drained and chopped fine
1 (4-ounce) can green chilies, drained and chopped

Preheat the oven to 300 degrees. Lightly coat a medium-large baking dish with vegetable oil cooking spray.

Bring 6 cups of water to a boil in a heavy or nonstick saucepan. Add the grits and salt, stirring constantly. Cook until thick, about 15 minutes. If using instant grits, follow package directions.

Combine the margarine, cheese, egg substitute, pimiento, and green chilies, stirring to mix well.

Add the cheese mixture to the grits. Pour into the prepared baking dish. Bake uncovered for 1 hour.

EGGPLANT FINGERS

3 grams fat entire recipe

SERVES 4

PREPARATION :20

COOK :35

STAND :00

TOTAL :55

1 tablespoon salt
1 medium-size eggplant
1 1/2 cups cornflake crumbs
1/2 cup fine dry bread crumbs
1 teaspoon Mexican oregano or regular oregano, crushed
1/2 teaspoon ground mild green chilies (optional)
1 teaspoon Mexican seasoning
1 cup egg substitute

Preheat the oven to 400 degrees. Spray a large baking sheet with vegetable oil cooking spray.

In a medium-large mixing bowl, combine the salt and about 1 quart of water. Peel the eggplant and cut into fingerlike strips about ½ inch thick. Put into the bowl of salt water; if water does not cover the eggplant, continue to add more until covered. Let stand while you prepare the rest of the recipe.

Combine the cornflake crumbs (I use the type already prepared in a box—zero fat grams), dry bread crumbs (also prepared commercially), and seasonings. Mix well. Pour half the mixture into a shallow bowl such as a pie plate. Place the egg substitute in a similar bowl.

Take a few eggplant pieces at a time out of the water and lay them on a paper towel or kitchen cloth to drain. Dip into the egg substitute and then the crumb mixture, coating evenly.

Place the strips in a single layer, not touching, on the prepared baking sheet. Spray the tops lightly with cooking spray. Bake 30 to 35 minutes, turning once halfway through baking time, or until tender and lightly browned.

Note: The salt water helps prevent the eggplant from turning dark.

ZESTY HEALTHY ROASTED POTATOES

Less than 1 gram fat per serving

SERVES 6

PREPARATION	:15
COOK	:40
STAND	:00
TOTAL	:55

1 teaspoon Mexican seasoning
1 tablespoon dried rosemary
1 tablespoon garlic powder
1 tablespoon onion powder
1/2 cup fat-free Miracle Whip dressing
2 pounds small red potatoes, quartered

Preheat the oven to 400 degrees. Spray a large baking sheet with vegetable oil cooking spray.

In a large mixing bowl, combine the seasonings with 1 tablespoon of water; mix well. Stir in the Miracle Whip. Add the potatoes, tossing to coat evenly. Arrange the potatoes in a single layer on the baking sheet.

Bake for 35 to 40 minutes or until golden brown, turning after 15 minutes.

Making mashed potatoes: Many flavors can be added, leaving out the whole milk and butter. Try fat-free cottage cheese or low-fat buttermilk; add baked garlic, a variety of spices, chopped chives—use your imagination. Fat-free cheeses are also a great addition. Your family and guests will never know they're eating something that's good for them; don't tell them and just reap the praises. You know, a lot of what people don't know is not going to hurt them.

POTATO SPEARS

Very slight trace of fat

SERVES 4

PREPARATION	:10
COOK	:30
STAND	:00
TOTAL	:40

These are wonderful to serve at a party, with a nice dip or with salsa. Cut a little thicker, they are excellent with fish.

2 tablespoons fat-free sour cream
2 tablespoons fat-free mayonnaise
1 tablespoon lime juice
1 tablespoon Tabasco jalapeño sauce (green), or dash of regular Tabasco
1 teaspoon Mexican oregano or regular oregano, crushed
2 large baking potatoes, unpeeled

Preheat the oven to 400 degrees. Prepare a baking sheet by spraying it very lightly with vegetable oil cooking spray.

In a medium-size bowl, make the coating sauce by combining the sour cream, mayonnaise, lime juice, Tabasco, and oregano. Stir with a wire whisk to blend thoroughly. Set aside while preparing your potatoes.

After scrubbing the potatoes, pat them dry with a paper towel. Cut lengthwise into wedges, usually 8; the thinner wedges get crisper than thicker ones. I make wedges thicker when serving with a meal.

Dip your potato wedges into the bowl, not too many at a time—two or three—and coat totally with the sauce. Lay each one on the baking sheet in a single layer, not touching. Spray very lightly with vegetable oil cooking spray.

Bake for 15 to 20 minutes; turn each potato with long tongs or a spatula and continue to bake until nice and brown.

POTATOES DOWN MEXICO WAY

We always had potatoes on the table at every meal when I was growing up, usually ones that Dad had grown. Read the potato story on page 135 of my first book, So Fat, Low Fat, No Fat.

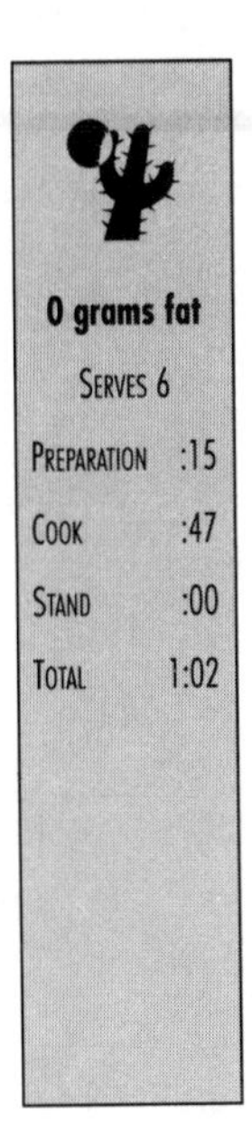

3 medium-size potatoes
2 fresh Anaheim chilies
3/4 cup chopped white onion
1/2 cup finely chopped green onions
1 clove garlic, crushed with garlic press
3 sprigs fresh cilantro, minced (optional)
Salt and fresh ground pepper to taste

Wash your potatoes, leaving the skins on, place them in a large saucepan, and add water to come about 3 inches over the tops. Bring to a boil, lower the heat to medium, a nice even boil, without overflowing your pan, and let cook about 30 minutes, or until tender to the fork test. Drain and, when cool enough to handle, peel and dice them into bite-size pieces.

While the potatoes are cooking, roast the Anaheim chilies following the instructions on page 40. While the chilies are steaming in the bag is a good time to dice your potatoes. You can organize your steps: prepare while cooking, cooking while preparing. Peel and chop the Anaheims fine. (You could use canned chopped green chilies if fresh ones are not available, but the aroma of the roasting chilies in your home is worth every minute of the roasting time.)

Sauté the white and green onions, garlic, and chopped Anaheim chilies in about 2 tablespoons of water over medium-high heat, stirring frequently, for 4 or 5 minutes. Stir in the warm potatoes and cilantro. Reduce the heat to low, cooking and stirring occasionally for about 2 more minutes. Add salt and pepper to taste, and serve immediately.

0 grams fat

SERVES 4

PREPARATION	:12
COOK	:22
STAND	:00
TOTAL	:34

GARLIC MASHED POTATOES

4 medium-size red potatoes (or your choice)
1 or more large cloves garlic
2 to 4 tablespoons skim milk or skim buttermilk
$1/2$ teaspoon Mexican oregano or regular oregano, crushed
Salt and pepper to taste

Peel the potatoes and cut them into $1\frac{1}{2}$-inch chunks. Place in a large saucepan, and cover with water; add 1 teaspoon of salt. Bring to a boil; reduce the heat to a steady simmer and cook for 15 minutes or until tender. While the potatoes are cooking, roast the garlic.

Place the unpeeled garlic in a small microwave-safe dish; microwave until soft, about 3 to 4 minutes, according to the power of your oven. Check to see if soft; if not, cook a little longer. Remove the peel; set the garlic aside.

When the potatoes are tender, drain off the water. Add the garlic and mash the potatoes with a potato masher or an electric mixer. Add the milk, a small amount at a time, until the potatoes reach the consistency desired. Add the oregano just before you are finished mashing the potatoes. Add salt and pepper to taste if desired. Serve immediately or keep warm until serving time.

A study of onions and garlic has produced strong evidence that adding garlic in your cooking can lower the risk of colon cancer by 35 percent and the risk of stomach cancer by as much as 40 percent.

POTATO SALAD

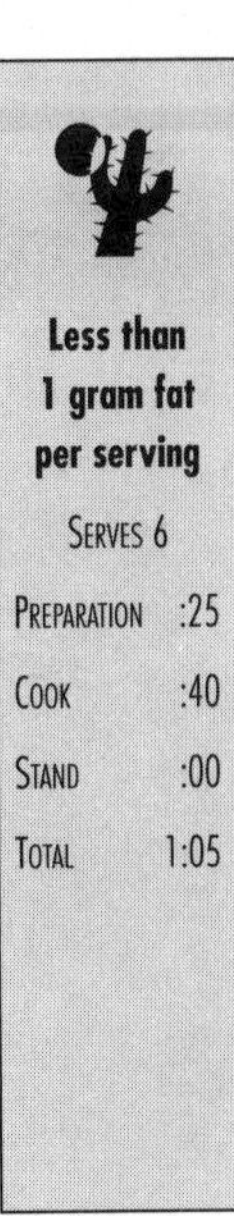

6 to 8 medium-size red potatoes, scrubbed
2/3 cup fat-free plain yogurt
1/3 cup fat-free mayonnaise
1/2 cup spiced vinegar, such as red wine with garlic vinegar
1/4 teaspoon lemon pepper
Salt to taste
2 tablespoons prepared mustard
1 (11-ounce) can shoepeg corn kernels, drained (see Note)
1 cup chopped celery
1/2 cup chopped green onion
1 tablespoon minced fresh parsley

Place the scrubbed potatoes in a 6-quart pan, cover with water, and bring the water to a boil over medium-high heat. Lower the heat to medium and boil the potatoes for 20 to 25 minutes, until tender when pierced with a fork.

Meanwhile, prepare the other ingredients. In a small bowl, combine the yogurt, mayonnaise, vinegar, lemon pepper, salt, and mustard. Blend well. Set the dressing aside.

In a larger mixing bowl, combine the corn, celery, and onion. When the potatoes are done, drain. Cover them with cold water and let stand for about 3 minutes. Drain. When cool enough to handle, peel and chop them into bite-size pieces.

Add the potatoes to the celery mixture, then pour the dressing over and toss lightly until evenly mixed. Sprinkle with the parsley and serve.

Note: You may substitute 1 cup of regular yellow corn kernels for the shoepeg corn. I prefer the small white shoepeg because it gives your salads a crunch. On the other hand, the yellow looks prettier.

MEXICAN TWIST POTATO SALAD

Less than 1 gram fat entire dish

SERVES 6

PREPARATION	:35
COOK	:25
STAND	2:00
TOTAL	3:00

1 1/2 pounds red or new potatoes
1 cup fat-free mayonnaise
2 tablespoons canned chopped green chilies (see Note)
1 tablespoon lemon or lime juice
1/2 teaspoon ground cumin
Salt to taste if desired
1 1/4 cups chopped celery
1/2 to 3/4 cup green or red bell pepper
1/2 cup chopped onion

Wash the potatoes, place them in a large saucepan, and cover with water. Bring to a boil, lower the heat, and simmer briskly until tender, about 20 to 25 minutes depending on how large your potatoes are. Drain, cool, and peel. Cut the potatoes into chunks about 2 inches in size, or any way you like your salad.

In a large mixing bowl, combine the mayonnaise, chilies, lemon or lime juice, cumin, and salt if using. Stir to blend; add the potatoes, celery, bell pepper, and onion. Toss carefully; cover and refrigerate for at least 2 hours to let the flavors blend.

Note: Before adding the green chilies, first taste them. The "heat" can be stronger in some than in others, so always taste and adjust the amount of heat you desire in each dish.

ZESTY POTATO SALAD

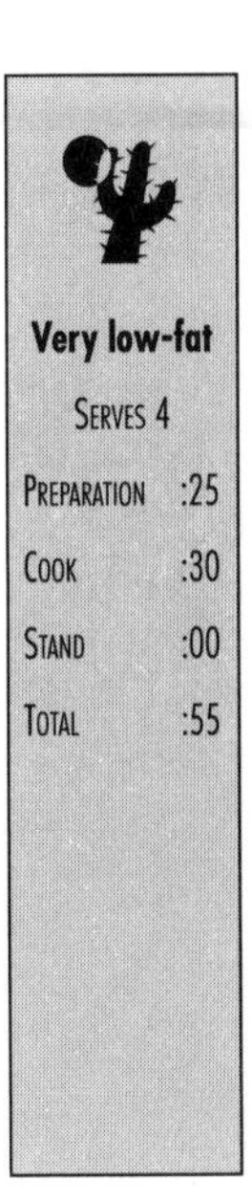

4 to 6 medium-size new potatoes
2 green onions
1/2 cup chopped red onion
3/4 cup chopped celery
1/2 cup fat-free cottage cheese
1 teaspoon Mexican seasoning
Salt and pepper to taste
1/2 cup fat-free yogurt
3 slices turkey bacon
1/2 teaspoon chopped parsley for garnish

Wash the potatoes well. Place in a deep saucepan and cover with water. Boil 20 to 30 minutes, until tender. Drain and, when cool enough to handle, peel the potatoes and cut them into small cubes.

While the potatoes are cooking, chop the onions and celery. Set aside.

To make the dressing, combine the cottage cheese, Mexican seasoning, salt and pepper, and yogurt in a blender or use a whisk to blend until smooth.

Cook the bacon on paper towels in the microwave until crisp. Crumble it and set aside. Combine the chopped vegetables and the potatoes in a bowl. Pour dressing over all and stir gently to combine and coat the potatoes. Garnish with the crumbled bacon and parsley.

ACORN SQUASH RINGS

2.5 grams fat entire dish

SERVES 4

PREPARATION :35

COOK :35

STAND :00

TOTAL 1:10

These are sweet enough to serve for dessert with a dip of fat-free ice cream or yogurt in the middle. Drizzle a little maple-flavored or fat-free butterscotch ice cream topping over. Yum yum.

4 acorn squash
3 tablespoons packed brown sugar
3 tablespoons skim milk
3/4 cup egg substitute
3/4 cup freshly made fine bread crumbs (about 2 1/2 slices bread)
1/2 cup cornmeal
2 teaspoons ground cinnamon
1/2 cup pourable fat-free margarine, such as Fleischmann's

Preheat the oven to 400 degrees. Lightly spray one or two large baking sheets with vegetable oil cooking spray.

Wash the squash and trim off the ends. Leaving the peel on, cut the squash crosswise into 3/4-inch-thick circles. Remove the seeds. In a shallow bowl, combine the brown sugar, milk, and egg substitute. In another shallow bowl, combine the bread crumbs, cornmeal, and cinnamon. Dip the squash slices into the egg mixture, then coat with the bread crumb mixture. Repeat with all slices.

As they are coated, arrange the slices on the prepared baking sheets, and drizzle with the margarine. Bake for 30 to 35 minutes or until the squash is tender when pierced with a fork.

ZUCCHINI SAUTÉ

0 grams fat

SERVES 6

PREPARATION :12

COOK :12

STAND :00

TOTAL :24

1 medium-size onion, sliced thin
2 teaspoons chili powder
1 teaspoon cumin seeds
1 teaspoon mustard seeds
1 small carrot, cut into matchstick strips
1 1/2 pounds zucchini, ends trimmed, cut into matchstick strips
Salt and pepper to taste

In a medium-size nonstick skillet or wok, heat about 4 tablespoons water; add the onion, sautéing until crisp-tender, about 4 or 5 minutes. Stir in the chili powder, cumin, and mustard seed.

Add the carrot and zucchini. Stir-fry until the carrot is just tender to the bite, about 5 or 6 minutes. Season to taste with salt and pepper.

SPICY FRIED GREEN TOMATOES

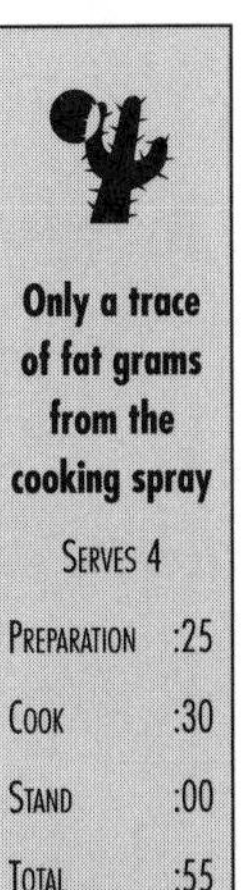

I have told you how to do fried green tomatoes in previous _So Fat, Low Fat, No Fat_ cookbooks, I do not mean to be repeating recipes, but I can't leave this out. Some of you may have missed it.

4 firm green tomatoes
1/2 cup canned chopped green chilies
3/4 cup egg substitute
2 tablespoons skim milk
1/2 cup cornflake crumbs (or yellow or blue cornmeal)
1 tablespoon minced fresh basil, or 1 teaspoon dried
1/2 teaspoon ground red chile pepper or Mexican seasoning
Salt and pepper to taste

Preheat the oven to 375 degrees. Spray a large baking sheet with vegetable oil cooking spray.

Wash the tomatoes and cut a thin slice off the top and bottom ends. Cut into ½-inch-thick slices.

Put the chopped chilies in a shallow bowl and beat with a hand-held electric mixer; this will make the pieces smaller and help them stick to the tomatoes. Add the egg substitute and milk and beat slightly to lighten up the mixture.

In another shallow bowl, such as a pie plate, combine the cornflake crumbs or meal, whichever you choose. Add the basil, ground red pepper or Mexican seasoning, and salt and pepper. Stir with fork to blend.

Start dipping the tomato slices one at a time, first in the egg mixture, turning to coat evenly, then in the cornflake mixture, turning and shaking to be sure all is covered.

Place in a single layer without touching on the baking sheet. Spray the tops lightly with cooking spray; this will help them brown and look and taste more like fried tomatoes. Bake for about 15 minutes; turn with a flat spatula and continue to bake for 15 more minutes or until brown and crispy on both sides.

Serve with salsa or sour cream, fat-free of course. You may like to serve with both.

Variation: To use these as appetizers, cut them into strips like french fries. Follow the same routine; place the strips in a single layer, not touching, on a baking sheet, turn them as above, and serve with fat-free sour cream to dip in.

ROASTED MIXED VEGETABLES

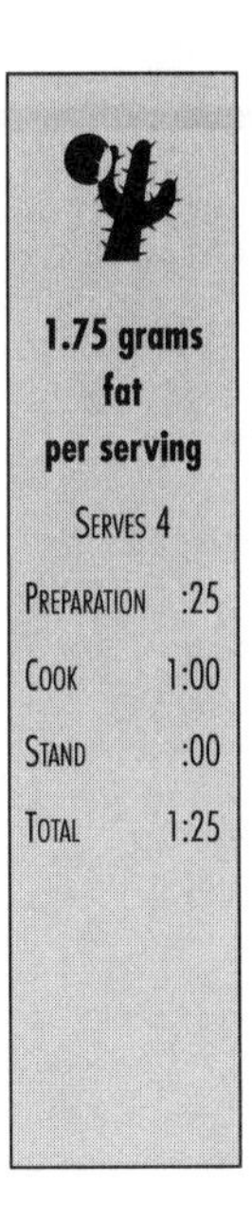

A Romertopf (terracotta dome-lidded baking dish) is nice for these vegetables, but a regular roasting pan will do.

1 teaspoon Mexican oregano or regular oregano, crushed
1 teaspoon chopped fresh cilantro
½ teaspoon Mexican seasoning
1 teaspoon vegetable oil (lightest available)
3 medium baking potatoes, washed and cubed
12 whole baby carrots
1 medium bell pepper, cut into chunks

If using a Romertopf, soak it in water about 1 hour.

Mix the oregano, cilantro, Mexican seasoning, and oil in a small bowl and set aside. Preheat the oven to 400 degrees.

Clean and prepare the vegetables; place them in a mixing bowl, pour the seasoning mixture over, and toss to cover nicely.

Spray the inside of the roasting pan you are using very lightly with vegetable oil cooking spray. Pour the prepared seasoned vegetables into the roaster. Cover and bake for 50 to 60 minutes or until the vegetables are tender, stirring once or twice during the baking period. Stir carefully so as not to crush the vegetables.

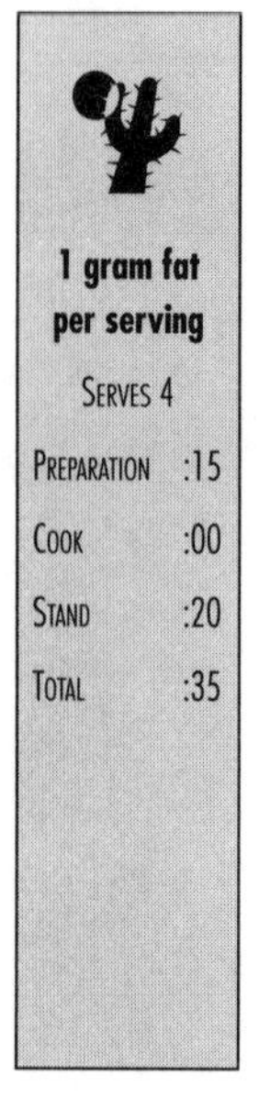

RICE SALAD

Serve this with a nice hot Mexican casserole, chips, and fruit.

2½ cups cold cooked rice
3 medium-size ripe tomatoes, peeled, seeded, and chopped
3 sweet banana peppers, seeded and chopped
1 (15-ounce) can Great Northern beans, drained and rinsed
¼ cup chopped onion
2 tablespoons chopped green chilies (canned)
1½ tablespoons Tabasco jalapeño sauce (green) or 1 dash regular Tabasco
½ teaspoon Mexican seasoning
Salt and pepper to taste

In a medium-size bowl, combine the rice with the tomatoes, chopped banana peppers, beans, and onion. Add the chilies, Tabasco, Mexican seasoning, and salt and pepper to taste. Toss to combine. Let the salad stand for about 20 minutes to absorb the seasonings.

Cooked rice: I usually double the amount needed of rice, cooking a double batch. Keep leftover cooked rice in a zipper-locked plastic bag in the freezer. You can unzip and warm it in the microwave right in the bag. It makes a great filler for any number of dishes, and stretches your dish if unexpected guests arrive. Very good and good for you.

MEXICAN CONFETTI RICE

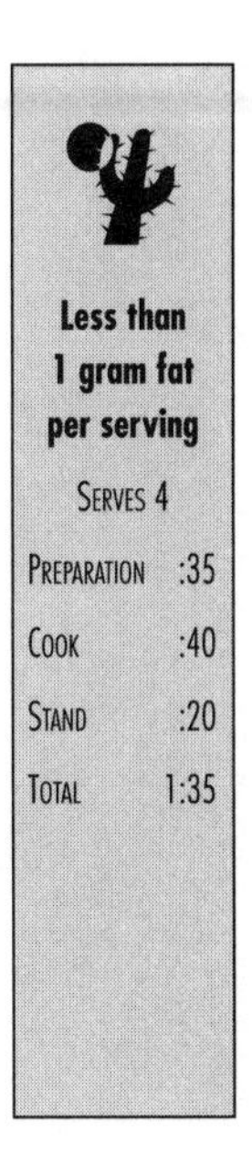

This is a wonderful main dish as well as a side dish for a great Mexican meal.

2 cups regular long-grain white rice
½ cup chopped onion
1 clove garlic, chopped fine
2 tablespoons chopped green chilies (or 2 serrano chilies, stemmed and chopped, if available)
4 cups (two 15½-ounce cans) fat-free chicken broth
1 medium-size ripe tomato, peeled, seeded, and chopped
½ cup frozen green peas
½ cup finely diced carrot

Soak the rice in hot water for about 15 minutes. Drain in a colander and shake well to remove excess water. Heat a large nonstick skillet and toast the rice until it starts to color, stirring constantly. Add the onion, garlic, and chilies; continue stirring until the rice is golden around the edges.

Add the chicken broth, tomato, peas, and carrot; bring to a boil. Reduce the heat, cover, and simmer without disturbing for 15 to 20 minutes. Remove from the heat and let stand, covered, an additional 15 to 20 minutes. Fluff with a fork before serving.

Less than 1 gram fat per serving

SERVES 4

PREPARATION	:35
COOK	:40
STAND	:00
TOTAL	1:15

STIR-FRIED RICE WITH VEGETABLES

This is a very quick meal or side dish.

½ (16-ounce) package Spanish flavor rice, such as Vigo yellow rice dinner
1 medium eggplant, peeled and sliced into thin julienne strips
1 medium-size red onion, quartered and sliced thin
1 tablespoon chopped green chilies, canned or fresh
1 medium bell pepper, chopped
3 cloves garlic, chopped (2 teaspoons)
Fresh slices of tomato and shredded fat-free cheese for garnish if desired

Cook the rice according to package directions, leaving out any oil or margarine called for. While the rice is cooking, prepare your stir-fry vegetables.

Peel and cut the eggplant, place it in a bowl of water with about 1 tablespoon of salt added, and let soak while you are working with the remaining vegetables.

Heat a large nonstick skillet or wok over medium-high heat; start to sauté the onion, chilies, and bell pepper—no water or oil needed; they will cook in their own juices.

Drain the eggplant and blot dry with kitchen towels. Add the garlic and eggplant to the skillet. Continue to stir and fry until the eggplant is just tender—do not overcook.

When the rice is done, add it to the stir-fry and mix in gently. Stop the heat at this point; the vegetables and the rice are already cooked.

Pour into a nice serving dish or casserole, top with slices of fresh tomato, and sprinkle with shredded fat-free cheese if desired.

I like to serve this alongside steamed broccoli and Mexicali Grilled Fish, page 70.

MEXICAN FRIED RICE

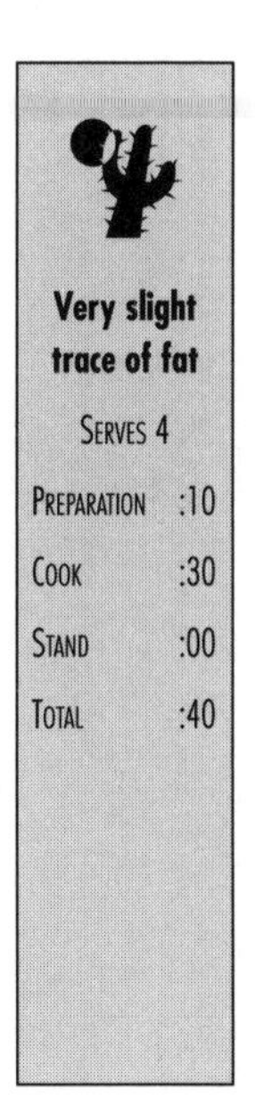

3 cups fat-free chicken broth or vegetable broth
1 1/2 cups long-grain white rice
1/2 teaspoon salt
1 cup V-8 juice or Spanish-style tomato sauce or Bloody Mary mix
2 tablespoons chopped green bell pepper
1 tablespoon minced onion
1/4 teaspoon minced garlic
2 tablespoons canned chopped green chilies

In a medium-size saucepan, bring the broth to a boil. Add the rice and salt, stir, cover, and cook over slightly lowered heat for about 15 minutes, until just tender but not mushy and stuck together.

Spray a wok or large nonstick skillet with vegetable oil cooking spray. Pour the rice in and stir-fry for 8 to 10 minutes, adding the V-8 juice when the rice starts to dry out. Add the green pepper, onion, chilies, and garlic; stir to mix evenly, and cook about 5 minutes more, stirring 2 or 3 times. Serve hot.

Less than ½ gram fat per serving

SERVES 6

PREPARATION :12

COOK :39

STAND :04

TOTAL :55

RICE WITH GREEN CHILE-CHEESE SAUCE AND CREAM

1 (10¾-ounce) can fat-free chicken broth
⅛ teaspoon garlic powder
2 cups uncooked instant rice
1 cup shredded fat-free Cheddar cheese
½ cup fat-free sour cream
1 (4-ounce) can chopped green chilies, drained
Pinch ground red pepper (cayenne) for garnish

In a saucepan, bring the broth and garlic powder to a boil; add the rice and lower the heat to simmer for about 1 minute or less. Remove from the heat, cover, and let stand for 15 minutes.

Stir in the cheese, sour cream, and chilies. Stir and place on low heat for 10 minutes, stirring not to burn, until heated through.

Place in a serving bowl; garnish with a very light sprinkling of ground red pepper.

QUICK FIESTA RICE

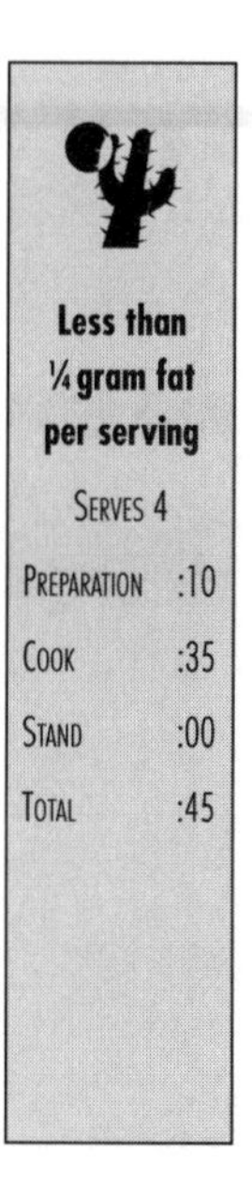

1 cup chopped onion (use frozen for time and effort's sake)
1 cup chopped green pepper (resort to the frozen again)
1/8 teaspoon minced preserved garlic
1 cup uncooked rice, long-grain if available
1 (11-ounce) can Healthy Request Fiesta tomato soup
1/4 cup chopped canned green chilies
2 cups water

In a large nonstick saucepan, over medium heat, sauté the onion, pepper, and garlic in 2 tablespoons of water until crisp-tender. (If you are using frozen vegetables, there is no need to add any water; enough moisture will cook out of the frozen vegetables to keep from sticking.)

Add the rice; cook about 45 seconds, stirring constantly. Stir in the soup, green chilies, and water. Heat to boiling; reduce the heat to low, cover, and cook for about 25 minutes, or until the rice is tender and most of the liquid is absorbed.

LAZY DAZE BAKED RICE

1 gram fat per serving

SERVES 2

PREPARATION :10
COOK 1:00
STAND :00
TOTAL 1:10

3/4 cup uncooked rice
1 1/2 cups chopped onion
1 cup chopped bell pepper
1/2 cup canned chopped green chilies
2 tablespoons chopped jalapeño pepper
1 teaspoon sugar (optional)
1 1/2 cups water
1 cup shredded fat-free cheese

Preheat the oven to 350 degrees. Spray a medium-size baking dish or casserole with vegetable oil cooking spray.

Combine the rice, onion, bell pepper, green chilies, jalapeños, sugar, and water in the baking dish and stir to mix. Cover with a lid or foil and bake for 50 minutes. Remove from the oven, top with the shredded cheese, and bake uncovered for an additional 10 minutes.

Chapter 8

Salsas and Sauces

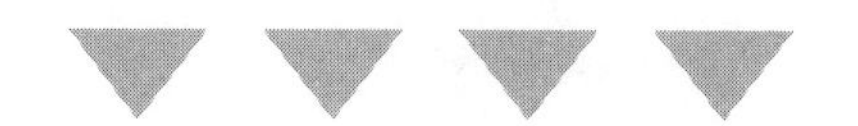

0 grams fat

SERVES 4

PREPARATION :20

COOK :00

STAND :30

TOTAL :50

FRESH SALSA

2 cups chopped fresh tomato (drained)
1/4 cup chopped green onions
2 tablespoons chopped fresh cilantro (optional)
1/4 cup lime juice
1/2 jalapeño pepper, seeded and minced, about 2 tablespoons
1 clove garlic, minced

Combine all the ingredients in a small mixing bowl; stir to blend. Let stand at least 30 minutes before serving to let the flavors blend.

Make salsas and chilis a day ahead. This lets the spices marry well and produces a better flavor. It also helps with time when coming home from work or when entertaining.

MARTHA'S FRESH SALSA

1.75 grams fat per 1-cup serving

SERVES 8

PREPARATION	:45
COOK	:00
STAND	1:30
TOTAL	2:15

Martha always makes this salsa when we bring her tomatoes in the summer at the lake. These are large portions—1 cup per serving—which is a lot, but no one can eat just 1/4 cup.

1 large cucumber
1 tablespoon canola oil
3/4 cup red wine vinegar
1 (16-ounce) can tomato sauce
4 packages artificial sweetener
1 bunch green onions, minced very small
1 large green bell pepper, minced very small
4 celery ribs, minced small
2 to 4 tomatoes, peeled and minced small
1 (10-ounce) can Ro-Tel diced tomatoes and peppers, drained
Dash of Tabasco (see Note)
Ground black pepper, garlic salt, and canned chopped jalapeños to taste (optional)

Peel and cut up the cucumber. Place in a blender with the canola oil, vinegar, tomato sauce, and sweetener; blend on low speed for 4 seconds. Watch out—you can't get soup to stay on your chip.

Put the mixture in a bowl; add the minced onion, bell pepper, celery, fresh and canned tomatoes, and the Tabasco. Season to taste with pepper, garlic salt, and jalapeños. Taste and, if desired, add more Tabasco—but just a little bit at a time.

This keeps up to two weeks in the refrigerator, tightly closed.

Note: My brother used to say, "If it doesn't make your head itch and forehead break out in a sweat, it's not hot." You be the judge on the temperature you desire.

VIDALIA ONION SALSA

0 grams fat
MAKES 2½ CUPS

PREPARATION	:25
COOK	:00
STAND	2:00
TOTAL	2:25

This can also be made with regular onions of any type or mixed. Vidalias or other sweet onions are great when in season.

2 cups finely chopped sweet onion (Vidalia, Maui, or Texas sweet)
1 medium-size ripe tomato, chopped fine
2 green onions, chopped
1/4 teaspoon ground red pepper (cayenne)
1 clove garlic, minced
1/4 cup lime juice
1 tablespoon finely chopped fresh cilantro
1 teaspoon low-sodium soy sauce
2 tablespoons red wine vinegar

Mix all ingredients in a bowl with a cover. Cover and refrigerate for at least 2 hours before serving. Also good to make a day ahead.

PEPPERY PINEAPPLE SALSA

0 grams fat
SERVES 4

PREPARATION	:20
COOK	:00
STAND	1:00
TOTAL	1:20

May also be served as a fruit salad on the side.

1 small fresh pineapple, peeled and diced into 1/2-inch cubes (2 cups)
1/4 cup minced red onion
1 tablespoon finely chopped fresh cilantro
2 tablespoons lime juice
3/4 cup finely chopped red bell pepper
1 small chile, seeded and chopped fine, or 2 tablespoons chopped canned chilies

In a medium-size mixing bowl, combine all ingredients; stir carefully to blend. Cover with a lid or plastic wrap and let stand at least an hour.

SPICY BLACK-EYED PEA SALSA

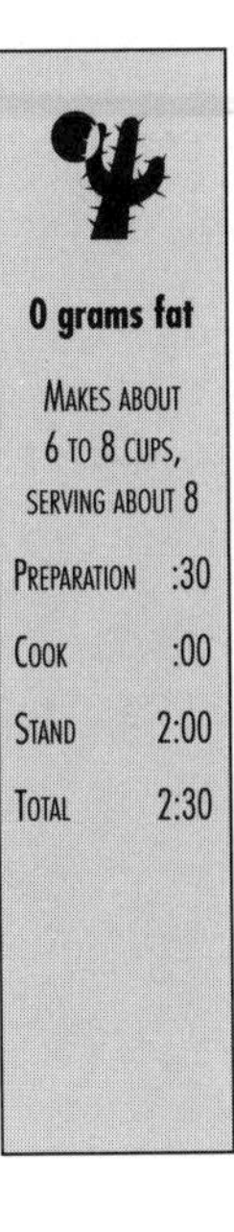

Make this a day ahead.

2 (15-ounce) cans black-eyed peas, drained
2 large ripe tomatoes, chopped
1 small red onion, chopped fine
1 cup minced celery
1/2 green bell pepper, chopped small (1/3 cup)
2 rings jalapeño pepper, chopped very fine
1 tablespoon lemon juice
1 tablespoon lime juice
1 (10-ounce) can diced tomatoes and green chilies, drained
1 clove garlic, chopped fine
1/8 teaspoon Mexican seasoning
1 cup tomato sauce
2 tablespoons vinegar
1/2 teaspoon Mexican oregano or regular oregano, crushed
Few drops Tabasco

In a large mixing bowl with a cover, combine the drained peas, chopped tomatoes, onion, celery, green pepper, jalapeño, drained tomatoes and chilies, and garlic. Toss lightly to mix well.

In a small bowl, add the Mexican seasoning to the tomato sauce; stir to blend. Add the vinegar, oregano, lemon juice, and lime juice. Pour over the pea mixture; stir gently to blend well, but don't crush the vegetables.

Start adding the Tabasco one drop at a time until you have the heat level you desire. Be really careful—you may want to wait an hour or so to let the other flavors blend, then taste to see how much Tabasco if any is needed. Remember the taste-and-add method.

Cover tightly and store in the refrigerator for 2 hours or more before serving. Can also be made the day ahead.

THREE-BEAN SALSA

0 grams fat

SERVES 8

PREPARATION	:35
COOK	:00
STAND	:30
TOTAL	1:05

1 (15-ounce) can pinto beans, rinsed and drained
1 (15-ounce) can black beans, rinsed and drained
1 (15-ounce) can ranch or chili beans, partially drained
1 (11-ounce) can shoepeg white corn, drained
1 (14½-ounce) can diced Just for Chili brand tomatoes, partially drained
1 cup chopped fresh green bell pepper
2 tablespoons chopped canned green chilies
1 cup finely chopped celery
1 cup chopped fresh onion
½ teaspoon garlic seasoning or salt
1 cup shredded fat-free Mexican cheese, such as Healthy Choice
¼ teaspoon Mexican oregano or regular oregano, crushed
1 tablespoon lime juice
1 tablespoon vinegar
¼ teaspoon Tabasco jalapeño sauce (green)

Pour the pinto and black beans into a colander, rinse, and set aside to drain. In a medium-size mixing bowl, combine the ranch or chili beans, the corn, and tomatoes. Stir gently to mix. Mix in the other two beans, pinto and black. Gently toss to combine.

Add the green pepper, chilies, celery, and onion; gently toss to mix well. Add the garlic seasoning, cheese, oregano, lime juice, vinegar, and Tabasco jalapeño sauce. Be careful when adding jalapeño sauce; just add a drop or two at a time, and taste. Some like it hot, some not. Let stand for at least 30 minutes.

Serve as a dip with low-fat or fat-free chips, or serve as a salad with dinner.

NEW MEXICO CHILE SAUCE

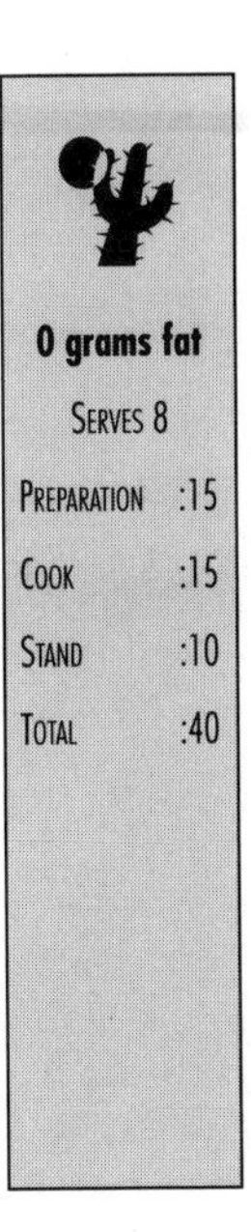

0 grams fat

SERVES 8

PREPARATION :15

COOK :15

STAND :10

TOTAL :40

3 ounces dried New Mexico red chilies, crushed
4 green onions, chopped
2 cloves garlic, minced
2 cups fat-free chicken broth (14-ounce can)

Combine the chilies, green onions, garlic, and broth in a medium saucepan. Bring to a boil, lower the heat, cover, and simmer for about 15 minutes. Let stand until slightly cooled. Place in a blender and blend until very smooth. Serve immediately or store in the refrigerator if made a day ahead.

Color: This is one of the most important points in cooking. Your presentation adds so much to the dish, making it much more appetizing as well as delightful to look at. It helps the flavor if the presentation is done in style. Use pretty bowls or dishes. That also adds to the delightfulness of the dish.

COUNTRY TOMATO SAUCE

0 grams fat

SERVES 4

PREPARATION	:35
COOK	:40
STAND	:00
TOTAL	1:15

4 to 6 medium to large tomatoes
1 medium onion
2 cloves garlic
1 to 2 small jalapeño chilies, seeded and cored (see Note)
1/4 teaspoon Mexican oregano or regular oregano, crushed
1/4 teaspoon salt
2 tablespoons water

Place the tomatoes in a deep pan of boiling water and let stand until the skins start to slip, about 40 seconds. Plunge into a bowl of ice cold water, remove the cores, and slip the skins off. Chop the tomatoes, onion, garlic, and chilies fine.

Combine all ingredients in a nonreactive saucepan and cook over medium heat, stirring occasionally, until the tomatoes and onions are soft. Refrigerate in a tightly covered container. Use within 6 to 8 days.

Note: Use fresh or canned chilies—just be careful not to get this too hot. You can always add more pepper, but once it is in there you can't take the fire out. *Caution:* When handling chili peppers, use rubber gloves.

SPICY TOMATO SAUCE

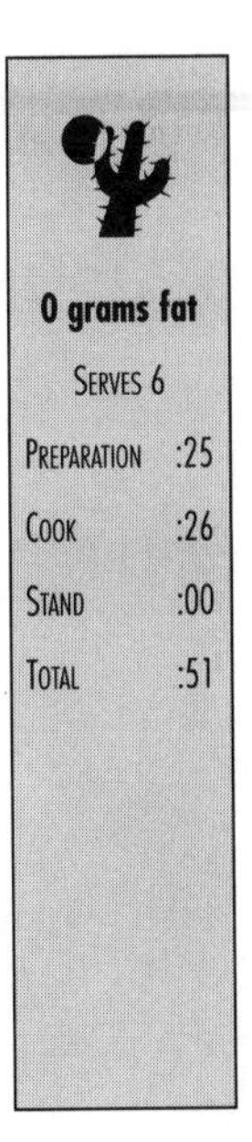

2 (15-ounce) cans stewed tomatoes, undrained
1 cup chopped onion
1 tablespoon minced garlic
2 tablespoons chili powder (Chimayo if available)
2 teaspoons ground cumin
2 teaspoons Mexican oregano or regular oregano, crushed
1 teaspoon ground cinnamon
1/4 teaspoon crushed dried red pepper
1/4 teaspoon ground cloves

Place the tomatoes, juice and all, in a blender and process until finely chopped. In a nonstick saucepan, sauté the onion and garlic in 1 tablespoon of water; stir to keep from burning the garlic. Cook and stir about 4 to 5 minutes or until the onion is tender.

Add the chili powder, cumin, oregano, cinnamon, red pepper, and cloves. Continue to stir and cook about 1 minute longer. Add the tomatoes, bring to a boil, and reduce the heat to a simmer. Cook uncovered about 20 minutes or until the sauce is reduced to about 3 cups.

SAUCE FOR SPOON BREAD

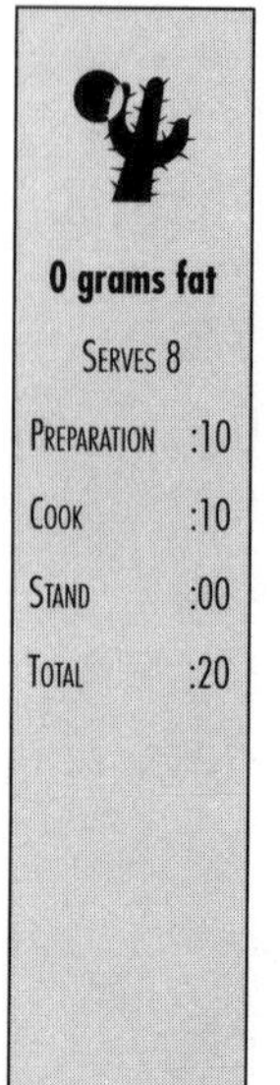

1 (28-ounce) can chopped or stewed tomatoes
1 (8-ounce) can tomato sauce
1 (4-ounce) can chopped green chilies
1 teaspoon salt
Dash of ground black pepper
1/2 teaspoon Mexican oregano or regular oregano, crushed

In a medium-size saucepan, combine all the ingredients; place over medium heat until very hot, but not boiling.

Serve alongside Mexican Spoon Bread (page 208) in small individual bowls.

Calcium sources: Here you need to have your watch-out eye open. Most items high in calcium are also high in fat. Our dietary allowance of calcium is 800 to 1200 milligrams per day, depending on your age (unfortunately I require more each day). Some suggestions: low-fat or fat-free skim milk, fat-free ice milk, or frozen yogurt in place of ice cream; low-fat or fat-free yogurt in place of whole-milk yogurt; low-fat or fat-free cottage cheese instead of regular; low-fat or part skim cheese in place of high-fat cheese. Other sources of calcium are canned salmon, sardines (with bones), cabbage, collards, kale, bok choy, and Brussels sprouts.

MULTI-PURPOSE MEXICAN SAUCE

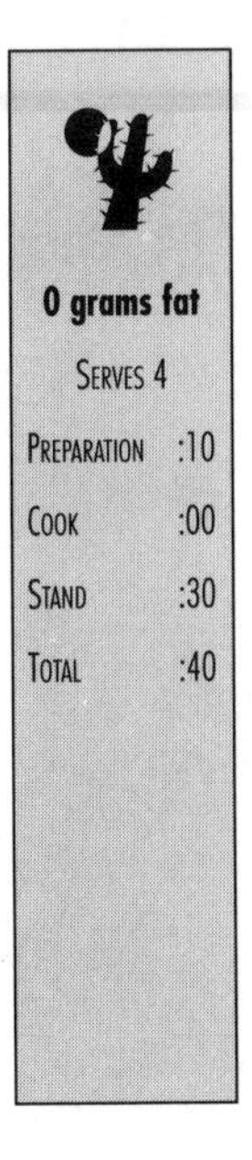

Although this sauce was created for Three Bean Bake, page 120 in *So Fat, Low Fat, No Fat*, it is also great to keep in your refrigerator for various last-minute quick fixes. Use it on salad, salsa, casseroles, meat dishes, or at cookouts. It will keep up to two weeks tightly closed in the refrigerator

1/8 teaspoon ground cumin
1/8 teaspoon thyme leaves, crushed
1 cup barbecue sauce, commercially prepared
1 teaspoon lime juice
1/4 teaspoon Tabasco jalapeño sauce (green)
1/8 teaspoon Mexican oregano or regular oregano, crushed
Touch of garlic seasoning

Mix all the above-listed ingredients in a small bowl with a cover. Blend with a wire whisk to mix seasonings thoroughly. Cover tightly and let stand about 30 minutes.

This is a good time to try your hand at creating. If you like sauces a touch spicier or hotter, add more of the cumin or the jalapeño sauce, but just a drop at a time. Don't get it so hot that others can't tolerate it—many people can't handle very spicy foods.

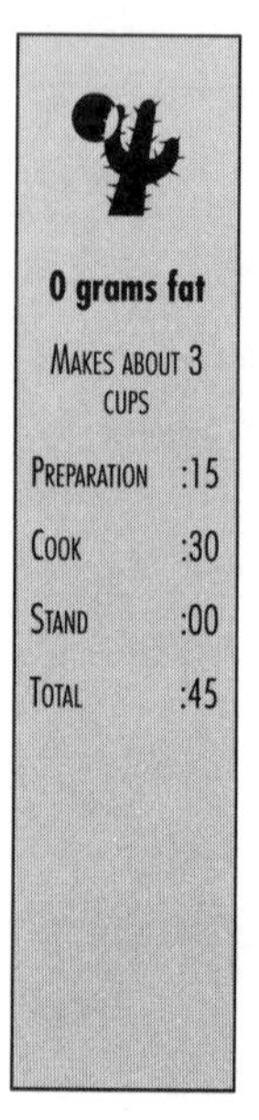

0 grams fat

MAKES ABOUT 3 CUPS

PREPARATION	:15
COOK	:30
STAND	:00
TOTAL	:45

TOMATILLO–GREEN CHILE SAUCE

2 (18-ounce) cans whole tomatillos
1 (4-ounce) can diced mild green chilies, drained
1/2 teaspoon ground cumin
1 teaspoon Mexican oregano or regular oregano, crushed

Drain the tomatillos and place them in a blender along with the chilies, cumin, and oregano. Blend until smooth. Turn the mixture into a nonreactive saucepan over medium heat and bring to a boil, stirring occasionally. Serve hot.

Many flavors and spices can be added to match the desired theme. Hot, sweet, chocolate, cookie, appetizers—use your imagination.

Breads

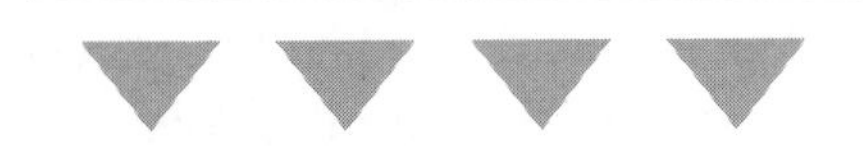

BEER MUFFINS

1.3 grams fat per muffin

MAKES 12

PREPARATION	:15
COOK	:30
STAND	:00
TOTAL	:45

3 cups self-rising flour
2 tablespoons sugar
1/2 teaspoon Mexican seasoning
1 (10-ounce) can light beer
2 tablespoons (1/4 stick) low-fat light margarine, melted

Preheat the oven to 350 degrees. Prepare two 6-cup muffin tins by spraying each cup with vegetable oil cooking spray. Set aside.

Combine the flour, sugar, and Mexican seasoning in a mixing bowl and stir with a whisk to blend.

Make a well in the center and add the beer and melted margarine. Stir quickly just until the flour is moistened—the batter should be lumpy.

Fill muffin tins about 3/4 full. Sprinkle Mexican seasoning over tops very lightly before baking. Bake for 20 to 30 minutes or until the muffins are golden brown and feel done to the touch.

When measuring out ingredients, do not measure directly over your mixing bowl. Measure into a spoon or cup, then put into the bowl. This ensures that any spills will not ruin the entire dish.

FIESTA CORN MUFFINS

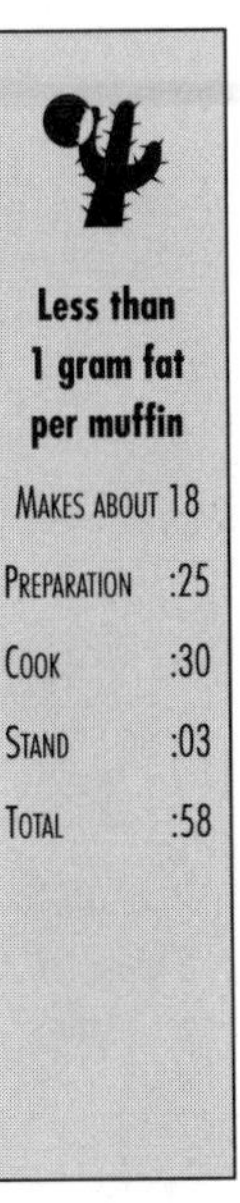

1/2 cup chopped fresh or frozen onion
1/2 cup Mexicorn (canned corn with red and green peppers)
2 tablespoons canned chopped green chilies
2 1/2 cups, self-rising yellow cornmeal mix
1/2 cup egg substitute
1 1/4 cups fresh or canned skim milk
1/4 cup water
1 (8-ounce) can cream-style corn
Mexican seasoning (such as McCormick)
1/2 cup shredded fat-free Cheddar cheese

Spray the bottoms only of three 6-cup muffin tins with vegetable oil cooking spray. Preheat the oven to 375 degrees.

In a nonstick skillet, sauté the chopped onion in about 1 tablespoon of water for 1 minute. Add the Mexicorn and chopped green chilies; continue to sauté for 1 minute more. Remove from heat.

In a medium-size mixing bowl, combine the cornmeal mix, egg substitute, milk, and water. Stir with a wire whisk until blended well. Stir in with a long-handled spoon the cream-style corn, the Mexicorn mixture, and 1 teaspoon of Mexican seasoning. Mix well; fold in the shredded cheese.

Spoon the batter into each muffin cup, filling about 3/4 full. Sprinkle a tiny bit of Mexican seasoning on top of each muffin. Bake for about 25 minutes, until the muffins are golden brown and feel done to the touch. Let stand about 3 minutes, then remove to a serving basket.

Variation: For Corn Cakes, prepare the batter as instructed. Preheat a griddle or large nonstick skillet; spray with cooking spray. When hot enough so that a drop of water dances on the surface, ladle portions of the batter onto the cooking surface just as if you were making pancakes. Let cook until the corn cakes are raised and bubbly on top; turn and continue to cook until both sides are nice and brown and the cakes are done to the touch.

These are fast and easy to do, especially in the summer when heating the oven will also heat your kitchen more than you desire.

Less than 1 gram fat per serving

SERVES 6

PREPARATION :20

COOK :30

STAND :05

TOTAL :55

CORNBREAD

1 cup yellow cornmeal
1 cup all-purpose flour
1/2 teaspoon salt
2 teaspoons baking powder
1/2 cup egg substitute
1 cup skim milk

Preheat the oven to 375 degrees. Place a medium-size cast-iron skillet in the oven to heat, or if you do not have a cast-iron skillet, spray a regular 8 x 8-inch baking dish lightly with vegetable oil cooking spray and set aside.

In a large mixing bowl, stir together the cornmeal, flour, salt, and baking powder. Beat the egg substitute and milk together; add all at once to the dry ingredients and stir with a wire whisk to blend well. If too stiff add a tablespoon or two of water.

If using a cast-iron skillet, at this time remove it from the oven and spray with cooking spray. Pour the cornbread mixture into the skillet and return it to the oven. Bake for about 30 minutes. Check for desired doneness and bake up to 10 minutes more if desired. The cornbread should be set and lightly browned on top. Remove from the oven and let stand for about 5 minutes before removing to a serving dish. Serve hot.

If using a baking dish, proceed with the same instructions. When the cornbread is done you will not need to turn this onto a serving dish as you did with your skillet. Just cut into squares and serve hot.

Variation: This is an excellent cornbread for stuffing. It makes about 7 cups.

GREEN CHILE CORNBREAD

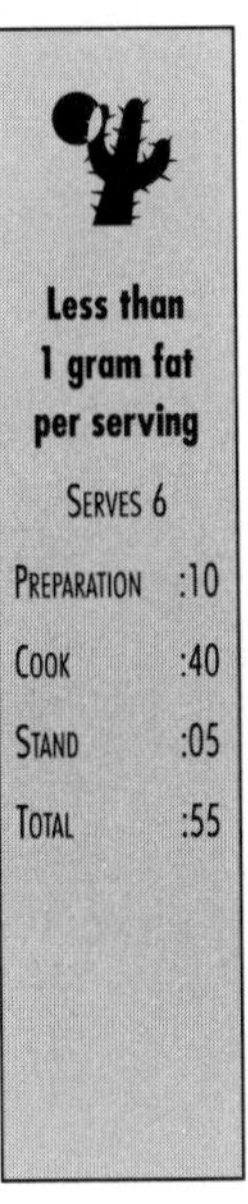

2 cups yellow cornmeal mix (not with buttermilk)
1/2 cup egg substitute
1/2 cup water
1 cup skim milk
1 cup cream-style corn
2 tablespoons canned chopped green chilies
3 tablespoons chopped onion
1/2 cup commercial salsa (medium hot)

Spray an 8 x 12-inch baking pan with vegetable oil cooking spray. Preheat the oven to 375 degrees.

In a medium-size mixing bowl, combine the cornmeal mix with the egg substitute, water, and milk. Stir to start mixing, then add the corn, chilies, onion, and salsa. Continue stirring until well mixed. The batter will be just a little thick; this is a moist, heavy, spicy cornbread.

Turn the batter into the prepared pan and bake for 35 to 45 minutes, until a toothpick inserted near the center comes out clean. Cool for 5 to 8 minutes, then cut into squares and serve hot.

MEXICAN SPOON BREAD

Less than 1 gram fat per serving

SERVES 8

PREPARATION	:15
COOK	:45
STAND	:10
TOTAL	1:10

1 (16-ounce) can cream-style corn
1 cup cornmeal
1/3 cup pourable fat-free margarine, such as Fleischmann's
1/2 cup egg substitute, slightly beaten
1 teaspoon salt
1/2 teaspoon baking soda
1 (4-ounce) can chopped green chilies
1/2 cup shredded fat-free Cheddar cheese

Preheat the oven to 400 degrees. Lightly spray a 9-inch square baking dish with vegetable oil cooking spray.

In a mixing bowl, combine the corn, cornmeal, margarine, egg substitute, salt, and baking soda. Mix well. Add the chilies and half the cheese; stir to mix. Pour into the prepared baking dish.

Sprinkle the remaining cheese over the batter. Bake for 45 minutes. Let stand for 10 minutes before serving.

HOECAKE

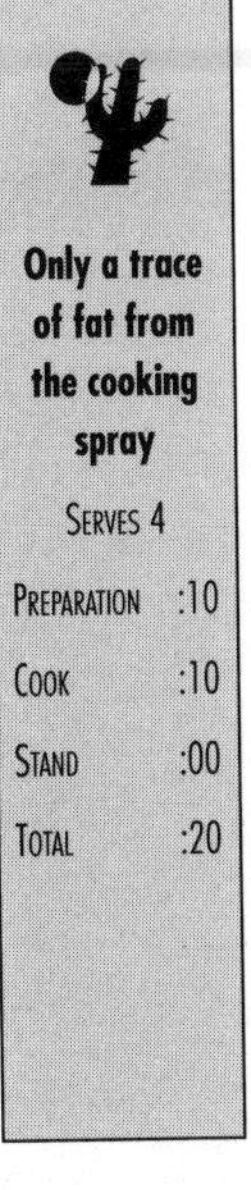

This recipe comes from deep, deep in the South. It originated when people really worked in the field, hoeing cotton or such crops. They would mix these cakes up, I would hope at home, and take them with them, or on the spot, build a little fire. They would actually hold their hoe (washed, of course) over the flame until it was hot, and cook the little cakes on their hoe over the open fire. That was what they had to eat; there was no McDonald's at the end of the row in the fields. I did not make these on a hoe—I did use my Jenn-Air and a griddle. I have done my share of hoeing the crops when I was growing up, but not too much. Dad just wanted me to be sure and know what work is. Well, believe me I do!

1½ cups coarsely ground cornmeal
1 teaspoon sugar (optional)
Pinch of salt (optional)
½ cup boiling water
1½ tablespoons skim milk, canned or fresh
½ cup cold water
½ teaspoon crushed caribe chile (optional)
1 tablespoon chopped green chilies (optional)

Combine the cornmeal, sugar, and salt in a medium-size mixing bowl. Add the boiling water slowly, stirring constantly, then stir in the milk and cold water. Stir in the crushed chile and green chilies. These may be a little spicy for you; you may choose to use only one or the other.

Heat a griddle or nonstick skillet to medium hot, or until a drop of water dances on the surface. Spray the griddle lightly with vegetable oil cooking spray.

Form the batter into cakes by rounded handfuls, then mash them down to ½ to ¾ inch thick. If necessary, dip your hands in cold water to keep the batter from sticking. Bake on one side until brown; turn and brown the other side. The cakes are already cooked from the hot boiling water. You are now browning for presentation.

Chapter 10

Breakfast and Brunch Dishes

CRUSTY FRENCH TOAST

1 gram fat per serving

SERVES 4

PREPARATION :10

COOK :08

STAND :00

TOTAL :18

If you are entertaining or it is a holiday, try adding 1/4 cup of finely chopped nuts. This makes a wonderful festive and tasty breakfast. Remember when you add the nuts to be careful and go lightly; they will add fat grams.

3/4 cup egg substitute
3/4 cup crushed corn flakes (not too fine) (see Note)
4 slices low-fat bread (1 gram of fat per slice or less)
Confectioner's sugar, for garnish

Place the egg substitute in a shallow bowl or pie plate. Do the same with the corn flake crumbs.

Dip the bread slices in the egg substitute, then coat evenly with crumbs. Spray lightly on one side with vegetable oil cooking spray. Place oiled side down on a hot griddle or nonstick skillet; spray the tops lightly, and cook until lightly browned. Turn and continue to cook until the bread is lightly browned and the egg mixture is done, just as you would any regular French toast.

Sprinkle with confectioner's sugar if desired. Serve with warm syrup of your choice and fresh fruit.

Note: I usually use the corn flake crumbs already prepared in a box, but for this recipe I use regular corn flakes and crush them myself in a zipper-lock plastic bag so as not to crush them so fine.

"GOOD MORNING" PANCAKES

1 cup skim milk
1/2 cup egg substitute
2 tablespoons drained chopped green chilies
1/8 teaspoon Mexican seasoning
2 cups reduced-fat baking mix, such as Bisquick

Stir together all ingredients in a medium-size mixing bowl until blended. Heat a griddle or large flat nonstick skillet to hot—until a drop of water dances on the surface.

Pour batter onto the cooking surface by the ladleful (about a scant 1/4 cup) or make the pancakes any size you desire. You might prefer to make silver dollar pancakes.

Cook until the edges are dry. Turn and cook until golden brown. Place on a plate to keep warm while cooking more.

Serve with a nice syrup—any flavor you prefer. One suggestion: Melt pepper jelly in a pan, add a little light corn syrup to thicken, and spoon on. That will get you attention!

2.14 grams fat per serving

SERVES 7

PREPARATION	:05
COOK	:28
STAND	:00
TOTAL	:33

Oats are an all-time favorite. They are high in fiber, low in fat and sugar, and have no cholesterol or sodium. They're known to help lower the levels of artery-damaging cholesterol. No wonder Grandma and Grandpa always had oats for breakfast! And I thought it was only because they were old and the oatmeal was soft. Maybe the reason they were old was the amount of soy products, grains, vegetables, and fruits they ate over the years, and the slower pace they kept. I bet that has a lot to do with our life expectancy.

SOUTHWESTERN-STYLE SCRAMBLED EGGS

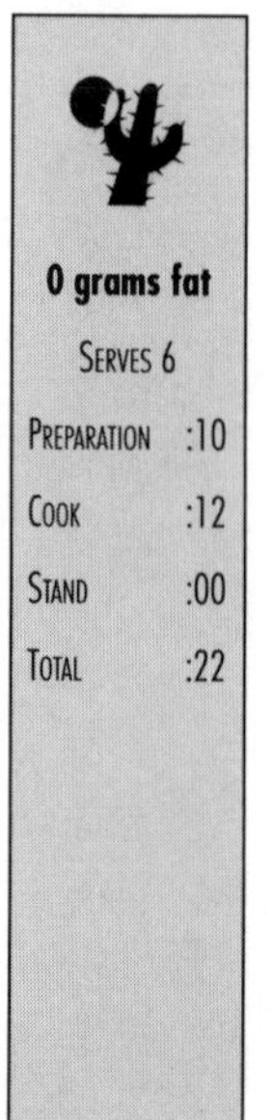

3 cups egg substitute (equivalent of 12 eggs)
1 small green chile, chopped fine (2 tablespoons canned)
1 small tomato, chopped fine and drained
1/2 cup shredded fat-free cheese, such as sharp Cheddar, Monterey Jack, or muenster (optional)
Salt and pepper to taste
Warm tortillas and salsa

In a large mixing bowl, beat the egg substitute with a whisk for about 1 minute. Add the chile, tomato, cheese, and salt and pepper to taste. Stir vigorously with a fork until blended.

Heat a large nonstick sauté pan and coat it with vegetable oil cooking spray. Add the egg mixture, and cook over low heat, using a plastic-coated spatula or wooden spoon to push the eggs gently from the outside (where they cook first) to the center of the pan, until firm but still creamy. Serve with warm tortillas and salsa on the side.

Store oats in a tightly sealed container, away from heat and light. They will last up to a year.

MEXICAN OMELET

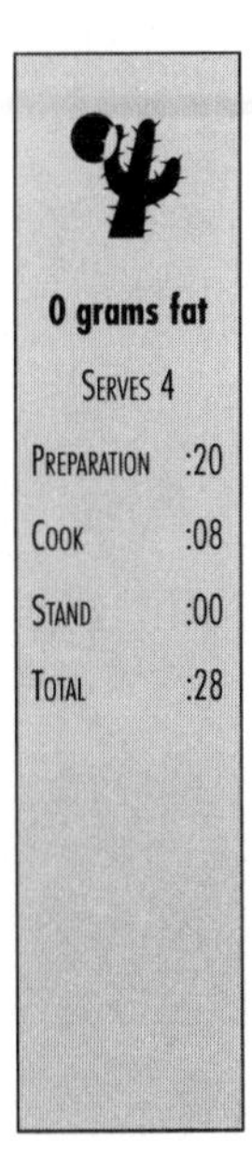

These omelets are cooked one at a time. You will need to allow about 4 to 5 minutes for the cooking of each omelet. Part of the cooking time listed in the time schedule is for the tomato sauce and chile.

10 ounces egg substitute (equal to 5 eggs)
1/4 cup tomato sauce, spicy or Mexican if available
1 fresh Anaheim chile, seeded, washed, and sliced thin
1/2 cup finely sliced green onions
2 sprigs fresh cilantro, minced (optional)

Allow the egg substitute to stand at room temperature for a short period of time while you are preparing this dish.

Combine the tomato sauce and Anaheim chile in a small saucepan over medium heat and bring to a boil. (If you do not have or cannot find Mexican tomato sauce, you might want to add a half teaspoon of dry Mexican spices.) Reduce the heat to low. Let simmer for a few minutes.

Prepare a nonstick skillet by spraying the entire bottom with vegetable oil cooking spray, to prevent the eggs from sticking. Place the prepared skillet over medium-high heat. Meanwhile, whip the eggs in a small bowl until well blended and a little fluffed. Reduce the heat under the skillet, pour in one-fourth of the eggs, and spread with a spatula to cover the bottom of the skillet. Lift the edges of the omelet and tilt the pan a few times to let the uncooked egg run to the bottom. Continue to cook until the omelet is creamy and set. Salt and pepper if desired at this time.

Evenly spread one fourth of the Mexican tomato sauce and 2 tablespoons of the green onions and cilantro across the flat omelet. Fold the omelet in half by lifting one side over to cover the filling. Using a spatula to loosen the omelet from the skillet, slide it from the skillet to a warmed serving plate. Cover loosely with foil and keep warm in a 200 degree oven.

Repeat the process until all four omelets are cooked. Garnish with remaining green onions and fresh minced cilantro. Serve immediately.

SPANISH-STYLE POTATO OMELET

Less than 1 gram fat per serving

SERVES 6

PREPARATION	:35
COOK	:40
STAND	:00
TOTAL	1:15

1 (24-ounce) package frozen diced potatoes with peppers and onions
2 tablespoons chopped green chilies
1/4 teaspoon crushed dried red chilies
Salt to taste
3 cups egg substitute
Chunky commercial salsa for garnish

Heat a large nonstick skillet. Spray lightly with butter-flavored vegetable cooking oil.

Put the potatoes along with the chopped green and dried red chilies in the hot skillet. Sauté or fry quickly until lightly browned and the potatoes are crisp-tender but not mushy, 15 to 20 minutes. Sprinkle with salt if desired.

Add the egg substitute to the skillet and stir to blend with the potato mixture. Cook over medium heat, gently pushing from the edge to the center, without scrambling, until almost completely set, about 10 minutes. Cover and continue to cook over very low heat until firm, 3 to 5 minutes. Remove to a serving dish and top with salsa if desired. Cut into pie-shaped pieces.

POTATO OMELET

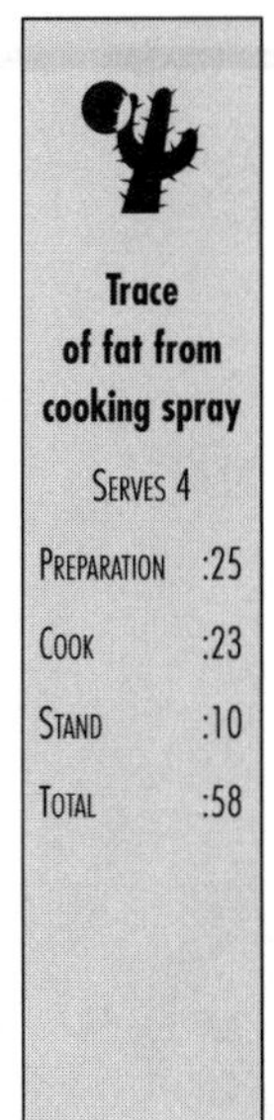

3/4 cup chopped red or white onion (red is prettier)
1 clove garlic, put through a garlic press
2 1/2 cups frozen shredded hash brown potatoes or 2 medium-large fresh potatoes, peeled, thinly sliced (see Note)
Salt and pepper (optional)
1/4 cup skim milk
2 cups egg substitute (equivalent of 8 eggs, 2 per person)
1 teaspoon ground hot or mild chili powder
1 (4-ounce) can chopped green chilies
1/2 cup mixed shredded fat-free Monterey Jack and Cheddar cheeses

Coat a large nonstick skillet lightly with vegetable oil cooking spray; set over medium-high heat for about 2 minutes. Put the onion in the hot skillet and sauté for 4 or 5 minutes or until crisp-tender. Add the garlic during the last minute of cooking the onion. Add the potatoes; continue to cook, turning occasionally with a large flat spatula; do not stir, just turn over so as to brown the top and bottom evenly. You may desire to season at this time with salt and pepper to taste.

When the potatoes are tender and slightly browned, remove the pan from the heat and set aside to cool while preparing the eggs.

In a large mixing bowl, combine the milk and the egg substitute; stir, add the ground chili powder and additional salt and pepper if desired. Beat the egg mixture with mixer for a couple of minutes or until it starts to fluff slightly. Stir in the green chilies and cooked potato mixture.

Using the same skillet (don't dirty a second one), apply an even coating of cooking oil spray. Heat for just about 1 1/2 minutes over medium-high heat.

Pour in the egg mixture. As it starts to set on the bottom, loosen the edges with a spatula and tilt the pan slightly to let the excess egg run under and to keep the omelet from sticking. When almost done, invert a plate over the skillet;

turn the skillet over to flip the omelet onto the plate. Now place the skillet back over the heat and gently slide the omelet back into the skillet, uncooked side down. Briefly cook this side, 2 to 3 minutes. (Or you could place your skillet under a preheated broiler for 2 or 3 minutes.)

Sprinkle the shredded cheese on top, cut into wedges, and serve with salsa.

Note: Most of you, like myself, do not have time to *not* use convenience foods, as busy as the world and families are today, and if we had time, who wants to?

SOUTH OF THE BORDER QUICHE

2 grams fat per serving

SERVES 4

PREPARATION :25
COOK :45
STAND :10
TOTAL 1:20

1 (10-ounce) package 98% fat-free breakfast sausage, such as Jimmy Dean brand
1/3 cup chopped onion
1/3 cup chopped green bell pepper
3 cups frozen hash brown potatoes, chunky style
1 1/2 tablespoons mild red enchilada sauce, canned, such as Old El Paso brand
2 tablespoons chopped canned or fresh green chilies
1 3/4 teaspoons Mexican oregano or regular oregano, crushed
2 (8-ounce) boxes egg substitute
1/2 teaspoon Mexican seasoning, such as McCormick
3/4 cup shredded fat-free Cheddar cheese or your choice
Salsa

In a medium-size nonstick skillet, lightly coated with butter-flavored vegetable oil spray, brown the sausage, crumbling or breaking it apart into bite-size pieces as you stir.

Add the chopped onion, bell pepper, and potatoes. Continue browning, using a flat utensil such as a spatula or pancake turner. Be careful not to use metal in your nonstick skillet, to prevent scratches to the surface.

When the sausage appears done and the pink is all gone,

stir in the enchilada sauce, 1 tablespoon of the green chilies, and 1 teaspoon of the oregano. If the mixture seems dry, add a few tablespoons of water. Scrape the bottom of the pan with the spatula to loosen the browned bits. When the potatoes are soft and the meat is all browned, remove the skillet from the heat; set aside.

Preheat the oven to 350 degrees. Spray a quiche pan or deep pie plate with vegetable oil cooking spray; spoon in the meat and potato mixture. Shake the egg substitute well and pour it over the meat mixture. Sprinkle on the remaining enchilada sauce, green chilies, crushed oregano, and Mexican seasoning.

Bake for 30 to 35 minutes. Sprinkle cheese evenly over the quiche for the last 5 minutes of baking time. The quiche is done when a knife inserted near the center comes out clean. Let stand about 10 minutes before serving.

Serve with prepared salsa on the side, a green salad, and unbuttered toast or low-fat chips.

MEAL-IN-ONE BURRITOS

2.5 grams fat per serving

SERVES 4

PREPARATION	:15
COOK	:08
STAND	:00
TOTAL	:23

12 ounces egg substitute (equivalent of 6 eggs)
1 (10-ounce) package 97% fat-free breakfast sausage, such as Jimmy Dean brand
1/4 cup chopped frozen or fresh white onion
2 green onions, chopped or sliced thin
1/4 cup chopped frozen or fresh green bell pepper
1/2 cup chopped fresh or canned mushrooms
2 tablespoons minced fresh cilantro (optional)
1/4 cup chile sauce, red or green
2 tablespoons skim milk
Salt and ground black pepper to taste
3 (6-inch) fat-free flour tortillas, warmed
1 cup shredded fat-free Cheddar cheese or cheese of your choice
Salsa

Let the egg substitute stand at room temperature for a few minutes while you are preparing your ingredients.

In a medium-large nonstick skillet, crumble and brown the sausage. When it's about two-thirds done, add the white and green onions, pepper, and mushrooms. Continue to cook until the sausage has lost its pink color and is slightly browned, and the onions are crisp-tender. Reduce the heat to low. Stir in the cilantro, if using, and the chile sauce.

Pour the egg substitute into a medium to small bowl; whip until light and well blended. Add the skim milk to fluff them just a little.

Pour egg mixture over the meat and vegetables in the skillet; reduce the heat to low. Gently stir the eggs to mix until set. Don't stir too briskly—use a flat spatula or pancake turner to push the meat mixture and eggs gently. When set to your individual taste, add salt and pepper if desired.

Place ⅛ portion down the center of each warmed tortilla. Sprinkle ⅛ of the shredded cheese down the center of each burrito. Fold the bottom up just about ½ to ¾ inch; fold the sides toward the center to overlap. Serve immediately, with salsa on the side.

Suggested serving accompaniments:

Serve with fresh fruit, juice, and coffee or tea, in the morning, followed by a low-fat fruit bread or a warm muffin with pepper jelly. For lunch or brunch, serve with a small green salad and fat-free dressing, or a small plate of fresh vegetables such as celery, carrots, broccoli, cauliflower, with fat-free sour cream to dip in, or pepper jelly mixed with fat-free cream cheese. Follow with small individual bowls of cut-up fresh fruit, with a scoop of sherbet or sorbet in the middle.

BREAKFAST CASSEROLE

1.25 grams fat per serving

SERVES 8

PREPARATION	:30
COOK	1:00
STAND	12:00
TOTAL	13:30

Prepare this the night before—it's good for early entertaining. For a holiday brunch, a mixture of red and green bell peppers is a nice touch.

1 pound 97% fat-free breakfast sausage, such as Jimmy Dean brand
3/4 cup chopped onion, green or white or red
3/4 cup chopped green bell pepper
1/2 cup chopped green chilies
1 cup sliced and halved fresh mushrooms
2 cups egg substitute (equivalent of 8 eggs)
2 cups skim milk
1/2 teaspoon dry mustard (or use prepared)
Salt and ground black pepper
1/2 teaspoon Mexican seasoning
1/8 teaspoon ground red pepper (cayenne or Chimayo)
2 cups dried bread cubes
2 cups shredded fat-free cheese, Cheddar or mixed

Prepare a 13 x 9-inch baking dish by spraying lightly with butter-flavored cooking spray.

Heat a large nonstick skillet and coat it lightly with cooking spray. Crumble the sausage into the pan and brown over medium heat, stirring often to break up lumps. When the meat is starting to lose its color, add the onion, green pepper, chilies, and mushrooms. Cook and stir until the meat is browned and the vegetables are crisp-tender.

Meanwhile, combine the egg substitute and milk in a mixing bowl. Add the mustard, salt and black pepper to taste, Mexican seasoning, and red pepper. Beat just until foamy.

When the meat-vegetable mixture is done, transfer it to a colander and run very hot tap water over to remove any excess fat. Shake the excess water off.

Start assembling the casserole: Spread the bread cubes

evenly over the bottom of the baking dish. Stir the cheese into the sausage mixture, then pour over the bread cubes, spreading to make an even layer. Pour the milk and egg mixture over the sausage layer.

Cover the casserole with foil and refrigerate overnight. Next morning remove the foil and allow the casserole to stand at room temperature while you preheat the oven to 350 degrees. Place in the oven and bake for 45 to 60 minutes, until a knife inserted near the center comes out clean.

Serve with salsa if desired, along with warm low-fat tortilla chips, juice, hash brown potatoes or grits, coffee, and a smile.

2.58 grams fat per serving

SERVES 6

PREPARATION	:25
COOK	:57
STAND	:00
TOTAL	1:22

BELIEVE IT OR NOT SAUSAGE BAKE

1 pound 98% fat-free light breakfast sausage, such as Jimmy Dean brand
2 green onions, chopped
1/3 cup chopped white onion
2 tablespoons chopped green chilies
2 1/4 cups frozen hash brown potatoes (loose pack shredded)
1 1/4 cups shredded fat-free Mexican Cheddar cheese
1 cup egg substitute
1 cup light or low-fat Bisquick
1/4 teaspoon salt
1/8 teaspoon ground black pepper
1 3/4 cups skim milk
1 green onion and 1 small fresh tomato for garnishes
Salsa

Preheat the oven to 400 degrees. Coat a 10 x 1½-inch pie plate or solid-bottom quiche dish with vegetable oil cooking spray.

Heat a nonstick skillet over medium heat; spray lightly

with cooking spray. Crumble the sausage into the pan and cook, stirring, until it begins to brown.

Add the onions, both green and white, and the green chilies; continue stirring and breaking the sausage apart until the sausage is brown and the vegetables are crisp-tender. Remove to a colander; rinse with the hottest water available to remove excess fat. Shake all the water off.

In your prepared pie plate, mix the sausage, potatoes, and 1 cup of the cheese. Toss gently to mix well.

In a mixing bowl, beat together the egg substitute, Bisquick, salt, pepper, and milk until smooth. Pour into the pie plate.

Bake for approximately 40 minutes or until a knife inserted near the center comes out clean. Sprinkle the remaining ¼ cup of cheese over and bake an additional 2 minutes.

Garnish with fresh tomato, chopped very fine and drained, and 1 green onion, chopped fine. Or use a sprig of fresh rosemary or cilantro. Serve a small dish of salsa to each guest, or spoon a tablespoon on top.

Chapter 11

Desserts

0 grams fat

SERVES 6

PREPARATION	:15
COOK	:00
STAND	1:00
TOTAL	1:15

WINE-MARINATED FRUIT DESSERT

This is fast, easy, and convenient for a light summer-evening dessert to serve out on the deck with a nice cold drink.

1 (8-ounce) can chunk pineapple, undrained
1/2 cup orange juice
1/4 cup dry white wine
1/8 teaspoon ground cinnamon
Dash of grated nutmeg
2 medium oranges, peeled and sectioned
1 medium pear, cored and sliced (peel left on)
1 cup halved fresh strawberries
Fat-free whipped frozen topping, thawed, for garnish
6 small sprigs fresh mint, for garnish

In a medium-size mixing bowl with a cover, combine the pineapple and its juice with the orange juice, wine, cinnamon, and nutmeg. Very carefully and lightly toss the fruit just to coat. Add the orange sections, pear slices, and berries. Continue to gently, *I mean very gently,* mix the fruit to coat evenly with the juice and wine mixture. Cover and chill for at least 1 hour.

Serve in footed fruit or dessert dishes; top with a little whipped topping and place a sprig of mint on top of each for garnish; or sprinkle a tiny bit of nutmeg or cinnamon for presentation along with the mint.

DESSERT TOSTADAS

If you want a little Mexican kick to this, add 1 ring of jalapeño pepper, seeded and minced, or more if desired.

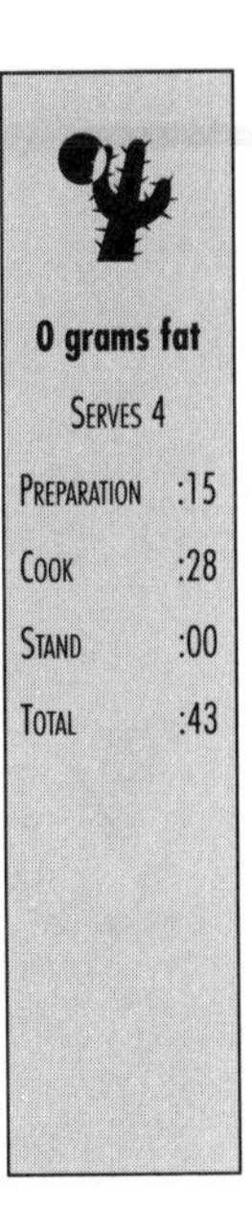

4 (10-inch) fat-free flour tortillas
1 cup fat-free ricotta cheese
1/3 cup nonfat vanilla yogurt
1/4 cup lemon juice
1 1/2 tablespoons sugar
1 teaspoon grated lemon peel
1 teaspoon vanilla extract
1 large ripe mango
1 tablespoon chopped fresh mint (or cilantro or basil)
1 firm ripe banana, sliced into 1/4-inch rounds
1 cup quartered fresh strawberries

Preheat the oven to 375 degrees. Place each tortilla flat on the center rack and bake for 6 or 7 minutes, until lightly browned. Remove to a wire rack or platter.

Combine the ricotta, yogurt, 1 tablespoon of the lemon juice, the sugar, lemon peel, and vanilla in a mixing bowl. Mix well with a wire whisk; set aside.

Prepare the mango: Cut the fruit away from the pit; chop half the fruit into ½-inch cubes. Place the remaining pieces of mango in the blender; add 2 tablespoons of lemon juice and the mint. Process until puréed.

Place the cubed mango, the banana, and the strawberries in a bowl along with 1 tablespoon of lemon juice. Toss very gently to coat.

Assemble the tostadas just before serving them: Spread about ¼ of the ricotta mixture on each tortilla. Spoon ¼ of the cut-up fruit over the ricotta; drizzle ¼ of the puréed mango evenly over the fruit. Serve immediately.

Note: If you do not care to purée the mango, you may drizzle a fat-free chocolate sauce over all. It is great.

Variation: This may be made without the mango, using banana and strawberries, with chocolate sauce or a caramel sauce. You could add any type of fruit in season. This is the great thing about my recipes, I live in a small town and can't always get items called for, so I substitute. Your imagination is your most exciting friend.

FRESH FRUIT TOSTADAS

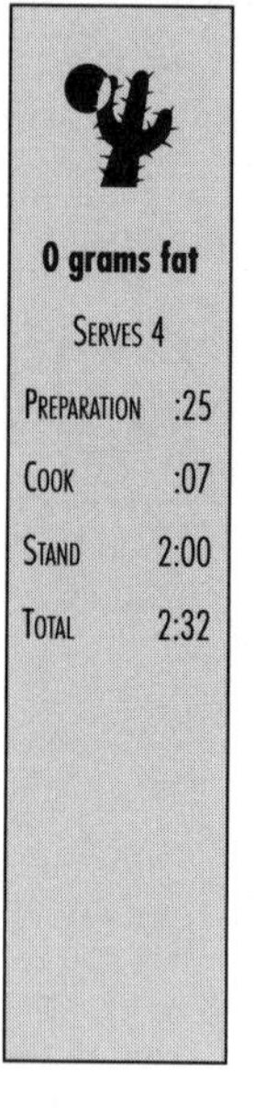

4 (10-inch) fat-free flour tortillas
4 cups mixed fresh fruits, such as watermelon balls, cantaloupe chunks, small pineapple chunks, berries in season, banana rounds
2 tablespoons fresh lime juice
2 tablespoons honey
3 cups fat-free whipped topping
Ground cinnamon or grated nutmeg or chocolate for garnish

Preheat the oven to 375 degrees.

Combine the prepared fruit in a mixing bowl. Mix the lime juice and honey in a cup and pour over the fruit. Very carefully stir to blend the juice and the fruit. Don't smush your fruit. We don't want fruit juice tostados, do we? Cover and refrigerate for at least 2 hours.

Place each tortilla flat on the center rack and bake for 6 or 7 minutes, until browned. Cool on a wire rack.

When ready to serve, place a tortilla flat on a plate, top with 1/4 of the fruit, and cover the fruit with about 3/4 cup of topping. If desired, sprinkle a tiny bit of cinnamon, nutmeg, or chocolate over the topping just for presentation. You could also top with one of the berries (reserved dry). Raspberries are always beautiful.

RICE PUDDING

1/2 cup uncooked long-grain white rice
2 cups hot water
1 cup sugar
1/2 teaspoon ground cinnamon
4 cups skim milk
1/2 cup raisins (optional)
1/2 cup egg substitute

Soak the rice in the hot water for about 15 minutes. Drain in a colander; rinse with cold water.

In a medium-large saucepan, combine the sugar, cinnamon, and milk. Bring to a boil, lower the heat, and add the rice. Cover and cook over low heat for 15 to 17 minutes or until the rice is quite soft but the mixture is fairly liquid. Stir in the raisins and egg substitute; continue cooking uncovered until the pudding just begins to boil again. Remove from the heat. Serve warm or chilled.

1 gram fat per serving

SERVES 6

PREPARATION	:10
COOK	:40
STAND	:00
TOTAL	:50

Don't trust the words Lite and Light—read your labels. Many times they are only 1 gram or so below the regular fat content count.

Less than 1 gram fat per serving

SERVES 6

PREPARATION :10

COOK :25

STAND :05

TOTAL :40

PRALINE RICE PUDDING

2½ cups fresh skim milk
1 (12-ounce) can evaporated skim milk
½ cup egg substitute (equivalent of 2 eggs)
¼ cup pure maple syrup
4 to 5 drops imitation maple flavoring
1 (3-ounce) package cook-and-serve vanilla pudding mix (not instant)
1 cup instant rice (not cooked)
¼ cup packed brown sugar
Ground cinnamon and grated nutmeg for garnish (optional)

In a medium saucepan, combine the fresh and evaporated skim milk, the egg substitute, maple syrup, and maple flavoring. Stir with a wire whisk to blend well. Continue stirring with the whisk, adding the pudding mix in three portions. Stir to mix well.

Pour in the instant rice. Over medium heat bring to a boil, stirring constantly. When the mixture reaches a full boil, remove from the heat; add the brown sugar, stir until the sugar has melted. When no more sugar can be seen, cover and let stand 5 minutes, stirring twice during the standing time.

Pour the pudding into serving dishes; sprinkle the tops lightly with cinnamon and nutmeg. Be careful: very lightly.

Variation: Toasted nuts ground very fine would be nice to garnish the tops of your individual puddings. Try propping a stick of cinnamon in the pudding's side.

LIME PIE

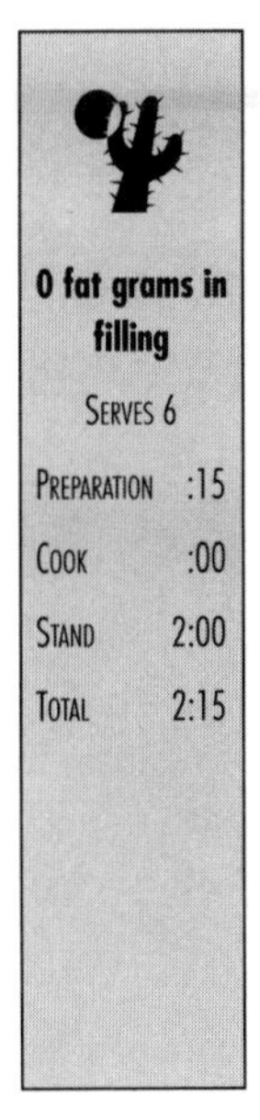

Shop for a low-fat graham cracker crust or make one yourself. This pie is so easy, quick, and good you will love it.

- 1 (8-ounce) tub frozen fat-free whipped topping, thawed
- 1 (14-ounce) can fat-free sweetened condensed milk, such as Eagle Brand
- 1 (6-ounce) can frozen limeade concentrate, thawed
- 2 to 3 drops green food coloring
- 1 low-fat graham cracker pie crust (see Note), or Cookie Crust recipe, page 232

In a glass mixing bowl, combine the whipped topping and condensed milk; with a wire whisk, fold and blend the two together. Stir in the limeade concentrate. Continue to blend, adding food coloring one drop at a time until the color of lime green you desire.

Pour into the pie shell. Chill for at least 2 hours before serving.

Note: You may choose to skip the fat grams in the crust and serve this in a footed dessert dish, with a slice of lime twisted onto the edge of the glass.

> Lime and lemon juice are used widely in Mexican cooking, as well as by many other nationalities. Using a wood reamer is a great quick way to extract juice. Bottled juice is fine, but often we like to add a special touch with fresh juice, which enhances the recipe greatly. I use bottled for time and convenience many times, but if I have a couple of extra minutes, fresh is best.

COOKIE CRUST

Very low-fat

MAKES 1 CRUST

PREPARATION :20

COOK :20

STAND :30

TOTAL 1:10

6 ounces low-fat graham crackers (about 26 squares)
2 large egg whites
1/4 teaspoon cream of tartar
3 tablespoons sugar

Break the crackers into large pieces. Place in a blender. Pulse to make chunky crumbs. Or do the same with a rolling pin in a zipper-lock plastic bag.

Beat the egg whites and cream of tartar on high speed in an electric mixer until foamy. Add the sugar, about 1 tablespoon at a time. Beat until soft peaks form. Gently fold the cracker crumbs into the whites. Spray a 9-inch pie plate lightly with butter-flavored cooking spray. Pour the cookie crumb mixture into the pan and gently spread over the bottom and sides of the pan.

Bake at 350 degrees for 20 minutes or until dry to the touch and lightly browned. With a metal spatula, loosen the crust from the sides of the pan, then slide the spatula under the crust a little at a time to loosen. Let cool completely in pan, then place in the freezer until cold, at least 10 to 15 minutes. Fill the crust or freeze for up to two weeks.

MARGARITA PIE WITH PRETZEL CRUST

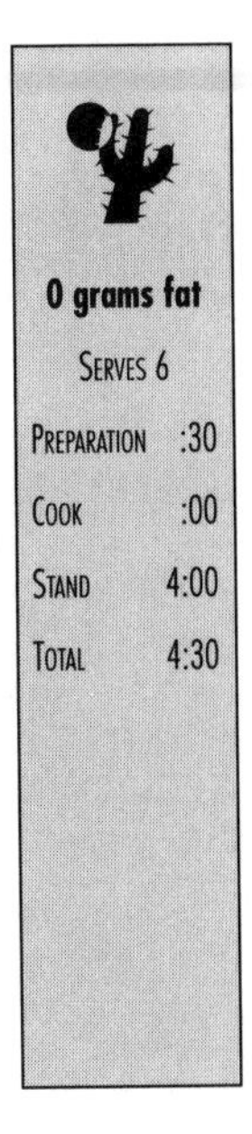

Yum yum.

1 1/2 cups crushed fat-free pretzels (crush in a food processor or with a rolling pin and a zipper-lock plastic bag)
2/3 cup fat-free pourable margarine, such as Fleischmann's
1/4 cup sugar
1 (14-ounce) can sweetened condensed skim milk, such as Eagle Brand
1/3 cup lime juice
2 tablespoons triple sec or other orange-flavored liqueur
1/4 cup tequila
1 (8-ounce) tub frozen fat-free whipped topping, thawed
6 slices of lime, cut thin, or fresh mint, for garnish

Spray a 9-inch pie plate lightly with vegetable oil cooking spray.

Combine in a mixing bowl the crushed pretzels, margarine, and sugar. Mix with a fork until well blended and thoroughly moistened. Press the crumbs onto the bottom and up the sides of the pie plate. You may need to wet your fingers with a tiny touch of cold water to keep the crumb mixture from sticking. Refrigerate the crust while you make the filing.

Combine the sweetened condensed skim milk, lime juice, triple sec, and tequila in a mixing bowl; stir to blend well. Fold in the whipped topping. Pour into the chilled crust. Lightly cover; refrigerate for at least 4 hours, or freeze for 2 hours. If frozen, soften the pie in the refrigerator for about 45 minutes before serving. At serving time, twist lime slices in half figure 8s and use for garnish, or lay a few fresh mint leaves along the edges.

2.1 grams fat per slice

SERVES 8

PREPARATION	:25
COOK	:56
STAND	:10
TOTAL	1:31

LEMON BREAD

4 tablespoons (1/2 stick) low-fat light margarine, softened
2/3 cup plus 1/2 cup sugar
1 large egg white
1/4 cup egg substitute
1 tablespoon grated lemon rind
1/4 teaspoon lemon extract
2 1/4 cups all-purpose flour
2 teaspoons baking powder
1/2 teaspoon baking soda
1 (8-ounce) carton fat-free lemon yogurt
1/2 cup lemon juice, for topping

Preheat the oven to 350 degrees. Spray a 9 x 5 x 3-inch loaf pan with vegetable oil cooking spray.

In a large mixing bowl, cream the margarine with an electric mixer until light. Gradually add 2/3 cup of sugar, continuing to cream until the mixture is fluffy. Add the egg white and egg substitute, lemon rind, and lemon extract; continue beating until well blended.

In a separate bowl, combine the flour, baking powder, and baking soda. Beat the flour mixture alternately with the yogurt into the cream mixture, beginning and ending with flour. Pour the batter into the prepared loaf pan.

Bake for about 55 minutes or until a toothpick inserted near the center comes out clean.

Remove from the oven and place the pan on a wire rack. Mix the remaining 1/2 cup sugar and the 1/2 cup lemon juice in a small saucepan. Bring to a boil and cook for about 1 minute. Remove from the heat. Take a large fork and punch holes in the top of the lemon bread in several places. Pour the lemon sauce over the bread and allow it to cool in the pan for another 10 minutes. Remove from the pan to the rack until completely cooled.

SPICY SPICE CAKE

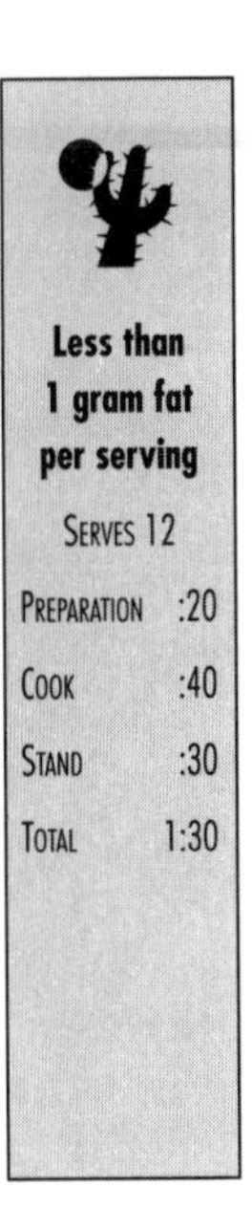

2 1/4 cups all-purpose flour
1 1/2 cups sugar
4 teaspoons baking powder
1 teaspoon baking soda
1 1/2 teaspoons ground allspice
1 teaspoon ground cinnamon
1/2 teaspoon ground cloves
1 (10 3/4-ounce) can low-fat tomato soup
1/2 cup applesauce
1/2 cup egg substitute
1/4 cup water

Lightly spray a 9 x 13-inch baking pan, or two 8-inch round or 9-inch square baking pans with vegetable oil cooking spray. (A somewhat expanded version of the round cake is shown on the cover.) Preheat the oven to 350 degrees.

In a large mixing bowl, combine the flour, sugar, baking powder, baking soda, allspice, cinnamon, and cloves. Stir with a wire whisk to blend well. Pour in the soup, applesauce, egg substitute, and water. Mix with an electric mixer on low speed until blended. Scrape down the sides of the bowl and mix at high speed for 3 to 4 minutes, continually scraping from the sides of the bowl.

Pour into the prepared baking pan; bake 20 minutes for two pans and 35 to 40 minutes for one large pan or until a toothpick inserted near the center comes out clean. Cool in the pan for 10 minutes, then remove from the pan onto a wire rack and cool completely. Frost with Cream Cheese Frosting (page 236).

CREAM CHEESE FROSTING

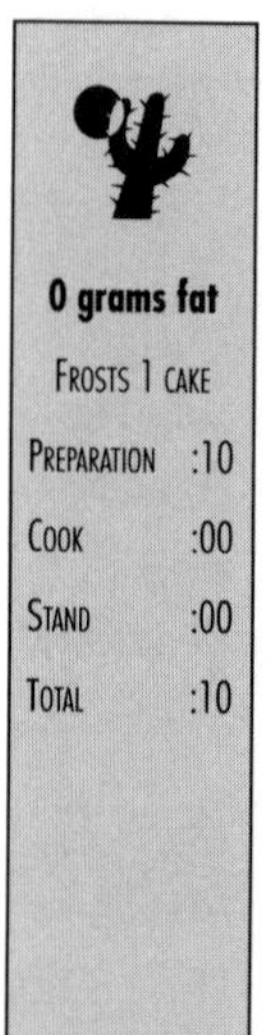

1 (8-ounce) brick fat-free cream cheese, at room temperature
2 tablespoons skim milk
1 teaspoon vanilla extract
1 (16-ounce) package confectioner's sugar (about 4 to 4 1/2 cups)

Place the cream cheese in a bowl. Take a wire whisk and gently start to cream; if you stir too briskly it will break down and be too thin. Add the milk and vanilla; continue to cream while you start adding the sugar, very slowly and carefully. Continue to whisk softly until all the ingredients are blended.

Use this recipe to frost any baked cake or sweet bread. You may garnish with a touch of cinnamon, nutmeg, or cocoa sprinkled on top, or toast a small amount of pecans to crumble and sprinkle over. Pecans do have fat, so be cautious.

Apples in anything cooking or baking always make your home smell and feel so warm and homey. If you plan on trying to sell your own home, try baking something with apples; it will help to make your prospective buyers feel right at home.

APPLE COFFEE CAKE

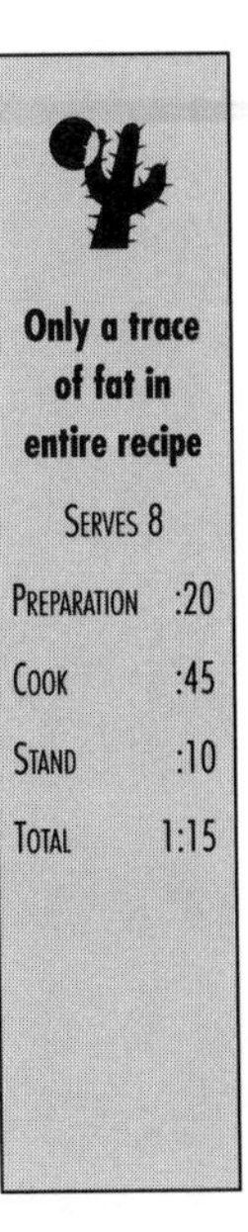

2 baking or Granny Smith apples
1/4 cup lemon juice
1/2 cup applesauce
1 cup plus 3 tablespoons sugar
1 cup egg substitute
2 3/4 cups all-purpose flour
2 teaspoons baking powder
1/2 teaspoon salt
1 cup skim milk
1 teaspoon ground cinnamon, for topping

Preheat the oven to 350 degrees. Lightly spray an 11 x 7-inch baking pan with vegetable oil cooking spray.

Peel and core the apples. Cut them in half from top to bottom, lay them cut side down, and slice into half moons. Toss in lemon juice to keep the apples from turning dark. Set aside.

In a mixing bowl, combine the applesauce and 1 cup of sugar. Add the egg substitute and beat well. Whisk together the flour, baking powder, and salt in another bowl. Add the flour mixture to the applesauce mixture alternately with the milk, beginning and ending with flour and beating after each addition.

Spread the batter in the prepared pan. Arrange the sliced apples in an attractive design (such as rows) over the batter; push very slightly down into the batter but do not submerge. Combine the remaining 3 tablespoons of sugar and the cinnamon; sprinkle over the apples. Bake for 40 to 45 minutes or until the cake shrinks slightly from the sides of the pan. Serve warm with coffee, or for an evening snack or dessert with fat-free ice cream or yogurt. A sugar glaze drizzled over is also nice.

2 grams fat per serving

SERVES 10

PREPARATION	:25
COOK	:40
STAND	:15
TOTAL	1:20

PINE-APPLE COFFEE CAKE

BATTER:

2 1/3 cups light Bisquick
1 cup fresh or canned skim milk
1/2 cup sugar
1/2 cup egg substitute, or equivalent of 2 eggs
1/8 teaspoon ground cinnamon
1 (20-ounce) can apple pie filling
1 (20-ounce) can crushed pineapple, drained

CRUNCHY TOPPING:

1/2 cup uncooked oats
1/2 cup packed brown sugar
1/2 teaspoon ground cinnamon
1/3 cup light Bisquick
1/4 cup pourable fat-free margarine, such as Fleischmann's
1/3 cup finely chopped nuts (optional)

Preheat the oven to 350 degrees. Spray the bottom of an 8 x 12-inch baking dish with vegetable oil cooking spray. Set aside.

Make the batter: In a medium-size mixing bowl, combine the 2 1/3 cups of Bisquick, the skim milk, sugar, egg substitute, and 1/8 teaspoon cinnamon. Mix until all is moistened. The batter will be slightly lumpy; this is OK.

In a separate small mixing bowl, combine the apple pie filling and the drained pineapple; stir to mix well. Measure out 1/2 cup of the mixed fruit and stir it into the batter. Stir to blend well, but do not beat with a mixer. (You may want to chop the pieces of apple a little smaller in this particular 1/2 cup, but it is not necessary for the remaining fruit.)

Put the batter in the prepared baking dish. Top with the remaining mixed fruit, adding a spoonful at a time and making sure that you have it divided evenly all over and not dumped the entire mixture in the middle of the batter.

In another small bowl, combine the topping ingredients: the oats, brown sugar, ½ teaspoon cinnamon, ⅓ cup Bisquick, and ¼ cup margarine. Mix with a fork until moistened and crumbly. Add the nuts at this time if desired.

Scatter evenly over the entire cake. (Be careful not to dump this all in the middle of the cake—then we would have to call it Middle Cake instead.) Bake in the preheated oven for 35 to 45 minutes or until a toothpick inserted near the center comes out clean. Let stand for 15 minutes before serving.

Serve warm with fat-free ice cream for dessert any time; it does not need to be only a breakfast cake. Excellent for brunch or ladies' lunches.

TROPICAL FRUIT DELIGHT OLÉ JOSÉ

This is named for two friends: Jerry named everything "Delight" and Jean said name everything "Olé."

1.2 grams fat per serving

SERVES 15

PREPARATION	:40
COOK	:35
STAND	1:00
TOTAL	2:15

1 (18.25-ounce) box Key Lime–flavor cake mix
3/4 cup egg substitute
1 1/3 cups water
1/3 cup applesauce
1 (14-ounce) can fat-free Eagle brand condensed skim milk
1/3 cup fat-free pourable margarine
4 tablespoons shredded coconut
8 (reduced-fat) Oreo cookies, crumbled
1 (16-ounce) can crushed pineapple, juice and all
1 (22-ounce) can lemon pie filling
1 (8-ounce) container frozen fat-free whipped topping, thawed

Spray a 13 x 9-inch baking dish lightly with vegetable oil cooking spray. Preheat the oven to 350 degrees.

In a medium-size mixing bowl, combine the cake mix, egg substitute, water, and applesauce. Blend with an electric mixer on low speed for 1 minute; turn to medium high and blend for another 2 to 3 minutes, or until smooth. Pour into the prepared baking dish, smooth out evenly and bake for 25 to 30 minutes, until a toothpick inserted near the center comes out clean. Set aside to cool for a few minutes.

Meanwhile, in a small saucepan, combine the condensed milk, margarine, and coconut. Heat just until hot; remove from the heat and let stand until needed.

In a food processor, crumble the cookies until they are the size of grains of rice.

Punch holes in the cake with a fork. Pour the crushed pineapple and its juice evenly over the cake.

On top of the pineapple, evenly pour the milk and coconut mixture.

Over the coconut mixture, evenly spread the lemon pie filling.

Over the lemon filling, evenly spread the whipped topping.

Over the topping, evenly sprinkle the crushed cookies.

Refrigerate until time to serve, at least 1 hour. Yum yum!!

Chapter 12

Beverages

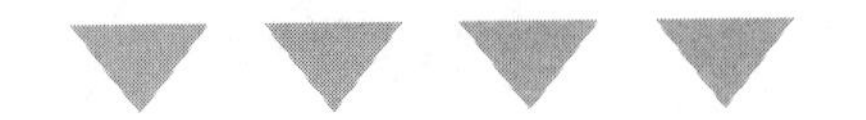

0 grams fat

SERVES 1

PREPARATION	:10
COOK	:00
STAND	:00
TOTAL	:10

MARGARITA

Juice of ½ lime (1½ tablespoons)
Coarse salt (optional)
½ cup crushed ice
1½ ounces (3 tablespoons) tequila
½ ounce (1 tablespoon) triple sec, or any orange-flavored liqueur

After squeezing the lime, rub the rind around the rim of a chilled cocktail glass. Dip the rim into a saucer generously sprinkled with coarse (kosher) salt, if desired. If time permits, place the glass in the freezer for 30 minutes to frost it.

Place the ice in the glass. Pour in the lime juice, tequila, and triple sec. Stir briskly and serve immediately.

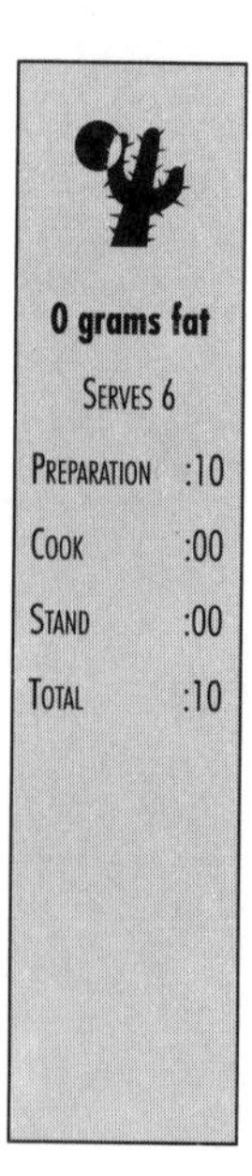

0 grams fat

SERVES 6

PREPARATION	:10
COOK	:00
STAND	:00
TOTAL	:10

MEXICAN-STYLE BLOODY MARY

2 quarts tomato juice
1⅛ cups tequila
¼ cup lime juice
Tabasco to taste—add 1 drop at a time
Pinch of ground red pepper (cayenne)
Dash of onion juice
Lime slices for garnish

In a pitcher, combine the tomato juice, tequila, lime juice, Tabasco (just a small touch), cayenne pepper, and onion juice. Pour into tall glasses with ice cubes; garnish each glass with a slice of lime.

MEXICAN SANGRÍA

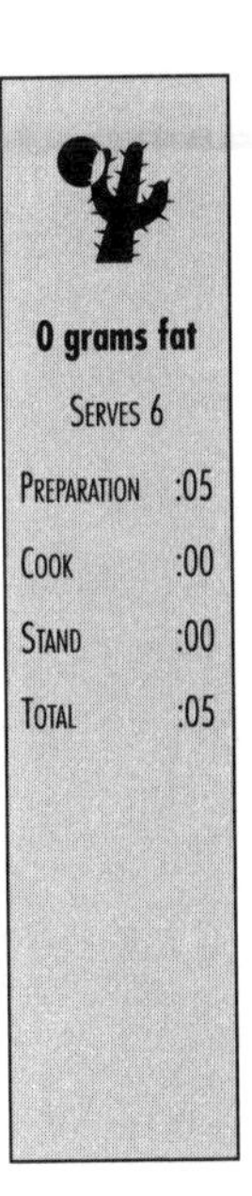

1 cup fresh orange juice
½ cup lime juice
½ cup sugar
2¼ cups red wine
2 cups crushed ice
Lemon or lime slices for garnish

In a nice pitcher, combine the orange juice, lime juice, and sugar. Stir to dissolve. Stir in the wine. Fill tumblers about ½ full of the crushed ice, pour the wine mixture over the ice, garnish with a slice of lemon or lime.

Tea drinkers are half as likely as non-tea drinkers to develop cancer of the esophagus. Where is the tea?

INDEX

Metric Equivalencies

LIQUID AND DRY MEASURE EQUIVALENCIES

CUSTOMARY	METRIC
¼ teaspoon	1.25 milliliters
½ teaspoon	2.5 milliliters
1 teaspoon	5 milliliters
1 tablespoon	15 milliliters
1 fluid ounce	30 milliliters
¼ cup	60 milliliters
⅓ cup	80 milliliters
½ cup	120 milliliters
1 cup	240 milliliters
1 pint (2 cups)	480 milliliters
1 quart (4 cups, 32 ounces)	960 milliliters (.96 liters)
1 gallon (4 quarts)	3.84 liters
1 ounce (by weight)	28 grams
¼ pound (4 ounces)	114 grams
1 pound (16 ounces)	454 grams
2.2 pounds	1 kilogram (1000 grams)

OVEN TEMPERATURE EQUIVALENCIES

DESCRIPTION	°FAHRENHEIT	°CELSIUS
Cool	200	90
Very slow	250	120
Slow	300–325	150–160
Moderately slow	325–350	160–180
Moderate	350–375	180–190
Moderately hot	375–400	190–200
Hot	400–450	200–230
Very hot	450–500	230–260